REFLECTIONS ON
THE UNIVERSAL DECLARATION OF HUMAN RIGHTS

Reflections on the Universal Declaration of Human Rights

A FIFTIETH ANNIVERSARY ANTHOLOGY

Published under the auspices of
THE NETHERLANDS MINISTRY OF FOREIGN AFFAIRS

Edited by
BAREND VAN DER HEIJDEN & BAHIA TAHZIB-LIE

MARTINUS NIJHOFF PUBLISHERS
The Hague / Boston / London

A C.I.P. Catalogue record for this book is available from the Library of Congress.

ISBN 90-411-1046-1

Published by Kluwer Law International,
P.O. Box 85889, 2508 CN The Hague, The Netherlands

Sold and distributed in North, Central and South America
by Kluwer Law International,
675 Massachusetts Avenue, Cambridge, MA 02139, USA

In all other countries, sold and distributed
by Kluwer Law International, Distribution Centre,
P.O. Box 322, 3300 AH Dordrecht, The Netherlands

Cover illustration by Lawrence Gerner

Kluwer Law International incorporates the publishing programmes of Graham & Trotman Ltd., Kluwer Law and Taxation Publishers, and Martinus Nijhoff Publishers.

Printed in the Netherlands, on acid-free paper.

To all victims of human rights violations

and

in support of all human rights defenders

DISCLAIMER

The facts and views presented in the essays and poems contained in this volume are the sole responsibility of the contributors and do not necessarily reflect the opinions of the Netherlands Ministry of Foreign Affairs.

Contents

Contents

At the request of the Netherlands Ministry of Foreign Affairs, the Dutch illustrator Lawrence Gerner has illustrated each article of the Universal Declaration of Human Rights. The illustrations can be found on the following pages:

The illustration of *Article 3* has been reproduced on the cover, the illustrations of *Articles 20 and 28* on the endpapers.

JOZIAS VAN AARTSEN
Netherlands Minister for Foreign Affairs

Foreword

This year marks the fiftieth anniversary of the Universal Declaration of Human Rights. It is an anniversary that deserves our full attention, for a number of reasons. I am therefore extremely pleased that so many celebrities were willing to contribute to this publication, and share their thoughts with us. The fact that we managed to collect fifty essays was no more than a happy coincidence, but we can also see it as a sign that this anniversary is too special to let it pass unnoticed. I should like to thank my predecessor, Hans van Mierlo, for encouraging and supporting this worthwhile project. The proceeds from the sale of the book will be donated to two funds which play an essential role in combating certain violations of human rights and their effects.

Fifty years ago, when memories of the atrocities of the Second World War were all too fresh, the world succeeded in laying the foundations for civilised relations between states and their citizens. However, politics often dictate the reality in which the ideals in the Universal Declaration have to be realised. The fiftieth anniversary is the perfect opportunity to assess what has been achieved for human rights, what has changed and how we should now proceed. A great deal has been achieved, particularly in terms of standard setting. And much has changed, not only in geopolitical terms. For instance the process of globalisation has led to a change in the role of government as the sole guardian of human rights. Non-state actors have now entered areas previously considered to be the exclusive domain of the state. This has directed the focus of the debate towards the issue of accountability for human rights violations by non-state actors.

Unfortunately, we are also forced to conclude that we still have a long way to go. Despite a host of instruments and good intentions, all over the world human rights are being violated on a massive scale every day. It will take much greater commitment than we have shown in the past if we are to get even close to the ideals enshrined in the Universal Declaration. Those working towards this ideal world deserve our unfailing support and protection. We must not only promise those who have, directly or indirectly, suffered human rights violations that we will improve the situation, we must also show them that we really mean it. I hope this commemorative book will help more people to realise that human rights are essential to human wellbeing – not only our own, but that of all people, wherever they may be.

BAREND VAN DER HEIJDEN
BAHIA TAHZIB-LIE

Preface:
Commemoration or Celebration?

For many people, anniversaries are a time for reflection, an opportunity to share thoughts about the past, present and future. This year, 1998, the world community is observing the golden anniversary of the Universal Declaration of Human Rights. On the eve of this momentous occasion, our then Minister for Foreign Affairs invited selected members of the world community from various walks of life and backgrounds to share their views on the Universal Declaration and their experiences with human rights. The result is this collection of fifty essays, presented in alphabetical order by the author's name, alternated with poems and illustrations of each article of the Declaration. We, as editors, had the privilege and honor of working with the authors. Just before the publication of this book, however, we were shocked and saddened to learn that Dr Jonathan Mann had died in a plane crash on 2 September 1998.

In editing this book we have tried to present the contributions in such a way that they are immediately accessible – and hopefully a source of inspiration – to many people throughout the world. We have therefore, for instance, avoided the annotations that are common in many scholarly texts. We would point out that all the contributions were submitted before May 1998, and hence before the adoption of the Rome Statute of the International Criminal Court, which many consider to be a historic step forward in the protection of human rights.

The authors shed their own personal light on various aspects of the Universal Declaration, coming from different angles and perspectives. They not only take stock of what has been achieved over the past half century; they also look ahead to the challenges still facing the world community in the field of human rights. Amid the diversity of content and context, all the essays emphasize the fact that something very special and impressive occurred in 1948. Ever since the day of its adoption, the Universal Declaration has exercised a more powerful influence and played a more prominent and dynamic role throughout the world – at global, regional and national level – than those who drafted it could ever have imagined. Even though the Universal Declaration was not intended to be legally binding, some of the essays argue that it entails legally binding international obligations for states. Clearly, over the years, the Declaration has acquired a mythical force which is difficult to describe. And as 1948 recedes further and further into the past, our admiration for what was achieved then grows and grows. But the Universal Declaration itself, the almost living embodiment of our good intentions, barely seems to age.

Nonetheless, human rights violations continue to occur with alarming regularity. The devastating personal experiences of a number of the authors bear witness to this. The title of this short introduction 'Commemoration or Celebration?' is therefore somewhat ambivalent. We certainly have something to commemorate, and perhaps even to celebrate, but we must realize that we still have a long way to go, and much to do. The gap between words and deeds is still too wide. We, as editors, therefore hope that you will read the essays and poems in this volume with interest and learn from the experiences of the authors. We also hope that this book, part of whose profits will go to the UNFPA Trust Fund for the Elimination of Female Genital Mutilation and the UN Voluntary Fund for the Victims of Torture, will help in its own small way to improve the human rights situation in the world.

The many views expressed in these essays, which were all inspired by a desire to bring home to people the continuing importance of human rights, are like so many streams flowing in the same direction, but along different channels. This brings to mind a conversation between Siddhartha and the ferryman Vasudeva in Hermann Hesse's novel *Siddhartha*, about the many different voices of a running river:

> And once again when the river swelled during the rainy season and roared loudly, Siddhartha said: 'Is it not true, my friend, that the river has very many voices? Has it not the voice of a king, of a warrior, of a bull, of a nightbird, of a pregnant woman and a sighing man, and a thousand other voices?'
> 'It is so', nodded Vasudeva, 'the voices of all living creatures are in its voice'.

May this publication serve as a reminder that the voices of the victims of human rights violations, and of those who defend human rights, must be continually heard by all.

Geneva / The Hague, 14 September 1998   *The Editors*

Article 1

All human beings are born free and equal in dignity and rights. They are endowed with reason and conscience and should act towards one another in a spirit of brotherhood.

KOFI ANNAN

Message by the United Nations Secretary-General

Human rights are the foundation of human existence and coexistence. Human rights are universal, indivisible and interdependent. Human rights are what make us human. They are the principles by which we create the sacred home for human dignity.

When we speak of the right to life, or development, or to dissent and diversity, we are speaking of tolerance. Tolerance – promoted, protected and enshrined – will ensure all freedoms. Without it, we can be certain of none.

Human rights are the expression of those traditions of tolerance in all religions and cultures that are the basis of peace and progress. Human rights are foreign to no culture and native to all nations. Tolerance and mercy have always and in all cultures been ideals of government rule and human behaviour. Today, we call these ideals human rights.

It is the universality of human rights that gives them their strength. It endows them with the power to cross any border, climb any wall, defy any force.

The struggle for universal human rights has always and everywhere been the struggle against all forms of tyranny and injustice – against slavery, against colonialism, against apartheid. It is nothing less and nothing different today.

Young friends all over the world,

You are the ones who must realize these rights, now and for all time. Their fate and future is in your hands. Human rights are your rights. Seize them. Defend them. Promote them. Understand them and insist on them. Nourish and enrich them.

They are the best in us. Give them life.*

---

*Excerpt from a message of 5 December 1997 on the beginning of the 50th-anniversary year of the Universal Declaration of Human Rights (SG/SM/6414).

WISŁAWA SZYMBORSKA

Tortures

Nothing has changed.
The body is a reservoir of pain;
it has to eat and breathe the air, and sleep;
it has thin skin and the blood is just beneath it;
it has a good supply of teeth and fingernails;
its bones can be broken; its joints can be stretched.
In tortures, all of this is considered.

Nothing has changed.
The body still trembles as it trembled
before Rome was founded and after,
in the twentieth century before and after Christ.
Tortures are just what they were, only the earth has shrunk
and whatever goes on sounds as if it's just a room away.

Nothing has changed.
Except there are more people,
and new offenses have sprung up beside the old ones-
real, make-believe, short-lived, and nonexistent.
But the cry with which the body answers for them
was, is, and will be a cry of innocence
in keeping with the age-old scale and pitch.

Nothing has changed.
Except perhaps the manners, ceremonies, dances.
The gesture of the hands shielding the head
has nonetheless remained the same.
The body writhes, jerks, and tugs,
falls to the ground when shoved, pulls up its knees,
bruises, swells, drools, and bleeds.

Nothing has changed.
Except the run of rivers,
the shapes of forests, shores, deserts, and glaciers.
The little soul roams among those landscapes,
disappears, returns, draws near, moves away,
evasive and a stranger to itself,
now sure, now uncertain of its own existence,
whereas the body is and is and is
and has nowhere to go.

An Indonesian View on Human Rights

As the international community prepares to celebrate the 50th anniversary of the Universal Declaration of Human Rights, it is only appropriate that nations remain seized with the issue of the promotion and protection of human rights. I find it lamentable, however, that there is still a great deal of unnecessary heat and not enough illumination attending current international discussions on this vitally important issue.

Over the past few years, there have been occasions on which I have had to express concern at a trend in international mass media journalism promoting the impression that there is a clash of values between the developed countries advocating a concept of human rights that gives prominence to political and civil rights and the developing countries, mostly of East Asia, propounding a purportedly 'dissident' view that emphasizes both the need to take into account the diversity of socio-economic, cultural and political realities prevailing in each country and the indivisibility of all categories of human rights.

This depiction is not only erroneous but also unwarranted and therefore counterproductive. I can say in all truthfulness that neither Indonesia nor the other developing countries of Asia that signed the Bangkok Declaration on Human Rights have ever advocated an alternative concept of human rights based on some nebulous concept of 'cultural relativism' as spuriously alleged in some quarters.

On the contrary, as clearly stated in the Bangkok Declaration, we recognize that the observance and promotion of human rights 'should be encouraged by cooperation and consensus, and not through confrontation and the imposition of incompatible values'.

Among members of the United Nations, there can and should be no room for confrontation or acrimony on the issue of human rights, considering that we all proceed from the same basic premises: our shared view on the universal validity of these rights and freedoms, our common adherence to the Universal Declaration and our commitment to the UN Charter which enjoins us to cooperate in promoting respect for human rights for all without distinction as to race, sex, language or religion.

If this is the case, then I cannot see how or why anyone can oppose the central proposition that we in Indonesia have always advanced, namely that in considering human rights issues and in promoting and protecting such rights we should all do so in accordance with the UN Charter rather than on the basis of the particular perceptions or preferences of any one country or group of countries.

Moreover, human rights are by no means a new issue. As early as in 1945 they were enshrined in the UN Charter and since then the World Organization has developed a growing corpus of covenants, conventions, declarations and other instruments that constitute a veritable International Bill of Human Rights. In the process, commonly agreed concepts, principles, procedures and mechanisms have been established within the United Nations system. I therefore believe that the promotion and protection of human rights would be far better served if all of us were to adhere more conscientiously to those common understandings and procedures as already agreed upon over the years rather than allow ourselves to be diverted into a futile debate over wrongly perceived alternatives and dichotomies.

And while it may be true that the theoretical basis for the concept of human rights as embodied in the UN Charter and the Universal Declaration of Human Rights was first conceived in the West, it is neither unknown nor unappreciated in the countries of Asia and Africa. We in Indonesia are well aware that this concept sprang from the libertarian writings of such European political and legal thinkers as Thomas Hobbes, John Locke, Montesquieu, Jean Jacques Rousseau, Cesare Beccaria and John Stuart Mill – and from their idea of a 'social contract' and of the inherent, 'natural' rights of individuals vis-à-vis the powers of the state and the attendant civil and political rights of the citizen. And these were among the ideas that inspired the struggle of many new nations in Asia and Africa to cast off the yoke of colonialism, just as they helped ignite, in an earlier age, the French and American revolutions.

Thus, if today there still appears to be a debate on the concept of human rights, it derives not so much from any dispute between East and West or between North and South but, it seems to me, from the lingering echo of an earlier clash between two Western traditions, between the principle of individual liberty passionately espoused by Thomas Jefferson and the principle of strong, lawful authority just as passionately advocated by Alexander Hamilton. Since the time of Jefferson and Hamilton, however, many political thinkers have been able to resolve the conflict between these two traditions and principles by uniting them. It has rightly been pointed out that neither of them can be salutary without the other: by itself and unrestrained, freedom leads through anarchy to tyranny; alone and unlimited, authority leads through tyranny to rebellion and anarchy. But with these two principles balanced together, freedom supports the enactment of strong law and strong law endures because it preserves freedom.

Since we in the developing world well understand the genesis of the thinking and the motivation underlying present-day Western policies and views on human rights, we expect at least some reciprocal understanding and appreciation of the historical formation and experiences of non-Western societies and the attendant development of our cultural and social values and traditions. In general, developing countries, some endowed with ancient and highly developed cultures, have not gone through the same history and experience as the Western nations in developing their ideas on human rights and democracy. In fact, they have often developed different perceptions based on different experiences regarding the relations between man and society, man and his fellow man and the rights of the community as against the rights of the individual. This is not to say that countries with such a tradition are therefore proposing a separate or alternative concept of human rights. But there should be greater recognition of the immense complexity of the issue of human rights due to the wide diversity in history, culture, value systems, geography and levels of development among the nations of the world.

In our case in Indonesia, we are firmly committed to the promotion and protection of human rights on the basis of our commitment to the UN Charter, the Universal Declaration of Human Rights and the Vienna Declaration and Programme of Action adopted at the World Conference on Human Rights. Such commitment flows from the state philosophy of *Pancasila* (Five Pillars), from the provisions of our 1945 Constitution, from our national laws as well as from the values, customs and traditions of our people. As a people who suffered colonial oppression for centuries, we know only too well the vital importance of human rights.

This is not to claim that Indonesia has a perfect human rights record. No nation, no matter how enlightened, can make that claim. We are aware of the expressions of concern by a number of countries about alleged violations of human rights in Indonesia. Many of these charges have no basis in fact or have been grossly exaggerated by Indonesia's detractors but we do acknowledge that there have been incidents that have set back our government's efforts to protect and uphold human rights and fundamental freedoms. When such incidents did occur, as happened in Dili on 12 November 1991, we acted swiftly to correct them and to bring to justice those responsible, be they civilian or military personnel.

Moreover, we have a very active National Human Rights Commission that diligently investigates reports of alleged violations which, in a vast land of 200 million people, are bound to happen now and then. We do our utmost to take legal action against all violations, to address the root causes of such violations, and to protect and promote the human rights of all our people in a balanced and equitable way.

In this regard, Indonesia has finalized and is implementing a National Action Plan in the field of human rights. Designed to guide the Indonesian government in promoting and protecting human rights throughout the country, the Action Plan focuses on three sets of activities: the ratification of international human rights instruments, the dissemination of information and social education on human rights issues, and the implementation of ratified international conventions such as the Convention on the Rights of the Child and the Convention on the Elimination of All Forms of Discrimination Against Women.

In its relations with other countries, Indonesia has always been open to and has sought cooperation in the field of human rights on the assumption that all of us in

23

the international community are working on the basis of the same fundamental premises: our shared faith in the inherent and inviolable dignity of the human person, our common adherence to the Universal Declaration of Human Rights and our commitment to the UN Charter which enjoins us to cooperate in the promotion of human rights. Consistent with these premises, Indonesia has always maintained that the promotion and protection of human rights would be far better served if all of us were to adhere more conscientiously to the provisions of the UN Charter, to the large body of covenants, conventions, resolutions and declarations agreed upon over the years as well as to the concomitant procedures and mechanisms established in the United Nations system, rather than blindly accede to the particular perceptions, interpretations and preferences of any one country or group of countries.

Since we hold that the promotion of human rights should be the subject of international cooperation, we consequently maintain that cooperation presupposes equality among those cooperating. And in this spirit of cooperation and mutual respect there is no place for the practice that some countries often indulge in – of making peremptory judgments of or preaching self-righteous sermons to one another. We should simply agree to work together and engage in constructive dialogue as the most effective way of advancing human rights.

We seek this kind of positive dialogue not only with other governments but also with all interested parties at all levels. For while it is true that the responsibility for the promotion and protection of human rights rests primarily with governments, the preamble to the Universal Declaration of Human Rights correctly states that every individual and every organ of society shall strive through teaching and education to promote respect for human rights and freedoms and through progressive measures, national and international, to secure their universal and effective recognition and observance. This is a cardinal principle that guides us in our efforts to promote and protect human rights.

Another principle that gives direction to our efforts is the indivisibility of human rights – civil, political, economic, social and cultural, the rights of the individual and those of the community, the society and the nation. This implies that the promotion and protection of all these rights should be undertaken in an integral and balanced manner and that inordinate emphasis on one category of human rights over another will militate against the effort to promote all of them. It is therefore our view that in assessing the human rights conditions of countries, especially developing countries, the international community should take into account the promotion and protection of all human rights and not just one or two categories.

Particularly vital, in our view, is the balance that must be maintained between individual human rights and the obligations of individuals to their community. Without such a balance, the rights of the community as a whole can be subverted in such a way that instability or even anarchy will ensue. This is a peril to which developing countries are often exposed. We therefore believe that the rights of individuals must be balanced by those of the community, by the obligation to display equal respect for the rights of others, the rights of society and the rights of the nation. Indonesian culture as well as our ancient customary laws place a high priority on the rights and interests of society or the nation, without, however, in any way ignoring or minimizing the rights of individuals and groups. Indeed, the interests of the latter are fully taken into account in the traditional practice of *musyawarah mufakat* (deliberations to obtain consensus) which is firmly embedded in our national socio-political system and our political institutions.

We therefore support all initiatives promoting a more balanced approach to human rights. We note with interest the 19-Article Universal Declaration of Human Responsibilities proposed by the InterAction Council. We agree with former Australian Prime Minister Malcolm Fraser, Chairman of the InterAction Council, that if adopted by the international community, the Universal Declaration of Human Responsibilities, together with the Universal Declaration of Human Rights, could form twin pillars that would serve as an ethical base for a just world. Indeed, freedom without acceptance of responsibility can destroy freedom itself whereas when rights and responsibilities are balanced, freedom is enhanced. Without this fine balance, neither rights nor responsibilities can meaningfully exist.

Nor can they meaningfully exist without the promotion and protection of one vital human right: the right of all human beings to be free from poverty, ignorance and disadvantage, to have the opportunity to earn a decent and dignified living – the right to development. To any person denied this right, all other rights are meaningless. One who can neither read nor write, for instance, has little use for freedom of expression. If country's citizens are so poor that they must spend all their time eking a bare living, they cannot be reasonably expected to use their civil and political rights fully. Thus economic development and human rights are intimately linked and are mutually reinforcing: successful development that is people-centred will result in the flourishing of human rights and, conversely, the promotion and protection of human rights will ensure the success of the most important component of national development, the development of a nation's human re-sources. Herein lies the essential and broadly-gauged linkage between development and human rights. We therefore cannot accept the attempt of some countries to reduce this broad linkage and to make the promotion of human rights a narrow and one-sided conditionality for development cooperation. Such an approach is not only counterproductive, it is also a blatant denial of the human right to development.

Accordingly, we believe that the human person should be the focus of development, that people should not only be the beneficiaries but also the prime movers of their own development. This is the reason why, in Indonesia's national development efforts, great emphasis is placed on human resources development. To us, this too is a matter of human right, the right to development.

In spite of all past and current efforts of the international community, the human

25

race has a long way to go before it can be said that on a global scale, all human rights are promoted and protected as they should be. But we already have a growing body of concepts, instruments and international understandings and agreements to work with and to build upon. We should therefore all take up that task together with patience and perseverance, while shunning the temptation to remake the world in our own image and always opting for cooperation, compassion and mutual tolerance. If we adhere to this approach, I am confident that in time the international community will achieve a global ethic based on human rights as well as human responsibilities. The result will be a more peaceful, a more tolerant and a more just international order.

Everyone is entitled to all the rights and freedoms set forth in this Declaration, without distinction of any kind, such as race, colour, sex, language, religion, political or other opinion, national or social origin, property, birth or other status.

Furthermore, no distinction shall be made on the basis of the political, jurisdictional or international status of the country or territory to which a person belongs, whether it be independent, trust, non-self-governing or under any other limitation of sovereignty.

PHILIP ALSTON

The Universal Declaration in an Era of Globalisation

The Universal Declaration of Human Rights is the greatest ethical and normative achievement of the United Nations, and perhaps even of the international community as a whole in the course of the past fifty years. It constitutes a significant step forward in the history of humankind and will be one of the enduring legacies of the twentieth century to its successor. But the progress and enlightenment of which it should be the harbinger cannot be taken for granted. There is little automaticity in human affairs; movement towards a more humane world does not happen inexorably. Progress must be fought for and defended and the next steps cannot simply be left to chance. An effective defence of human rights requires an understanding of the dynamics which have given the Universal Declaration its status as a beacon of light in a fog of inhumanity.

The interplay of continuity and change is an integral part of those dynamics. Their dialectical relationship must be understood in order to appreciate the elements which influence the evolution of the theory and practice of human rights. Those who would set the Universal Declaration in concrete are as mistaken as those who would jettison it as being anachronistic.

Reconciling the Needs of Continuity and Change

Continuity is achieved by a process of repeated invocation, gradual entrenchment in both the minds of peoples and the laws of nations, application across an ever-widening sphere of influence, and reinforcement by other complementary trends and policies. The Universal Declaration has been the beneficiary of all of these developments. The almost transcendent status which it has achieved is perhaps best illustrated by the extent to which that status almost defies definition according to the traditional categories of international law.

Change is equally indispensable. No statement of human rights, no matter how compelling – even temporarily definitive – it might be, can afford to be treated as static, unchanging, or rigid. Thus, to take but one example, the Magna Carta, with which the Universal Declaration has been constantly compared since the moment of the latter's adoption in 1948, actually contains many provisions which are dated and long forgotten. The prohibition of fish reservoirs in rivers, for example, is no longer a matter of the highest principle and the right of a lord to impose a levy upon his 'free men [in order] to make his eldest son a knight and to marry his eldest daughter once' sits rather awkwardly beside today's human rights standards.

The challenge then is to reconcile the needs of continuity and change in such a way as to protect the *acquis* in human dignity while ensuring its capacity to respond to new challenges, changing circumstances and progress in shared values. While the Universal Declaration can never be the last word, it remains the benchmark against which all subsequent claims for such adjustment, adaptation, or perhaps more accurately evolution, must be measured. For the most part, that change can and should be achieved through an evolution in the accepted interpretations applying to the provisions of the Universal Declaration and through the development of complementary norms and instruments. The burden of proof upon those who would seek to formalise any such evolution is immense and the strength of the popular mandate for change must be compellingly demonstrated.

THE CHALLENGES POSED BY GLOBALISATION

As we commemorate the fiftieth anniversary of the Universal Declaration the process of globalisation poses a variety of challenges which demand our attention but have not been receiving it. Globalisation is a phenomenon which pre-occupies the international community, even though it is capable of multiple and diverse definitions. Leaving aside the developments in science, technology, communications and information processing that have made the world smaller and more interdependent in so many ways, globalisation has also come to be closely associated with a variety of trends and policies including an increasing reliance upon the free market, a significant growth in the influence of international financial markets in determining the viability of national policy priorities, a diminution in the role of the state and the size of its budget, the privatization of various functions previously considered to be the exclusive domain of the state, the deregulation of a range of activities designed to facilitate investment and reward individual initiative, and a corresponding increase in the role and even responsibilities attributed to private actors both in the corporate sector and in civil society.

None of these developments in itself is necessarily incompatible with the principles of the Universal Declaration or with the human rights obligations of governments. Taken together, however, and if not complemented by appropriate additional policies, globalisation risks downgrading the central place in world affairs accorded to human rights by the United Nations Charter and the Universal Declaration. Because there often seems to be little that can be done to change its course or slow its development, there has been a tendency to assume that the two issues of human rights and globalisation can, indeed should, be kept separate. This also reflects in part the pre-occupation of human rights proponents with the maintenance of the status quo in the name of preserving the continuity which is essential in the human rights area. But if taken to the extreme, that pre-occupation can blind us to the equally important need for change in order to respond to circumstances which are, in some ways at least, fundamentally different from those of 1948.

Globalisation is by no means a one way street in terms of human rights. There are clear benefits resulting from it. The freer flow of information has many positive ramifications. Similarly, there is much to be said in favour of the pressures upon governments generated by financial institutions and markets to respond to concerns about good governance and the rule of law through the elimination of corruption and cronyism and the upholding of a free and independent judicial system. But my aim is not to sing the praises of globalisation; a powerful chorus is already doing that. Rather, it is to point to the risks inherent in the enterprise in the form in which it is currently being pursued.

In relation to civil and political rights, the process of globalisation has called into question the sustainability of the traditional divide between governmental accountability for human rights violations and the non-accountability of private actors. As corporations assume an ever greater role in managing or even establishing prisons, hospitals, public parks, and shopping and recreation areas, and for providing much of the security available to citizens, so too must new and innovative ways be found to ensure respect for civil and political rights. The new political 'consensus' which has developed since the end of the Cold War has also seen a tendency to restrict international concern to a certain core of rights while giving governments a far greater benefit of the doubt to experiment with 'new' policies to combat crime, drug abuse, terrorist threats and anti-social behaviour in general. But many of these policies seem to be little more than throwbacks to an inhumane past, and little consideration is given to their compatibility with the notion of 'human dignity'. Yet, it is probably the single most important principle which underpins the Universal Declaration, from the assertion in Article 1 that '[a]ll human beings are born free and equal in dignity and rights', through the affirmation in Article 22 of 'economic, social and cultural rights [which are] indispensable for [the individual's] dignity and the free development of his personality', to the reference in Article 23 to 'the right to ... remuneration ensuring ... an existence worthy of human dignity'.

The actual or potential impact of globalisation and the values and approaches associated with it is especially significant in relation to economic, social and cultural rights. Thus, for example, respect for the right to work and the right to just and favourable conditions of work is threatened by an exclusive emphasis upon competitiveness to the detriment of respect for the labour standards recognised in the Universal Declaration. The right to form and join trade unions may be threatened by restrictions upon freedom of association which are claimed to be 'necessary' in a global economy, by the effective exclusion of possibilities for collective bargaining, and by the closing off of the right to strike for various occupational and other groups. The right of everyone to social security might not be ensured by arrangements which rely entirely upon private contributions and private schemes. While work-fare policies might be effective in many circumstances, they can be no substitute for the panoply of measures inevitably required to ensure respect for the right to an adequate standard of living.

Similarly, respect for the family and for the rights of parents to be with their children in an era of expanded global labour markets for certain individual occupations might require new and innovative policies rather than a mere laissez-faire approach. The introduction of user fees, or cost recovery policies, when applied to basic health and educational services for the poor can easily result in significantly reduced access to services which are essential for the enjoyment of the rights recognised in the Covenant. An insistence upon payment for access to artistic, cultural and heritage-related activities risks undermining the right to participate in cultural life for a significant proportion of any community.

Most, although perhaps not all of these risks can be guarded against, or compensated for, if appropriate policies are put in place. But it is clear that while much energy and many resources have been expended by governments on promoting the trends and policies that are associated with globalisation, insufficient efforts are being made to devise new or complementary approaches which could enhance the compatibility of those trends and policies with full respect for human rights. A fascination with simplistic one-shot policies (the social equivalents of the 'three strikes and you are out' approach to dealing with criminal recidivism) must not be permitted to wipe clean the slate of governmental responsibilities in relation to human rights.

The Role and Responsibilities of International Organizations

While governments bear the principal responsibility for ensuring respect for human rights, international organizations are an important instrument of policies which can either be conducive to human rights or can directly or indirectly undermine them. Those organizations, as well as the governments that have created and manage them, have a strong and continuous responsibility to take whatever measures they can to assist governments to act in ways which are compatible with their human rights obligations and to seek to devise policies and prescriptions which promote respect for those rights. It is particularly important to emphasise that the realms of trade, finance and investment are in no way exempt from these general principles and that the international organizations with specific responsibilities in those areas should play a positive and constructive role in relation to human rights.

In 1997 the UN Committee on Economic, Social and Cultural Rights sought to highlight this responsibility in one of its 'General Comments' when it insisted that even the Security Council, and even when it was acting on the basis of the draconian powers entrusted to it under Chapter VII of the UN Charter, was still subject to human rights requirements. In an important analysis the Committee wrote that these rights:

> ... cannot be considered to be inoperative, or in any way inapplicable, solely because a decision has been taken that considerations of international peace and security warrant the imposition of sanctions. Just as the international community insists that any targeted state must respect the civil and political rights of its citizens, so too must that state and the international community itself do everything possible to protect at least the core content of the economic, social and cultural rights of the affected peoples of that state (General Comment 8 (1997), paragraph 7).

This analysis has clear parallels in relation to the activities of those international organizations which are in the frontline of dealing with issues put in the spotlight by developments associated with globalisation. Thus, for example, the International Monetary Fund and the World Bank should pay careful attention to the human rights impact of their policies, albeit within reasonable bounds in light of their mandates and responsibilities. While the Managing Director of the Fund observed in May 1998 that 'human rights violations can never be accepted and are never a good thing for economic progress', neither the Fund nor the Bank has a clear, let alone comprehensive, policy relating to human rights. This includes policies designed to promote respect for economic, social and cultural rights, which should include explicit recognition of those rights, the identification of country-specific benchmarks to facilitate their promotion, and the development of appropriate remedies for responding to violations. Social safety nets should be defined by reference to these rights and enhanced attention should be accorded to such programs for the poor and vulnerable in the context of structural adjustment programs. Effective social monitoring should accompany the enhanced financial surveillance and monitoring policies accompanying loans and credits for adjustment purposes.

Similarly the World Trade Organization should devise appropriate methods to facilitate more systematic consideration of the impact upon human rights of particular trade and investment policies. Regardless of whether such policies should focus on the adoption of a 'social clause' linked to sanctions against non-complying countries, there are many other options which should be explored to enable the WTO to be a responsible partner in the international community's quest to give the fullest possible meaning to the commitments contained in the Universal Declaration of Human Rights.

As we enter the twenty-first century it is imperative that we acknowledge that human rights are the only bulwark that remains against a world whose 'values' are defined solely by reference to economic determinism, by the notoriously and in many ways appropriately selfish and narrow preferences of the market. We must therefore re-double our efforts to ensure that the real values enshrined in the Universal Declaration of Human Rights move closer to realization in the second half century of its existence than they have in the first.

AHMAD SHAMLU

The Banquet
*After the Epic of Siah-Kal**

NARRATOR
But
    a curved dagger
                alone
lies on a dish
across a lush feast table.

HOST
My Lords! My Lords!
Please,
    treat my home as your own!

NARRATOR
Into the guests' chalices
the slaves pour poison
from ancient decanters.
Their smiles tulips and lies.
With their aprons stretched out
they demand
        reward
for offering death with ease.

The dead are laid
upon far off shelves,
the living in chests.

Around the lush table
we stare at the bloodless faces
    of our fellow-guests:

---

*Mountainous forest where the first guerilla attack against the Shah's regime was launched. Some years later the notorious royal festivities followed.

Oh, wonder!
Who
      are we?-
We're neither dead
      laid on the far off shelves,
nor alive
      in the chests.

Only the bloody doorway
and the blood-stained carpet
bear witness that,
      barefooted,
we've walked upon a path of swords.

    CONTENDERS
... to sit at the table?
The women are gilded
with a sickly yellow slime!

    JESTER
The garden without cherubs
is an incomplete beauty!
Mocking laughter.

    VAGABOND
Hastens forward, and hastens past.
The bailiffs are saints.
The bailiffs are saints.
The bailiffs are saints.
The bailiffs are sain-
Cut with the sound of a bullet.
Long silence.
Mourners' drums and cymbals from far off.
Footsteps of slowly-moving mourners,
against the background of the eulogist's oration.
Now and then the drums and cymabals are faintly heard.

    EULOGIST
In an epic tone.
See him off with a sweet tune
for
    Satan was the Archangel

close and intimate.
        'No!',
he shouted heedlessly,
altough his wings were his immortality,
although he knew that the cry
was the hopeless scream
of a broken-winged falling bird.

He was not downcast
        nor ashamed of himself,
and did not pass in the cool shade:
        his way was through the sun
        even though blazing
        and tasting of blood.
His head he kept high and proud;
although
        he who keeps his head low
is immune
        to the dark curse of the gallows.

NARRATOR
With the same tone.
        'You *will* deny',
they said,
        'the song of the quail
        and the murmur of the water
        singing in freedom.'

VAGABOND
This seemingly-minute,
                however,
is the great truth of the world.

And the greatness of every sun
to the feeble-sighted seem
                like an asteroid,
and the moon
        like the paperish clipping
of a baby's fingernail;
and the ritual silver coin put in the baby's palm.

The moon,
the tiny fingernail,
and the silver farthing of deception!

But those who accept
deny themselves.
This is not the crown to be snatched from between two lions,
it's a kiss on the crown of the sun
and demands your life
together with your bone-ashes.

EULOGIST
The women
        brought forth their loves,
their frames fevered
with the heat of acceptance and nurturing;
desire flaming up
        from their waistlines.
And consummate beauty
was of chastity a cloak
            on their nudity.

WOMEN IN LOVE
Aside, lamenting
The root
        the deepest root
calls aloud from the heart of the earth:
            'The scent of the farthest flower bud
            must turn into honey!'

EULOGIST
Mothers,
        in their search for you,
have revived forgotten loves,
for
    your spilt blood
was a noble experience.

MOTHERS
The root
        the deepest root
calls aloud from the heart of the earth:

'The scent of the farthest flower bud
        must turn into honey!'
Oh, children!
Warm little children of earth,
        who are killed innocent
to open up the chambers of Heaven
unto your parents!-
We're seeing those chambers
        right now on earth,
not in the quivering mirage of a deceptive heaven,
with walls of steel
and shade of stone
under shadow-casting trees
whose green scent is the reminder of your blood
running
        in the roots of a deep faith.

EULOGIST
Men are descending the green footpaths,
with love on their figures
inevitable like moss on a rock;
and wounds upon their breasts
their eyes affection and hate,
their teeth
        in a smile of determination
are the hanging curved dagger of the moon
in the bandit night.

From the grim density
            into the darkness
they bore a cold tunnel
(where beech and maple have grown in vain
and growing is a task
        fulfilled by the yawning soil
even though the sun
with her shining blade
        every morning cuts
            a seedling's umbilical cord,
in an era when honour
                is an astounding rarity
that disturbs the quiescence of the dead
not the repose of the living.)

ORATOR

Oh, message fabricators, messengers!
What need is there
to imitate the saints
by sitting against the back-drop of a setting sun
in such a slow-passing day
and putting your head
in the sun's golden platter?
What need is there
to sit in a way
so that the sun's halo be seen
       around your face?

That concealed-visible dagger
has already proclaimed
the 'rightfulness' of this 'divine' mission!
The four-beat rhythm of a drum from far away
It suddenly stops.
A long heavy silence.

NARRATOR

The Demon
       is sternly posing
upon an enormous pedestal of stone
with the spittle of a satisfied sneer
       running down his chin.
Envoys
       from sea to sea, all over the land
knock on every door in search
and criers announce:
Far and near doors are knocked on.

CRIERS

In changing numbers and from various distances.
                    'Virgins
                    worthy of the Lord!
                    Virgins worthy
                    of the Lord!'

JESTER
Aside
For the garden of decay
is a prized legacy!
The garden of decay.
The garden of decay.
The garden of decay...

NARRATOR
But
      a shuddering question
whirls around you:

CONTENDERS
They have testified
that you've perceived
the time's boundless extent
in the four-syllabled cycle of the year;
you've testified
that you've seen
the God's secret
      in human shape
and perpetuity
         in love.
Would the Spring smile
in the bitter scent of the burning leaves
when the sun is spelt
in the fluffy snow spangle?

JESTER
Yes,
      but just a sneer.
The bailiffs are saints!
The bailiffs
are saints!

CONTENDERS
... And the absolute truth of the world, now
is nothing but these two blood-dripping cynical eyes.

ONE CONTENDER
These two watchful eyes
        in this head
lurking behind glass and stone
observing you.

JESTER
I know!
And if I trusted the truthfulness of my eyes
I would have known long before
that the image mirrored in the clarity of the sky
is nothing but my own distant image.

ORATOR
You must keep silent
if your message is nothing
            but lies
But
    if you have the chance to moan
            in freedom
then thunder out the message
and power it with your life.

CHRISTIANE AMANPOUR

View from the Front

I was twenty years old before my conscience kicked in, before I understood the real meaning of words like freedom and human rights. I am now forty and the intervening years sometimes seem like an atonement for that early ignorant indifference. My introduction to human rights *and* violations, came with the Islamic Revolution in Iran in 1979. Suddenly my whole world spun around. People I had grown up admiring and respecting were put before firing squads, a beloved uncle was tortured to death in prison.

Today some two decades later, Iran under the new president Mohammad Khatami, not only promises Iranians rule of law, but for the first time promises Iran will properly cooperate with the UN High Commissioner for Human Rights. Past Iranian leaders used to dismiss outside complaints, saying each society, each country has its own specific values and ideas on human rights. Indeed many world leaders ignore the universality of human rights. *Stay out of our affairs … respect our sovereignty*, they say.

In Algeria civilians, men, women and children, are slaughtered on an almost daily basis. Yet the government allows no proper investigation..

In Iraq, the government blames international sanctions for the terrible hardships inflicted on its people. In fact the government itself siphons off its precious resources to build opulent presidential palaces. They are called *people*'s palaces, but the only time the Iraqi people are allowed in is when Saddam Hussein needs human shields in case of a military strike. Using human shields, by the way is not just a violation of human rights, but a *war crime* under the Geneva Conventions.

In Algeria, Iran, Cuba and elsewhere, at least people speak their minds to visiting journalists. In Iraq they are too terrified. They fear a government spook hovering at their shoulder. The government has succeeded so completely in removing basic human rights, that unless an Iraqi knows exactly who he is talking to, he won't say anything meaningful.

My eight short years as a foreign correspondent for CNN, sometimes seem like a guidebook to human rights violations. I have seen tyranny, oppression, slavery, torture, indignity, inequality, invasion of privacy, the denial of political rights, arbitrary arrest, imprisonment, torture and execution, the denial of free speech and of freedom of association and of worship, female genital mutilation, child slaves, child soldiers, not to mention genocide and crimes against humanity.

But what astounds and appals me most is the often blind, deaf, silent response from the free world, the very societies that helped *draft* the Universal Declaration of Human Rights.

The governments, mostly American and European, knew about the rapes, the ethnic cleansing, the genocide in Bosnia for four years before doing anything serious to end it.

They knew about the mass slaughter in Rwanda, yet the UN chose to *withdraw* peacekeepers and allow it to continue until as many as a million people were dead ... in three months.

They know about the Taliban in Afghanistan systematically robbing women of their rights, yet few seriously condemn the Taliban.

They have known for six years about the mass murder in Algeria, and yet no government has properly condemned Algeria for failing to allow UN or any other independent investigations. Is it for lack of political clarity, or because of political and economic interests?

I believe *journalists* have a duty, especially in human rights cases. I will focus on Bosnia, where I have spent the most time, and witnessed many of the worst crimes.

Covering Bosnia was a personal and professional coming of age. Like many of my young colleagues, I started out mostly looking for adventure. But in Bosnia it soon became apparent that we journalists were not covering just another story. Terrible crimes were being committed, the like we had learned in our history lessons, would never again be tolerated. But *never again* was happening, in Europe, at the end of the 20th century, in full view of the world's cameras.

Sarajevo was besieged, ordinary men, women and children, shelled, sniped, starved. The same was happening in towns and villages around Bosnia. Early on, in August 1992, journalists exposed the concentration camps. Civilians were being expelled from their homes because of their religious beliefs. A new word was coined for what was happening in Bosnia: ethnic cleansing.

Bosnia was not a war, it was a bloodbath. Yet, on New Year's eve 1992, four months after the discovery of concentration camps, the then UN Secretary General Boutros Boutros Ghali visited Sarajevo and stunned its citizens with this observation: 'You have a situation which is better than ten other places all over the world. I can give you a list of ten places where you have more problems than in Sarajevo'. Srebrenica, which later became synonymous with genocide, was dismissed then, by Boutros Boutros Ghali as but 'a village in Europe'.

I mention this because it illustrates the institutional indifference about Bosnia and the wholesale violation of human rights there, not just at the highest levels of the UN but also in Western capitals.

We journalists felt then we had a *duty* to keep reporting, to confront the official lies and get the true story out. The true story involved distinguishing between aggressor and victim. That introduced a moral dimension. I decided early on to examine the concept of objectivity and its meaning here. It was a struggle because objectivity is a journalist's golden rule. But I, and many of my colleagues realised that objectivity means giving all sides an equal hearing, it does not mean *treating* all sides equally. When you do that, when you cannot distinguish between victim and aggressor, rapist and victim, you enter the zone of moral–equivalence. And that in a clear case of genocide, and crimes against humanity, means you are but a step away from acting as an accessory.

I could not and would not do that. I took some hits, people complained I had lost my objectivity that I was siding with one faction. My answer is that I sought the truth, and I became aware of the moral dimension to our profession. I also became aware of the power of a journalist's words and the consequences they have.

World leaders, US and European governments, were trying to say that all sides in the Bosnian conflict were 'equally guilty', that the atrocities were a result of 'centuries of ethnic hatred'. This of course was untrue. It was designed to muddy the waters, confuse public opinion and avoid the necessity of intervening.

It was our job to make that clear. And I don't mind admitting that we as a profession, who had been derided as 'laptop bombardiers', felt vindicated when intervention in 1995 actually did end the war and set Bosnia on the road to peace.

Twenty years after discovering a conscience, I put it to use. I believed the way I reacted professionally in Bosnia would shape not only the way my reports were perceived, but would shape me forever as a person.

Having started out being told that any country, anyone, can tailor human rights to suit themselves, I discovered what human rights really are. From Bosnia to Somalia, from Cuba to Iran, from Afghanistan to Vietnam, I learned that people know and want their rights.

Having started out ignorant and somewhat indifferent, I have found that our profession can be a power for good, can advance universal rights, can expose those who would destroy them.

I would like to close with words from Edward R. Murrow, an American, a journalist, a giant. About television he said: 'This instrument can teach, can illuminate, yes, and it can even inspire. But it can do so only to the extent that humans are determined to use it to those ends. Otherwise it is merely lights and wires in a box'.

Article 3

Everyone has the right to life, liberty and security of person.

ABDULLAHI AN-NA'IM

The Universal Declaration as a Living and Evolving 'Common Standard of Achievement'

In the glorious language of its preamble, the Universal Declaration of Human Rights was proclaimed by the UN General Assembly in 1948 'as a common standard of achievement for all peoples and all nations....' In this tribute to the Universal Declaration on its 50th anniversary, I wish to reflect on the meaning and implications of this truly inspired characterization. The main thrust of my contribution is that, to be a common standard of achievement, the Universal Declaration must be a *living and constantly evolving* instrument of sustained and enlightened change so that all human beings are truly 'free and equal in dignity and rights', not only at birth as affirmed by Article 1, but throughout their lives.

Although the picture is mixed, and will probably remain so, there is no doubt that significant improvements have been made in the protection of human rights throughout the world. But it is precisely because of these advances, and recent spectacular changes in global political and economic relations, that, if it is to be a common standard of achievement, the Universal Declaration cannot remain trapped in the vision of its inception. The standard of achievement for humanity today cannot be the same as that of half a century ago. Each generation must determine the common standard of achievement of its time in relation to the causes and dynamics of injustice and oppression as understood and experienced by that generation.

For example, to those who drafted and adopted the Universal Declaration in 1948, decolonization and independent statehood probably appeared to lead automatically to the protection and promotion of the human rights of the peoples of Africa and Asia. In hindsight, we know that traditional colonialism has been replaced by other forms of exploitative and oppressive economic and political relations. We also have a better appreciation now of the risks and drastic consequences of internal colonialism within a country. A present-day under-standing of the meaning of the Universal Declaration as a common standard of achievement for human rights would clearly address these and other possible transformations of colonialism as sources of systematic and gross violations of human rights, by whatever name they are known.

A living and evolving standard of achievement must build on and promote the universality of human rights as proclaimed by the Universal Declaration, and should never repudiate its principles or diminish its relevance and efficacy. The essence of human rights is to protect individuals and groups against the excesses of their own state or society on the basis of internationally agreed standards that apply equally to all societies. In contrast, relativism claims that a state or society can only be bound by its own standards, and that it is free to treat individuals and groups as it pleases. In other words, relativism is the negation of the essence of universal human rights.

Yet the dangers of relativism must be taken very seriously because those who support it usually do so in the name of religious or cultural self-determination: the right of a people to govern themselves in accordance with their own norms and values. Such claims are difficult to challenge except by reconciling the norms and values of the society with its human rights obligation.

In Islamic societies, for instance, restrictions on the rights of women or religious minorities are usually justified as being required by Islam. Since any Muslim would find it difficult to openly challenge what is commonly believed to be required by Islam, restrictions on the rights of women and religious minorities can best be challenged by showing that they are not in fact required by Islam in the present context of Islamic societies. While previous generations of Muslims understood Islam to require such restrictions in accordance with their own historical context, this is no longer a tenable interpretation of Islamic scriptural sources. A purely secular justification of universal human rights is unlikely to prevail over Islamic objections, but an Islamic justification is both possible and more likely to be accepted by Muslims.

Besides such tactical considerations, there is a more principled reason for the need to engage the internal religious and cultural resources of different societies in the legitimation of the Universal Declaration. If the human rights it proclaims are truly universal, they must be recognized as such by different societies on the basis of their own world view, value system and practical experience. Although not a binding treaty, the Universal Declaration is generally accepted as the definitive founding document of the international human rights movement because of its moral force and practical resonance in the lives of all types of human societies around the world. This moral authority is unlikely to be accepted by societies if it is believed to be inconsistent with the established authority of their religion and practical experience.

It is true that engaging in discussions about religious and cultural justifications for human rights may support claims of relativism by conceding moral authority to religious and cultural considerations. But that is a risk human rights advocates have to face in any case, whether or not they try to justify universal human rights in religious and cultural terms. The main issue is whether to be assertive or defensive about the relationship between human rights, on the one hand, and religion and culture, on the other.

Because I have found these tactical as well as principled reasons to be valid in my own experience, I wish to share this insight with others who may be in a similar position in relation to their respective religion or culture. I was born in 1946 in a village on the Nile in Northern Sudan, the first of eleven children, three of whom died in infancy. Raised a Muslim male, I grew up believing my immediate community to be the universal norm of human dignity and rights. But the values and social relations of that community are hardly consistent with the 'inherent dignity and equal inalienable rights of all members of the human family' asserted by the preamble of the Universal Declaration. In fact, during my childhood and youth, there was little public awareness of the Declaration, and its liberating power was appreciated only by a few liberal intellectuals. Dynamic leaders on both the left and right of Sudanese politics (Marxists at one extreme and Islamists at the other) paid lip service to the ideals of the Universal Declaration, but each group added its own ideological qualifications. How does one break away from the authority of family and immediate community, as well as the prevailing intellectual and political climate, in order to affirm universal human rights?

Another difficulty is that the great liberating potential of the Universal Declaration does not seem to have been realized, or even be realizable, for the vast majority of Sudanese. They cannot see how it might affect the quality of their daily lives, which has not improved significantly since independence in 1956. It is therefore not surprising to find rather strong skepticism among the vast majority of the Sudanese people today about the relevance and efficacy of the Universal Declaration. It is the task of people like me, who claim to have a more concrete and immediate appreciation of the relevance and utility of the Declaration, to keep its promise of liberation alive.

The Universal Declaration has given me personally assurance of my human dignity and entitlement to rights at home, and the privilege of belonging to a global community of human rights advocates abroad. This global community of human rights advocates has helped me transcend the narrow affiliations of my childhood and youth, while securing my sense of identity and human dignity in being who I am – a Sudanese Muslim advocate of human rights. But I have come to this appreciation of the Universal Declaration through a personal transformation made possible by the fact that I could challenge supposed Islamic justifications for rejecting the universality of human rights by finding Islamic foundations for their universality. I was able to achieve this transformation through the life and work of the late *Ustadh* Mahmoud Mohamed Taha (see his book *The Second Message of Islam* and my book *Toward an Islamic Reformation*). Without that understanding of Islam as a source of legitimation of human rights, I would not have known how to reconcile my religious beliefs with my commitment to the universality of human rights. Faced with a stark choice between my faith and a purely secular justification of the universality of human rights, I might have chosen the former, or at least remained torn between the two. But the insights of *Ustadh* Mahmoud resolved that conflict for me.

Notwithstanding this personal transformation, however, my ability to persuade other Sudanese of the relevance and utility of the Universal Declaration is contingent upon its ability to remain a 'common standard of achievement' for matters that make a difference in their lives. Instead of hearing assertions of human dignity and rights in the abstract, what they want to know is how the Declaration can help them to combat the current sources of human rights violations. Can the Universal Declaration enable them to address the structural sources of economic deprivation and political powerlessness, and generally liberate them from the consequences of colonialism that still remain, long after the termination of direct colonial rule?

The question today is therefore whether the Universal Declaration is capable of empowering communities around the world to challenge the international economic order that oppresses them, and to achieve genuine development on their own terms. Can the Declaration help the poor and powerless masses of Africa, Asia and Latin America to realize the economic, social and cultural rights it affirms in Articles 22 to 28? Does the liberating potential of the Declaration apply to collective rights to development or protection of the environment? It can and must do all of this, I believe, but not if it is trapped in the vision that created it fifty years ago.

In my view, the mandate for an evolving vision of the role of the Universal Declaration in response to emerging challenges is clear, since every violation of human dignity or the rights of any person or group tells us that we are not doing enough to realize the objective of the Declaration in that regard. For example, Article 25 of the Universal Declaration provides that everyone has a 'right to a standard of living adequate for the health and well-being of himself and of his family, including food, clothing, housing and medical care and necessary social services....' If this provision means what it says, and I believe it does, then these economic and social rights are as much human rights as the right to life, liberty and security of person (Article 3), protection against torture, cruel, inhuman or degrading treatment or punishment (Article 5), equality before the law without discrimination (Article 7), and freedom of opinion and expression (Article 19). No one would suggest that torture or violations of freedom of expression should be condoned or tolerated, yet there is little objection to our failure to provide for the basic need for food, shelter and medical care for the majority of human beings around the world.

It should also be emphasized that violations of any of the rights provided for by the Universal Declaration must be condemned and redressed with equal vigor, regardless of their source or cause. There is nothing in the language of the Declaration that limits human rights to the model of civil and political rights which requires the identification of an individual victim, violator and judicial remedy. In fact, Article 28 provides that '[e]veryone is entitled to a social and international order in which the rights and freedoms set forth in this Declaration can be fully realized'. To the majority of human beings around the world whose right to an adequate standard of living is violated, whatever the source or cause of the violation may be, the promise of the Universal Declaration remains unfulfilled. It is not good enough to say to them that you do not have a human right to housing, education or health care because we are unable to identify a specific violator and effective judicial remedy since these rights are violated by the global economic and trade relations and the under-development of your own countries, and so on.

The difference between what the Universal Declaration has achieved in the past and can achieve now and in the future is a result of who controls its meaning and implementation. Those who wanted the Universal Declaration to focus exclusively on individual civil and political rights will not want it to become an effective instrument for the realization of economic, social and cultural rights or of collective rights. But the global acceptance of the Universal Declaration in itself means that control over its meaning and implementation must also be shared among all those who uphold it as a common standard of human achievement. Otherwise, the Declaration's universal end of protecting and promoting human dignity and rights would be defeated.

So far I have been talking about the Universal Declaration as if it were an independent entity. In fact, it is always what human beings everywhere make of it in its actual interpretation and implementation. Therefore, those who believe in its liberating force will always face the challenge of ensuring that the Declaration remains a living and evolving common standard of achievement. They have to find and apply appropriate responses against whomever and whatever is obstructing the liberating potential of the Declaration by preserving exploitative economic relations and oppressive political conditions, at both the domestic and international levels.

In this respect, the Universal Declaration is similar to other founding constitutional documents or initiatives throughout history, only at a global rather than local or national level. Such documents and initiatives are always the subject of dispute between conservative forces seeking to preserve their privilege under the status quo, and innovative forces trying to redress economic, political and social injustice. As can be seen from the experience of the most established constitutional orders of Western Europe and North America, intense disputes about the meaning and implications of founding documents and initiatives are not only a permanent feature of the democratic process, but are also likely to lead to mixed results as each side strives for popular political support.

Moreover, the sorts of arguments that are likely to be used in disputes about the meaning and implications of the Universal Declaration are often similar to those used in domestic struggles over national constitutions: assertions of the purported intention of the framers of the original document versus emphasis on the current meaning and implications of the original intention of the framers, claims of hierarchies among rights to justify postponing one set of rights until another set of rights is realized, calling one set of rights (civil and political rights) true rights in the legal sense of the term, while others (economic, social and cultural rights or collective rights) are only aspirations or benefits to be realized over time through the political, economic and social processes of society.

But does the similarity between the Universal Declaration and national founding documents and initiatives also extend to the methods and processes through which such disputes about meaning and implications are mediated or settled? In the domestic context, national constitutions are interpreted and applied through the political and judicial processes of the country, in which the protagonists act through the organs and institutions of the state, political parties and other non-governmental organizations and groups. Do similar mechanisms and processes exist, or can they be devised, for the mediation or settlement of disputes about the Universal Declaration at the global level? It would be an exaggeration to answer this question in the affirmative, but it is reasonable to say that corresponding mechanisms and processes are beginning to emerge for the mediation of disagreements over the meaning and implications of the Declaration at the international level.

The United Nations and regional systems can be seen as the framework within which governments and international non-governmental human rights organizations compete for political and quasi-judicial support for their interpretations of the Universal Declaration. With recent shifts in political and economic configurations around the world, developments in communication technologies, and the medium of major international conferences (like the ones in Vienna in 1993, Cairo in 1994, and Beijing in 1995) new alliances are being built around human rights issues on the basis of changing understandings of self-interest. Pressure from a growing international civil society is forcing transnational corporations to adopt codes of conduct or engage in participatory approaches to development that are more 'human rights friendly'. But, as can be expected, these mechanisms and processes are available to conservative and innovative forces alike, in support of their differing understandings of the meaning and implications of the Universal Declaration today.

In my view, the Universal Declaration is the fundamental embodiment of the most significant political and social idea of our time. For that same reason, the meaning and implications of this founding document are and will remain the subject of intense debate between different forces at both the domestic and global levels. I also believe that the Universal Declaration has already realized some of its liberating potential, though that is often taken for granted because of the subtle organic way in which the norms and values of the Declaration have been absorbed in the moral and ideological consciousness of most societies around the world. The Declaration has become so much a part of the world view and value systems of very diverse societies that most of us are unaware of its profound influence.

But the challenge persists, probably more than ever before, precisely because of the success of the Universal Declaration. As people around the world are now exercising their fundamental human rights more than ever before, there is even greater demand for additional ways of realizing new possibilities for fulfilling their human potential. Will the Declaration remain as relevant and effective as a 'common standard of achievement' for this eager and deserving humanity? The answer depends on the moral and political choices we all make, and the action we take, each in our own context and according to whatever means of participation are available to each of us.

In conclusion, I wish to emphasize that choices and action in favor of human rights should be guided by two considerations. First, there is the need to guard against the danger of complacency in thinking that a society is secure against regression in its level of human rights achievement. In any case, even societies with the best human rights record cannot claim to have exhausted the protection and promotion of human rights because the measure of success keeps rising with the level of achievement – the more each society achieves, the greater the possibilities of further advancement and refinement.

Second, those societies with a relatively good record of human rights protection have an obligation to assist others who are at a lower level of achievement. The clause in the preamble of the Universal Declaration quoted at the beginning of this essay proclaims the Declaration as a common standard of achievement '... *to the end that* every individual and every organ of society ... shall strive by teaching and education to *promote respect* for these rights and freedoms and by progressive measures, national and international, to *secure their universal and effective recognition and observance....*' (emphasis added). This is what a common standard of achievement is all about, and it is only by implementing it throughout the world that we can really pay tribute to the Universal Declaration of Human Rights.

VEDAT TÜRKALI

Seventh Year

Comrades decamped and left one by one
Some got entangled with home and kids
Others are marrying freshly
Yet others with bread worries
Settled at their stalls
Nowadays occasional letters open our doors
We learn
From newspapers books periodicals
About mankind the world our country
No matter how much we read
It's not a friend's smiling face
The world of dark black print lifeless writing

I last saw my wife at the train station
The gendarmes were good lads and let us be
She stood by my side
So close so distant from my hands
I said we're getting old approaching forty
She was sad kept smiling
Then the children
Thoughts grab a man and sweep him away
A cloud envelops the speaker
Two and a half months the boy was the day they took me off
Kept crying in his mother's arms
Today he is seven the girl past fourteen
For years we've watched the country
From prisons like this
As if we've been forgotten on a desolate island
In history's most enlightened age
The years have sailed past the horizon like so many ships

Every day doors become more of an enemy
The iron colder the bars monstrous
The walls ready to strangle you every day

Days when your eyes can't catch sleep
You're in prison
Those who love you forget if they can
Only the enemy surrounding you
Doesn't forget
You too will live a lifetime
Not forgetting the enemy for a moment

Besides all that
The country's fallen into the hands of the perfidious enemy
Our country is communal property
When you start your movement
Your heart must be so full
That the iron bars must bend
The walls must fear your majesty
What awaits us are not laments
Nor death in Yemen's deserts nor defeat in the Caucasus
Nor soldiers at barrack doors
Nor bread coupons
Not even villages and cities bombed by aircraft
But thermonuclear war
To be wiped off the face of the earth in an atomic hell

Nature that gives life to an egg
Melted and drained away in barren darkness
Babies ended up extinct
Hasan Barış Deniz
Our children
Are slipping down the side of a precipice into a void without hope
Before my eyes
My arms stone my arms shorn of strength
Every breath frozen
The enemy standing over me
Eyes seething with snakes
Ears at my door ambush on my path
The land is under a scourge
There is the sleep of death in the land
Death has established sovereignty
Peasants driven away from the land
Wait at labourers' markets
Workers vomit blood at their counters
They broke their hands with rifle butts

Tore their feet into pieces sliced up their backs
Only yesterday in Antep during an election game
They assaulted our honest people with tanks

They take me out to the garden these days
I've leant against the wall
Gendarme opposite me
For a long time now I stopped caring
That the sun is so bright
The sky spotlessly blue
An ant's nest under my foot
Sparrows chirping and chirruping as they play on the ground
An owl the ku-ku-mav bird

On the chimney same place as yesterday
When it comes like this every day and squats on the chimneys
All the inmates go mad
When it gets dark and the doors shut
The deep ugly strangulated ku-ku-mav sound
Strikes a man as really strange
My head is loaded with dark thoughts
I said ku-ku-mav bird
These days in our country
You're tailor-made for the roof over there
Are you expecting something more fearful
Than these dark days

Once mankind learned how to laugh
News came from beyond the horizons
From Asia Africa the Pacific
People like daisy fields
With guns in their hands against the darkness
Learned how to laugh
The darkness was confused
The darkness was hopeless
You're waiting in vain ku-ku-mav bird

Let the dungeoner hide it anyway he can
The horizons are covered with tumult and good news
Hands like olive branch dove's wing
Hands stretching from mines
From the China Seas to Berlin

From plains to atomic stations
Wrist fearlessly wiping the sweat from its brow
It did what it had to do without chains
Minds spreading light over counters
They did what they had to do to those who made us vomit blood

Let the dungeoner hide it anyway he can
The horizons are covered with tumult and good news
All that we produced in chains
Now overflows from warehouses railways
Now the ships are confused
The harbour stinks of goods
They confiscated and left rotting in locked storehouses
Before we could sate the hunger in our stomachs
Now those approaching step by step from the horizons
Make the stock exchanges tremble in their dreams
Denying us even a morsel
They ate until they burst

In their torn gullet every mouthful like fire
Now infinite ability sweat of the brow eye's radiance face you
You with bloody hands cut off at the wrist
So bewildered so alone
You the leprous emperor of the land of fears
Your lips mercilessly on our pink veins
You worm you leech stuck on the earth
Protect yourself if you can
From the hammering hoofs of
The rearing thoroughbred

Suddenly a rain of stones fell on the roof opposite
It chased away the ku-ku-mav bird
From the garden of the fifth block
We need to go in
Before the guard blows his whistle
Cold descends towards night
On the seventh year of imprisonment
There is joy too in thinking of these things
A winter's day in Anatolia
In the garden of a prison
At the foot of a wall
Facing the sun

AUNG SAN SUU KYI

Individual Human Rights and the World Community

It is now fifty years since the United Nations declared that there are inalienable human rights which constitute the foundation of freedom, justice and peace in our world. Freedom from want and fear is the most basic of these rights. Our human dimensions become stunted when we are subjected to the continuous assault of insecurity and terror. Under conditions where free thought and expression, initiative and creativity, are stifled, there is little room for growth and progress. Our very humanity can become debased in a struggle for survival within a climate of physical, mental and spiritual deprivation. It is thus essential for the future of our human race that strenuous efforts be made to protect and promote the belief that all human beings are born free and equal in dignity and rights.

Lack of respect for fundamental human rights inevitably leads to conflict within human society. The argument that insistence on individual human rights is inimical to the interests of the wider community fails to take into consideration the reciprocal nature of rights and obligations. Just as we are entitled to demand and defend our basic rights, so are we obliged to respect and concede the rights of others. Universal observance of human rights is the best prophylactic against violence and disorder. The infringement of the fundamental rights of a single individual is the seed for wider violations, violations that could spill across national borders and lead to widespread suffering and destruction. It is therefore of the utmost importance that the international community make a strenuous effort to secure the 'universal and effective recognition and observance' of the articles of the Universal Declaration of Human Rights.

Article 3 in the Universal Declaration states that '[e]veryone has the right to life, liberty and security of person.' Such an unarguably fundamental right. Yet this right is violated almost on a daily basis in Burma. There are so few of us who can be confident that our liberty will not be taken away from us at the whim of those in power. There are many who have already experienced the loss of their liberty, not because they have committed any crime but because they decided to follow the dictates of their conscience. There are some who have lost their lives because they decided to stand firmly by the democratic principles of freedom and justice. The right to life, liberty and security of person remains a mere dream for us and for other peoples ruled by dictatorial regimes that ignore the needs and rights of their citizens.

Lack of a sense of security constitutes the most destabilizing factor in any society. Seemingly unassailable authoritarian states have collapsed like a house of cards when repeated violations of human rights wore down the tolerance of the people and ate away at the foundations of development and prosperity. Unhappy, frightened citizens inhibit peace and progress; repressive governments that rule by fear prevent the emergence of strong, stable nations that are capable of living in harmony with their neighbours.

In this year of the golden anniversary of the Universal Declaration of Human Rights, I hope that all the free peoples of the world will be inspired to take united action to turn the dreams of their oppressed brethren into reality. By working for basic human rights we shall be working for the promotion of freedom, justice and peace on our globe and thus ensuring the happy survival of our human race.

Article 4

No one shall be held in slavery or servitude; slavery and the slave trade shall be prohibited in all their forms.

BISHOP CARLOS FILIPE XIMENES BELO

The Dignity of the Individual

Human Rights and Natural Law

There are some who trace the origins of human rights back as far as the Stoics, since their writings already emphasised the dignity of *all men* by virtue of the fact that they are men, regardless of race, nationality, etc. These were the first manifestations of *natural law*. The Ancients focused their concerns on the morality of the city, and not all were city-dwellers.....

However, it was not until later, through the influence of Christianity, that the idea of human dignity took root in our culture: the idea that all men were children of God ('there is neither Jew nor Greek, there is neither bond nor free, there is neither male nor female....'). *All men*, created in the image and likeness of God, were essentially equal and all were called upon to become children of God in Christ.

Man could thus come to know natural law, which was older and greater than positive law (in other words, temporal power and its laws). According to theologians, this natural law was the same *divine law* which was imprinted in the heart of man, and whose signs were a sense of morality and, above all, an unconditional perception of duty. Without explicitly invoking God as the source of this law, they all at the very least acknowledged *moral conscience* as the immediate norm for all human action and as something sacrosanct.

Clearly, the individual conscience, while it was the indispensable immediate norm for morally endowed action, was not the *ultimate* norm – whether because man was not the overall inventor of his own rational structure (much less the creator of existence) or because the individual conscience could be mistaken (see the problem of *erroneous conscience*). What this meant was this: while ethics – which lay at the origin of all law – could only emerge from *freedom*, freedom was not the last word, for it was always freedom *to do* something else which transcended it. Conscience, then, was always called upon to rectify itself through the *truth*; and so truth had precedence over freedom, just as *judgment* had precedence over *decision*.

The concept of the human dignity of *every man* was thus of divine (trinitarian and Christological) origin in Judaeo-Christian thought, or of purely moral origin in lay philosophical thought. So how did we get from the mere consideration of human dignity to human rights? The step from human dignity to human rights – from natural law to natural rights – was taken in the modern age, in which the autonomy of the human order came to the fore. With justice and reason shorn of their divine element, man was not seen – at least not directly – as the beneficiary of divine ordinance, but as an individual being *with rights*.

THE HISTORICAL CONQUEST OF HUMAN RIGHTS

Although human rights are inherent in man as such, it is only within a historical process that they are acknowledged, specified and made concrete; they are not merely a theoretical product, but are historically embodied in *norms and institutions* whose purpose is to define and protect the various aspects of the personality in the specific context of society.

The English-Speaking Countries. Before the modern sovereign state became established, the first historical affirmation of human rights took place through treaties – the most natural way of resolving issues of power. A famous example is the Magna Carta (1215), in which King John of England acknowledged certain freedoms by undertaking not to have people killed, banished or denied justice arbitrarily. However, this was not a normative acknowledgement of *rights*, but a kind of compromise; moreover, these freedoms were not so much freedoms as privileges granted to certain strata of society (aristocratic privileges, Church prerogatives, municipal freedoms) – rights, not of equality, but of inequality.

The rights secured in the course of England's 17th-century Puritan revolution were statements of a general nature. The Petition of Right (1628), the Habeas Corpus Act (1640) and the Bill of Rights (1689) – especially the latter – may be seen as 'constitutional' human rights, even though in their formulation they retained the empirical character of mediaeval treaties.

These rights were transplanted to England's colonies and were eventually to bear fruit in the American Revolution. The Declarations of Rights of the American states which were then formulated – the first of these were in Virginia, Pennsylvania and Maryland (all in 1776), the most famous being that of Virginia, drawn up by Madison – and later the federal Constitution (1787) and its various Amendments (particularly the first ten, also known as the Bill of Rights) already stated human rights in universal, solemn terms. Here Anglo-Saxon pragmatism joined hands with the rationalism so typical of the age, reinforced by an awareness that a new political society was being created. In a community marked by the experience of religious exile, Anglo-Saxon pragmatism claimed to provide an effective guarantee of rights (this is why Hegel, in his *Reason in History*, asserted that the United States would brook no compromise in matters of freedom, because of the religious conflicts which its people had experienced in Europe before moving to the New World).

The French Contribution. The French contribution to human rights is more recent but also more dramatic (and it should not be forgotten that, for good or ill, Portugal is very much the child of the French Enlightenment, which was very different from its English and German equivalents). The Declaration of the Rights of Man and of the Citizen of 1789, which overshadowed ensuing declarations made in 1791, 1793 and 1795, was the formal, solemn expression of a rationalist concept of natural law, and proclaimed a set of rights based on freedom, security and property as being inalienable natural rights of man. Profoundly marked by revolutionary sentiment, the Declaration was phrased in solemn, grandiloquent terms, and was more concerned to lay the *new foundations* of society than to protect freedom in practice against the specific dangers which threatened it.

This is why it is said that it was France which gave us a philosophy of freedom, but the English-speaking countries (especially the United States) which gave us the first examples of legislation designed to protect freedom.

The Conquest of Equality. The first stage in the formulation of human rights had come to an end, but the rationalist, self-sufficient, progressive optimism of the Enlightenment soon fell foul of reality. The framework of liberal thought guaranteed physical freedom and curtailed abuses of power for the common good, but only certain people were able to benefit from this; in decreeing economic freedom and *guaranteeing property as an absolute right*, it excluded vast segments of the population from participation in public life and abandoned the poor and the weak to their fate.

The conquest of human rights thus continued in accordance with the principles of fraternity and equality. Among the rights now claimed were rights of political participation (freedom of information, freedom to demonstrate, universal suffrage), workers' rights (the right to form trade unions, the right to strike, the right to periods of rest and to minimum conditions of health and safety), and the rights of disadvantaged groups (the right of the sick, the disabled, mothers, children and the elderly to receive care). These claims went hand in hand with the great social upheavals which shook the liberal states to their foundations and eventually led to the emergence of the welfare and socialist states (particularly significant in this connection are the 19th-century Marxist ideology and Pope Leo XIII's Encyclical *Rerum Novarum* – cf. Pope John Paul II's Encyclical Letter *Centesimus Annus*).

Thus, in addition to the traditional rights of freedom, there were now new *rights of political participation* and *economic, social and cultural rights*. Whereas the former had required the state to refrain from intervening, the latter required the state to take responsibility for creating the legal and material conditions needed in order for all people to enjoy their rights effectively. However, it should be noted that there was always to be tension between the interventionist and liberal facets of the state, especially in economic matters, and inconsistency between the *formal* character of freedoms and rights and their *practical implementation* ('real freedoms').

INTERNATIONAL PROTECTION OF HUMAN RIGHTS

Within each country, various forces (social, cultural, religious, etc.) worked to achieve legal and constitutional protection of basic human rights. However, there was a new development in the 20th century, particularly after the horrors of the Second World War (although the humanitarian doctrine had first emerged back in the 19th century, in the form of conventions against slavery and on the treatment of prisoners of war). The new development was that human rights began to be protected *worldwide*. This was symbolised by the Universal Declaration of Human Rights (1948), but since then there have been numerous other conventions designed to protect human rights.

Conventions. The International Covenant on Civil and Political Rights and the International Covenant on Economic, Social and Cultural Rights were signed in 1966 (they entered into force in 1976 and have since been ratified by some 140 countries). Other examples of global human rights conventions are the Geneva Conventions relative to the Treatment of Prisoners of War and to the Protection of Civilian Persons in Time of War, the International Convention on the Elimination of All Forms of Racial Discrimination, and the ILO Convention concerning the Abolition of Forced Labour. At the regional level we have the following examples: the American Convention on Human Rights (signed in San José, Costa Rica, 1969 – the USA, Argentina and Brazil were not among the signatories, entered into force in 1978), the European Convention for the Protection of Human Rights and Fundamental Freedoms (signed in 1950, entered into force in 1953, with eleven additional Protocols), the European Social Charter (signed in 1961, entered into force in 1965), and the African Charter on Human and Peoples' Rights (signed in Nairobi, 1981, entered into force in 1986).

The Effectiveness of Legal and Institutional Protection. It is true that the principle of respect for human rights has not yet been adopted by the international community as a *principle which is independent of the will of individual countries*. Nevertheless, the idea that human rights only concern the relationship between each individual and the country of which he is a national or a resident is now outmoded. This is because international public opinion has been alerted by such bodies as Amnesty International and the International Commission of Jurists; at the same time, many countries now accept the notion that their citizens may appeal *directly and individually* to international bodies whenever they consider themselves restricted in the enjoyment of rights laid down in the conventions ratified by those countries.

The Difficulties of Achieving Effective Universal Protection of Human Rights. The set of 'international' human rights claims to represent the common denominator of the different sensibilities of countries which differ, sometimes radically, in their manner of political, economic, religious or cultural organisation. This is why, in addition to individual rights, we must also consider the rights of peoples (it should not be forgotten that the theory of *ius gentium* – in terms of the right to self-determination and peace – was first formulated in the Iberian Peninsula).

This explains the lack of uniformity in the interpretation of the provisions laid down in the various conventions, the ways in which they are applied, and the severity of the punishments imposed if they are infringed. *We are dealing here with differing views of man and his basic rights*: the liberal (now liberal-social) view, the Marxist-Leninist view, Third World views, imperialist and fundamentalist views, etc. It is not surprising, for example, that the protection of human rights has progressed further in Europe, has run into obstacles in the USA (particularly in the economic and social spheres), is seriously hampered in Eastern countries (as far as civil and political rights are concerned), and is almost entirely lacking in many Third World countries, where not even the most basic individual rights are protected (as far as radical Islam is concerned, the *individual* as such does not even exist).

Awareness of this reality does not, however, permit an infinitely elastic interpretation of human rights (the notion of the *objectivity and universality* of human rights continues to be based on the profound *dignity of the individual*, which may not be infringed for any reason, be it economic, political or whatever; however, in today's world there are many countries, particularly ones outside the Christian tradition, that have yet to discover the sacrosanct, irreplaceable value of the individual – which can never be a means, but is always an 'end in itself').

Article 5

No one shall be subjected to torture or to cruel, inhuman or degrading treatment or punishment.

TONY BLAIR

The Universal Declaration as a Source of Inspiration

I was delighted to be asked to contribute to this publication commemorating one of the earliest and most important texts adopted by the United Nations. The Universal Declaration of Human Rights was the first definition by UN members of the human rights and fundamental freedoms they had pledged to promote. Its adoption in 1948 came in the aftermath of a world war that had brought unparalleled devastation and human misery. Its message then was inspirational. It remains so today.

The Universal Declaration of Human Rights is the basis of the entire international framework of human rights. It sets a common standard of achievement for all peoples and all nations. It lists numerous rights – civil, political, economic, social and cultural – to which people everywhere are entitled. Five decades on, it has lost none of its relevance to the lives of people around the globe.

Commemorative events in 1998 give us an opportunity to look back on what has been achieved over the last fifty years and to reflect on the challenges that remain as we enter the next century. Many of these challenges will be faced by the next generation. We should focus our commemorations on the Universal Declaration's relevance to young people.

We are not looking at standards that express the values of any single region, culture or religion. It is the universality of human rights that gives them their strength and moral force. As the United Nations Secretary-General said in December 1997:

> Human rights are universal not only because their roots exist in all cultures and traditions. Their modern universality is founded on their endorsement by all 185 members of the United Nations. The Declaration itself was the product of debates between a uniquely representative group of scholars, a majority of whom came from the non-Western world.

The significance of the Universal Declaration lies both in the text itself and in its wider impact beyond the United Nations. Many newly independent countries have cited it in their basic laws or constitutions. Its provisions have been referred to in courts of law. The principle of universality asserted in the Universal Declaration is reflected in regional instruments, including the American Convention on Human Rights and the African Charter on Human and Peoples' Rights.

Perhaps most importantly from Britain's perspective, it was the inspiration for the

European Convention on Human Rights. The widespread ratification of that Convention has significantly enhanced the protection of human rights on our continent. For over thirty years, people in the United Kingdom have been able to go to Strasbourg to enforce their rights in the Court there. The new Labour Government in Britain is now fulfilling the promise it made to the British people to make the European Convention part of British domestic law. It is one of the principal pillars of our constitutional reform programme to modernise Britain.

The Universal Declaration also helped shape the development of human rights treaties within the United Nations. In September 1948, Ernest Bevin, the British Foreign Secretary, called on the General Assembly to adopt the Declaration, describing it as 'this great instrument'. He said:

> If there were a definition agreed upon among us as to what human rights each should safeguard, if there were provision among us for the free movement of information as well as of individuals, the tension between us would be immediately relieved and misunderstanding between us would be ultimately removed.

The last part of that challenge has still to be met. But with the Universal Declaration as its starting point, the United Nations has indeed elaborated over the years what amounts to the international community's definition of human rights. With the participation of countries from all regions, we have seen the creation of a framework of human rights treaties, each with universal application. These include the international covenants on civil and political rights, and economic, social and cultural rights, a convention against torture, and conventions to eliminate racial discrimination and discrimination against women.

Let me take as an example the most recent of these, the Convention on the Rights of the Child. Its adoption in 1989 had a clear link to the Universal Declaration, in which the United Nations had proclaimed that childhood was entitled to special care and assistance and appropriate legal protection.

The Convention reaffirms the message that everyone has human rights, including children. It covers civil and political rights such as freedom of expression, thought, conscience and religion. And economic and social rights, including a child's right to proper standards of education, health and protection from harm. These rights apply to all children equally whatever their race, colour, sex, religion, language, disability, ethnic or social origin. It makes clear that on issues that affect children, they too have the right to have their views carefully considered by courts and other bodies.

The Convention sets out legally binding obligations on acceding states. Hundred ninety-one states have now accepted them, making it the most widely ratified human rights treaty. The main responsibility for implementation rests with governments, who are required to report progress to an independent expert committee. In Britain we are about to start work on our next report. We will have a process of extensive consultation and co-operation with the many agencies with an interest in children's rights and well-being. We will ensure too that children's contributions are included in our report.

The Convention is not simply a theoretical abstraction. It provides a starting point for countries to co-operate in tackling serious human rights problems affecting children. For example, Britain and other donors provide development assistance to help countries stamp out abusive child labour practices. The United Kingdom recently funded a partnership programme in Pakistan to provide practical alternatives to using children in the football stitching industry. In recent years too, there has been increased international action to combat the commercial sexual exploitation of children. We have passed new laws to crackdown on British citizens involved in such despicable acts. Our police have run training programmes in countries where children are involved in prostitution. In all these cases, we are helped in having common international standards to be applied and common obligations under the Convention.

The United Nations and child agencies have done much to publicise the Convention on the Rights of the Child in a way that is meaningful and of interest to young people. We face a similar challenge in publicising the Universal Declaration in its fiftieth year.

Whenever I meet young people at home and abroad, I am struck by their interest in the world around them. They want to get involved with global issues such as human rights. I want to tap that energy and creativity, so that the commemoration of the Universal Declaration is forward looking and seen as relevant to individuals' daily lives.

That is why in Britain the new Labour Government is working closely with the United Nations associations and human rights non-governmental organisations to direct the message towards young people. We have helped fund information packs on the Universal Declaration for schools, with practical ideas for project work and competitions. Around the country, lawyers have agreed to visit schools to give talks on human rights. There are also plans for inter-school debates modelled on the UN Commission on Human Rights. All of these activities, involving young people directly, should help to raise awareness of the Universal Declaration and its continuing relevance.

Human rights may sometimes seem an abstraction in the comfort of the West. But when they are ignored, human misery and political instability all too easily follow. Our message in 1998 should be clear. We should all pledge to redouble our efforts to ensure that the principles set out in the Universal Declaration are translated into daily practice around the world.

RENDRA

Song of the Full Moon

The moon rises from the sea,
unravelling her long, tangled hair.
Towards midnight,
her round face
shines on the cardboard shanties
of Jakarta.

The sky is crystal clear.
Thieves play on their guitars.
The prostitutes are getting on famously.
The bright night is a boon to taxi drivers
and a portent of good-fortune to the coffee stalls.

The full moon settles in a maidservant's hair.
Her radiant glow
makes her master tremble.

'Come here, you!'
'No sir. I'm afraid of madam.'
The night confuses him;
he steps into the kitchen
and seizes her.

The moon enters her belly
and slowly rises to her head,
forming beautiful dreams.

About two o'clock,
the moon comes down to the highway,
wearing a white satin frock
and a fragrant perfume.
The police take her
and offer her to a state visitor,
hungry for entertainment.

EMMA BONINO

Humanitarian Aid and International Policy

It is to the ethical and political sensibilities of Jacques Delors and Manuel Marin that the European Union owes the establishment in 1992 of the European Community Humanitarian Office (ECHO), through which the European Commission has managed, within the space of a few years, to affirm the presence of a united Europe in over sixty countries throughout the world. For some time Europe has been, and is set to remain, the main world donor of emergency aid and ECHO – whose annual expenditure varies between ECU 600 and 700 million – is much more than a new administrative structure designed to merge and rationalise the various flows of funding earmarked in the past for humanitarian aid.

The Humanitarian Office is now among the leading observers of the most difficult crises afflicting mankind. For this, the European Union owes a debt of gratitude to Delors and Marin who provided us – in the ongoing absence of a common foreign and security policy – with an 'ethical touchstone' that compels us to perceive certain international crises from the point of view of the human suffering they entail, which we must then seek to relieve. This is not always an easy task as ethics and politics do not always go hand in hand.

When I was appointed European Commissioner for Humanitarian Affairs, in the first few days of 1995, I was immediately reassured by the enormous flow of funds that Europe, through its taxpayers, channels into humanitarian aid. As time passed, I became aware of a less reassuring fact: the humanitarian policies of some European states are not always consistent with their diplomatic policy. Let me try to explain.

Humanitarian aid is a policy that is not really a policy. Saving human lives, relieving suffering, defending people's dignity and 'humanising war' (to use the words of the Red Cross) are worthy endeavours in themselves. However, in order to perform these worthy tasks, i.e. to provide humanitarian aid that is independent, impartial and free from any kind of external influence, a number of rules have absolutely to be respected, starting with those international conventions on human rights to which the member states of the United Nations are all signatories. Such respect is becoming less and less common.

We know from the reports that we receive on the major humanitarian crises of our time – from the former Yugoslavia to the African Great Lakes region, via the Caucasus and South-East Asia – that human rights are being systematically and deliberately violated and that those values to which we attach great importance are inexorably being eroded.

We might expect our politicians and diplomats, in their day-to-day endeavours to contend with these crises, to express their anxiety about the massive violations of human rights that unfailingly accompany violations of international law. This is not always the case. The system of gender apartheid that has been imposed for over a year on the women of Afghanistan has not stopped other governments – in that region and elsewhere – from entering into dialogue with the fanatical Taliban faction in power in Kabul. The saga of the United Nations Commission of Inquiry into the massacres that took place in the former Zaire, now known once more as the Congo, between 1996 and 1997 – a Commission openly boycotted and scorned by the new regime in Kinshasa – has not stopped the leaders of many democratic countries from making common cause with a government that is manifestly inimical to any form of justice. These are only some examples.

Every time a voice is raised against these contradictions in an attempt to place the ethical dimension at the centre of the debate on the conflicts by which our century has been beset, someone else explains that it is very difficult, if not impossible, to reconcile humanitarian action, based on abstract principles and values, and political action, governed – we are told – by the pursuit of realism. From this point of view, principles, however commendable they may be, do not provide a sound basis for tackling a crisis, since what is needed are realistic solutions.

I shall never be convinced by this argument. I am becoming more and more convinced that a diplomacy which is based solely on interests, and on a national and/or regional perception of these interests, is unsustainable. I continue to believe that Europe, and the rest of the world, has no alternative other than a foreign policy firmly anchored in morality and based on principles that start with respect for people's dignity. What we need are transparent political choices that we can explain with our heads held high to our national politicians, public and media.

Fortunately I am not the only person who believes that states have a duty to defend ideals as well as interests. In the USA, the school of *Realpolitik* is now being counterbalanced by the school of *Idealpolitik,* in which a diplomacy based on ideals is considered – in the long term – to be the most realistic form of diplomacy of all. Provided, of course, that its objectives are to extend the frontiers of peace, human rights and well-being.

I come from a political family that considers the respect of rights to be sacrosanct; a family that, under the slogan *There is no peace without justice,* launched a campaign for the establishment of a permanent International Criminal Court responsible for trying war crimes and crimes against humanity.

As long as diplomacy continues to lack any ethical or moral values, new 'monsters' are likely to come to the fore throughout the world: 'local' allies – chosen yesterday in the name of pragmatism or of national interests – whose ambition to become uncontrollable outlaws we discover far too late. The list is far too long, ranging from Saddam Hussein to the Taliban and including Jonas Savimbi in Angola and the unlamented Mobutu.

I am not so naive as to be unaware that the international community and its highest expression, the United Nations, is nothing other than a reflection of the will of the individual states that make up this community. What is needed, however, is for someone somewhere to state a very simple truth: that if a national or international authority tolerates the violation of established rules on a couple of occasions, it must be prepared to endure – sooner or later – the systematic violation of those rules.

Those of us who are concerned with humanitarian aid have no choice. There is no way that we can disregard the violations of human rights occurring before our very eyes. If we remain silent in the face of crimes against humanity, even if this silence is in the name of the impartiality of humanitarian aid, we risk becoming accomplices. Our duty to assist all victims of all conflicts does not mean that we cannot identify those who are oppressors and those who are oppressed, those who are persecutors and those who are persecuted.

The task of humanitarian aid is not to find solutions to crises or the means of doing so, but one thing is certain: without our testimony, without humanitarian aid workers on the spot (the same could also be said of the media) it becomes much more difficult to understand why conflict has arisen, to re-establish a minimum of justice and to find the way out of a crisis.

It will be impossible for Europe to export its values further afield as long as we do not have a common foreign and security policy able to provide our community with a single voice and a single political approach – at least on those occasions when it is most needed.

Article 6

Everyone has the right to recognition everywhere as a person before the law.

THEO VAN BOVEN

A Universal Declaration of
Human Responsibilities?

In early September 1997 a prominent group of elderly statesmen – former heads of state and government – assembled in the InterAction Council launched a proposal for a Universal Declaration of Human Responsibilities. It was suggested that the United Nations should adopt such a Declaration on 10 December 1998 on the fiftieth anniversary of the Universal Declaration of Human Rights. The proposed Universal Declaration of Human Responsibilities, the result of some ten years of work, consists of a preamble and nineteen articles and draws its inspiration, as regards form, structure and content, from the Universal Declaration of Human Rights. According to the introduction the InterAction Council regards the proposed Declaration as a necessary complement to the Universal Declaration of Human Rights, so as to balance freedom with responsibility, but also as 'a means of reconciling ideologies, beliefs and political views that were deemed antagonistic in the past'.

Given the prominence of its initiators and supporters, who were assisted by experts from a variety of backgrounds and disciplines, and considering the scale of their ambition to see their initiative consecrated by the United Nations on 10 December 1998, the proposal for a Universal Declaration of Human Responsibilities deserves due attention.

UNDERLYING MOTIVES

To illustrate the motives behind the proposal, the introduction relates the notion of human responsibilities to the globalization of the world economy. It states that '[g]lobalization of the world economy is matched by global problems, and global problems demand global solutions on the basis of ideas, values and norms respected by all cultures and societies'. Continuing in the same vein, in its letter recommending the adoption of the draft Universal Declaration the InterAction Council declared that '[i]n a world transformed by globalization, common ethical standards for living together have become an imperative, not only for individual behaviour but also for corporations, political authorities and nations'. And it argued that unbridled freedom operates at the expense of present and future generations and that as a consequence freedoms and responsibilities have to be brought into balance.

CRITICAL QUESTIONS

At first glance the proposed document evokes a sense of approval. The concerns of the former heads of state and government are certainly genuine and widely shared and the initiative of the InterAction Council would seem to deserve the recognition and gratitude of all who regard human rights and human responsibilities as interdependent and indivisible notions. However, after further reflection the proposal does raise a number of doubts and critical questions. In particular one starts to wonder whether the proposed Universal Declaration is an adequate response to the problems of globalization, as envisaged. Moreover, whether a Universal Declaration of Human Responsibilities should be devised as a sort of 'twin' of the Universal Declaration of Human Rights, with the same style and in similar wording, is open to question. Before reviewing these two important issues, it may be useful to take a brief look at existing texts which link human rights with human duties.

BALANCING RIGHTS AND DUTIES

At the time of the drafting of the Universal Declaration of Human Rights in the years immediately after the Second World War, many of the authors were clearly influenced by a deep sense of horror at the inhuman and cruel policies and practices of totalitarian regimes. With total disregard for all fundamental human rights and freedoms, these regimes demanded absolute and servile submission to the state, the party and the official ideology, with full emphasis on duties. It is well known that some of those who played a key role in the conceptualization of the Universal Declaration of Human Rights, notably René Cassin and Eleanor Roosevelt, were very mindful of the policies and practices of totalitarian regimes and were therefore not in favour of laying great emphasis on human duties. It was their objective that the International Bill of Human Rights, of which the Universal Declaration of Human Rights was to be a constituent part, should effectively ensure human dignity and guarantee human rights which had been threatened and trampled underfoot as a result of mistaken concepts of duties imposed by merciless oppressors. In the perception of the authors of the Universal Declaration of Human Rights and of successive international instruments, the promotion and protection of human rights was a matter for which states should primarily be held responsible. However, the emphasis on the rights and freedoms of individuals and on the duties of states to promote and protect these rights and freedoms did not mean that the authors of the Universal Declaration of Human Rights were entirely unaware of the notion of our duties towards our fellow human beings and the community.

The *travaux préparatoires* reveal that lengthy debates took place on the issue of duties and responsibilities and that a variety of proposals surfaced. The final result became Article 29, and in particular its first paragraph, which reads: 'Everyone has duties to the community in which alone the free and full development of his personality is possible'. This provision occupies a rather modest position in the Universal Declaration, as if it were some kind of afterthought. However, the debates in the UN Commission on Human Rights and in the UN General Assembly that preceded its adoption provide a different picture. The issue of duties was duly and thoroughly discussed. But the view that prevailed was that, while a balance between rights and duties must be attained, the need to guarantee rights as an international undertaking was more pressing than the need for a catalogue of duties. In the relationship between the individual and the state the balance of power usually tilts overwhelmingly on the side of the state and international human rights guarantees are designed precisely to protect the individual against the abuse of power and to help ensure a life of dignity for all.

American and African Texts

It is true, however, that certain regional human rights instruments do contain a catalogue of duties, in addition to rights. The American Declaration of the Rights and Duties of Man, adopted in Bogotá (Colombia) in May 1948, includes a list of no less than ten duties, but the subsequent American Convention on Human Rights of 1969 contains only the simple statement that every person has responsibilities to his family, his community and mankind. The African Charter on Human and Peoples' Rights of 1981 is a unique document in that its first chapter deals not only with the rights of individuals, but also with the rights of peoples, and its second chapter spells out certain duties of the individual. These texts refer to duties that are owed to the family, the national community and the state, including the duty to defend the security of and ensure the preservation of the state. One cannot help feeling some discomfort when human duties are so explicitly related to the state in an international instrument. In general the domestic constitutional order is the appropriate level for defining human duties and human responsibilities. If any case is to be made in favour of defining human duties and human responsibilities in some detail at the international level, then such a definition should clearly indicate the limits of the discretionary powers of the state. Unless these limits are set out, an international declaration on human duties and responsibilities might risk legitimizing totalitarian powers.

The Effects of Globalization

To return to the proposal by the former heads of state and government launched by the InterAction Council, one can in no way question their good intentions. Any suggestion that the proposed Universal Declaration of Human Responsibilities might be intended to support totalitarian ideologies or practices would certainly be misconceived, although the initiative may inadvertently have such an adverse side effect. Leaving aside this issue, however, there are other reasons why it would not be advisable for the United Nations to endorse the proposed document.

First of all, the introduction, in explaining the need for a Universal Declaration of Human Responsibilities, proceeds on the basis of the notion that the globalization of the world economy demands 'global solutions on the basis of ideas, values and norms respected by all cultures and societies'. In fact, it is quite appropriate to try to find responses to the globalization of the world economy, because of the profound impact it is having on the lives of many peoples and nations. One might even argue such a response is urgently needed. But one might also question whether the InterAction Council and its members and advisors are fully aware of its consequences for the enjoyment of human rights. In numerous countries the social and cultural rights of the most vulnerable groups in society are seriously threatened as a result of the effects of the unbridled market forces and the mass communication media which control the process of globalization. In this process, the interdependent and joint powers of national and international economic and financial actors, in particular transnational corporations and financial institutions, are gaining a great deal of strength and influence at the expense of the state, thus weakening the state's role as protector of social rights and social welfare. Due to the process of globalization, the imperatives of social justice aimed at promoting and protecting the rights of the weak and the marginalized are increasingly being jeopardized. The gap between the rich and the poor is becoming more pronounced, in both the North and the South.

NON-STATE ENTITIES AND CORPORATE RESPONSIBILITIES

The international system for the promotion and protection of human rights with the International Bill of Human Rights as its foundation is based on the premise that states are to be held accountable, in the legal and political sense, for the manner in which they implement human rights as an interdependent and indivisible whole. One of the consequences of the globalization of the world economy is, as noted above, a weakening of the role of the state and, on the other side of the coin, an increase in the powers and influence of non-state entities which are hardly accountable to anyone, except perhaps their shareholders. This evolution is having an adverse effect on the existing – unfortunately still very weak – legal and political human rights system which largely assumes the responsibility of states.

In all good conscience one may wonder whether the proposed Universal Declaration of Human Responsibilities is an effective response to the challenges of globalization, and in particular the weakening of the global human rights system. The text undoubtedly contains a number of commendable notions. It is organized in sections which cover fundamental principles of humanity, non-violence and respect for life, justice and solidarity, truthfulness and tolerance, and mutual respect and partnership. It entrusts people, individually and collectively, with the responsibility for and task of enhancing these excellent and essential ideals. One cannot fundamentally disagree with the principles and concerns outlined in the proposed document.

However, the text unfortunately fails to point to the economic and financial actors who, in the process of economic globalization, have become increasingly powerful and who should do their share when responsibilities and duties in the area of human rights are at stake. The recognition of human rights and the attribution of human responsibilities and duties can only be realized if political and economic powers and their leaders are made to understand and accept their responsibility for the general welfare, and, moreover, if their policies and practices are reviewed and adjusted accordingly. This essential dimension of corporate responsibility is largely overlooked in the proposed document, except insofar as it states that economic and political power must not be handled as an instrument of domination but in the service of economic justice and of the social order (Article 11). If the initiative of the InterAction Council is actually meant as a response to the globalization of the world economy, it should focus much more sharply on the effects of the market on rights, in particular the rights of the vulnerable, and on the accountability of non-state entities.

TWIN DOCUMENTS?

Another critical observation relating to the proposed Universal Declaration on Human Responsibilities touches upon the claim that it might become a twin document or a necessary complement to the Universal Declaration of Human Rights. This pretension is manifest in the solemn tone of the preamble and the final provision, which to a large extent copies the wording of the Universal Declaration of Human Rights. Moreover, the same pretension is apparent in the structure of the document and the wish to see it solemnly proclaimed by the United Nations General Assembly on 10 December 1998. As in the Universal Declaration of Human Rights, recognition of the inherent dignity and of the equal and inalienable rights of all members of the human family as the foundation of freedom, justice and peace in the world figures in the opening phrase. But immediately thereafter it is stated that the exclusive insistence on rights can result in conflict, division, and endless dispute, and the neglect of human responsibilities can lead to lawlessness and chaos. This statement may be very true, but by choosing the Universal Declaration of Human Rights as the frame of reference authors have unintentionally created the impression that the Universal Declaration of 1948 has contributed to excessive emphasis on human rights and fundamental freedoms.

Ambiguous Language

Given its scope and content, the Universal Declaration of Human Rights, couched in terms of rights, has evolved into a genuine international legal instrument. This quality has been widely recognized, notably in the Proclamation of Teheran (1968) which referred to the Universal Declaration as 'a common understanding of the peoples of the world concerning the inalienable and inviolable rights of all members of the human family and ... *an obligation for the members of the international community*' (emphasis added). The proposed Universal Declaration of Human Responsibilities suffers, however, from a troubling ambiguity. It wishes to convey common ethical standards but it is drafted in a language, partly borrowed from the Universal Declaration of Human Rights, which wavers between moral duties and legal obligations. As a result, in certain instances the text uses gentle admonitory or advisory language where, in view of the present state of international law, the strongest imperatives are actually called for. For instance, it states in Article 6 that '[n]o government *should* tolerate or participate in acts of genocide or terrorism, nor *should* it abuse women, children, or any other civilians as instruments of war' (emphasis added). In Article 15 it states that representatives of religions '*should* not incite or legitimize hatred, fanaticism and religious wars' (again, emphasis added). It is simply unthinkable that the United Nations General Assembly should associate itself with such soft, albeit well-intended, pronouncements where the strongest terms are actually required.

The Position and the Perspective of the Universal Declaration of Human Rights

It is not my intention to suggest that the Universal Declaration of Human Rights has no deficiencies and that there is no room and no reason for new emphases in response to developments and to present-day awareness of serious threats to humanity, such as the degradation of the environment, the dangers of genetic manipulation, the increase of racism and ethnic violence. Moreover, it cannot be denied that the Universal Declaration of Human Rights does not pay enough attention to the rights of collectivities, in particular the rights of peoples, minorities and indigenous populations and groups. However, these shortcomings have to a large extent been addressed by the United Nations and other international organizations through the adoption of new documents which are intended to supplement the International Bill of Human Rights, including the Universal Declaration of Human Rights. But it would appear a haphazard undertaking to model a Universal Declaration of Human Responsibilities on the basis of the pattern set out in the Universal Declaration of Human Rights. With all due respect to the authors and sponsors of the Universal Declaration of Human Responsibilities, their proposal aimed at the adoption and proclamation of this document on the fiftieth anniversary of the Universal Declaration of Human Rights on 10 December 1998 raises serious questions. I would certainly not go so far as to repeat, in connection with the Universal Declaration of Human Responsibilities what a 1949 American Bar Association report defiantly and erroneously stated about the Universal Declaration of Human Rights: 'A few people, with beliefs utterly foreign to each other, meet, debate, and by majority vote seek to determine how the people of the world shall live on a common pattern'. But I would submit that a deeper analysis and a bold and forward-looking re-assessment are needed in order to formulate an effective and appropriate response to the globalization of the world economy from the perspective of human rights. This perspective is not one that dominates, marginalizes and excludes people; on the contrary, it is a perspective that acknowledges, respects and embraces. It is in the light of this perspective that the values of the Universal Declaration of Human Rights should be reaffirmed.

JONI MITCHELL

The Magdalene Laundries

I was an unmarried girl
I'd just turned twenty-seven.
When they sent me to the sisters
For the way men looked at me
Branded as a jezebel,
I knew I was not bound for Heaven
I'd be cast in shame
Into the Magdalene laundries

Most girls come here pregnant
Some by their own fathers
Bridget got that belly
By her parish priest
We're trying to get things white as snow,
All of us woe-begotten-daughters,
In the steaming stains
Of the Magdalene laundries

Prostitutes and destitutes
And temptresses like me -
Fallen women -
Sentenced into dreamless drudgery …
Why do they call this heartless place
Our Lady of Charity?
Oh charity!

These bloodless brides of Jesus,
If they had just once glimpsed their groom,
Then they'd know, and they'd drop the stones
Concealed behind their rosaries
They wilt the grass they walk upon
They leech the light out of a room
They'd like to drive us down the drain
At the Magdalene laundries

Peg O'Connell died today
She was a cheeky girl,
A flirt
They just stuffed her in a hole!
Surely to God you'd think at least some bells should ring!
One day I'm going to die here too,
And they'll plant me in the dirt
Like some lame bulb
That never blooms come any spring,
Come any spring,
No, not any spring …

INA BROUWER

Human Rights: A Parting of the Ways

When I was small, human rights were something you took for granted. Well, I did at any rate. Everyone had a roof over their head, food, a school, parents who looked after them. I had no reason to think that things might be different elsewhere. That was how it was in my village, near Rotterdam, and in the village where my grandparents lived, and in the new housing estate to which my friend had moved. As far as my limited experience extended – and it stretched to holidays in Germany and Austria – the world was made up of villages like ours, with bustling metropolises like Rotterdam and safe new housing estates on the horizon. Nor was this impression contradicted by the recently acquired television set that stood in our living room. We mainly watched on Wednesday afternoons – the weekly slot for children – when the programmes were about tramps with dented hats and hearts of gold, and similarly kind-hearted village policemen.

Of course, the world was not perfect. I had heard of poverty, but the Red Cross was doing its bit to help the poor, and in the final analysis everyone's human rights were respected all over the world. Anyway, if there were any problems, I was going to help sort them out. I was going to be an explorer and my friend was going to be a doctor. Together we would drive into the African jungle in our jeep, looking for adventure while of course helping anyone who needed assistance along the way. When I was a child, adventure and solidarity went hand in hand. I acted out this scenario when school was out, leading expeditions through the barren wastes of the park close to my house. These journeys were full of danger, snow, wild beasts, bad guys and near starvation, but at the end of each of them, when you were at your last gasp, you found yourself in sight of the safe farm where we would find shelter, food, a warm bed and, best of all, my mother playing the part of the kind farmer's wife. Whatever the hardships of the journey it was always a case of 'all's well that ends well'.

I often wonder now not only how children survive in the killing fields of war and in dead-end slums, but how they can preserve in their minds a fragile flame of hope for the future. Violation of a child's rights shapes that person for the rest of their life.

The beautiful illusion of my youth was shattered by modern means, through television. I must have been about eight or nine when I saw, in those May days, images that would change my life. The Second World War was being commemorated with long sombre films full of the violence of war, the stamp of jackboots and the shouting of officers. Then the television screen showed a long line of railway trucks, and in the centre a frightened girl who was trying to catch a last glimpse of the station between two sliding doors. Her eyes were sad, the saddest eyes I had ever seen. I looked and looked, and hoped that the girl had ended up all right, that at the end of her harrowing journey she had found a farm, as I always did when I emerged from the park. But something told me that her journey had had a terrible end. My mother told me about it: the war, the concentration camps, the many innocent people who died, the hate and the violence ... and my image of the world split in two. Life before and after the girl. The expeditions through the park came to an end for good.

But why didn't anyone do anything, I asked. Why didn't a doctor or an explorer in a jeep, a sturdy farmer, a policeman or even a soldier do something to free that girl from the sadness that showed on her face? Someone had taken pictures, after all, had even made a film. I saw the train moving on the screen; why hadn't someone stopped it? The question hung in the air. It was an unanswered question that worried me for good.

A few years later, when I was fifteen or sixteen, the images of war touched me again. It was May once more. I wrote a poem, entitling it:

TO UNKNOWN HEROES

Streets, calm and clear
the sound of footsteps
soldiers appear

Silence broken
creaking boots
kicking doors open

Standing side by side
innocent men
helpless, as they abide.

A cry of grief
a mother sobs
her son will leave.

His eyes find her
a sorry smile
their last encounter.

Men in a row
injustice done
see them go.

> *Terrible sin*
> *guiltless men*
> *parting from kin.*
>
> *A crack, a cry*
> *a body tumbles*
> *the noises die.*

The poem describes the past war. In it I, a sixteen-year old child from a safe world, reflect on the events of war. The arbitrariness, the violence, the powerlessness and the treacherous silence. As of the time of writing the poem I realised how relative security is, and that human rights cannot be taken for granted. I realised how one person can make or break another person's security. I would never again regard security as a birthright, even if it seemed to be the case in my world. I had been promised great things: a good education, a house, a job, a successful husband and a glittering future, but these things had lost their magic ... for ever.

My rebellion followed shortly after. Another image, television again. It was 1968. Vietnam was burning after American bombings. Napalm bombs, houses destroyed by gunfire, fleeing, naked and burning children with mortal terror in their eyes. It was the same terror that I had seen in the eyes of the girl in the goods wagon. This time I knew who was responsible. Shockingly it was us, by which I mean the West. The Americans were our allies and so we, the Netherlands, were also indirectly responsible because we did not stop it – we even condoned it. With anger in my heart I debated with the American family with whom I was staying at the time. They retorted, 'But we liberated you Europeans! We're doing the same again now in Vietnam'. Liberating? By burning children? I would never accept that argument, would never accept the hardening of the heart that went along with it, the inhumanity of the reasoning that says if you do not happen to be born in the right place, at the right time or under the right regime it is your bad luck to be forgotten, tortured or killed. Later I realised that the state of being forgotten extended to many women in the so-called security of the home, placed by tradition at the mercy of a husband who regards a wife as his possession. Women such as these have never been able to take human rights for granted. They were born as second-class citizens.

Now, in 1998, I realise something else. When I refused to accept the prevailing logic of the times, I (and many of the generation of 1968) undertook a tremendous responsibility: to rid the world of misery. It is a responsibility that brings a new danger with it: the danger of concluding that this task is simply too great for a single individual, and thus of giving in to feelings of impotence and cynicism. Might it not be this feeling of powerlessness, coupled with the avalanche of information and bad news, that is the underlying cause of the lack of drive that at present afflicts politics and the atmosphere surrounding the UN? The world is so large, misery continues unabated, and the violation of human rights is all too visible. Human rights organisations and the United Nations are no more than Tom Thumbs, leaving a trail of breadcrumbs on roads destroyed by shelling. They simply do not have any other resources.

Is the predominating emotion, fifty years after the proclamation of the Universal Declaration of Human Rights, disappointment at our failure to achieve its lofty ideals? How often have we not heard it said that paper promises are easy to make, but that they are not doing much to make the world a better place? Anyone who sees the idealists of the United Nations, working hard in their antiquated offices in New York, backed by inadequate resources, in the midst of an increasingly fast-moving high-tech society, cannot help feeling depressed. Is this all that we are prepared to invest in human rights, fifty years after the solemn adoption of the Universal Declaration? Are we only prepared to invest in our human rights instruments when a world war has stunned us into action, or have we finally realised that investment of this type is just as necessary as investment in the economy?

A world community that has set itself a universal and humane goal cannot take a few steps back. There is no such thing as a bit of human dignity. Respect for human beings cannot be broken down into little pieces. We must therefore accept the considerable challenge of respecting universal human rights, even if the images on our television screens over the last fifty years have made painfully clear that these human rights are by no means flourishing. On the contrary, the picture is pretty bleak at times. It seems that the world's future is increasingly threatened by the greed and zest for exploitation displayed by a small section of humanity.

I was 21 when my search for the meaning of life took me to India. In a hospital there I met a girl of my own age. She was lying in bed under a roof supported on ramshackle walls, in an advanced stage of tuberculosis. 'She will die', I was told, 'we can do nothing'. I was amazed. After the girl with the sad eyes and the burning children in Vietnam, this was the third time that the reality of life had shocked me to the core. This time it was not about war, but about dying purely and simply because you were unfortunate enough to have been born poor, too poor to buy medicines. There she lay, written off, while Western tourists in the street outside registered poverty with their cameras in preparation for slide shows with their friends at home. Violence, repression, poverty and indifference; I had become aware of them, and felt a responsibility, as a child from a secure world, to do something about them. It was one of the reasons I entered politics and as of 1981 became one of the mouthpieces for human rights in the Dutch parliament.

I shall not, in this brief account, go into all the trials and tribulations I experienced during my parliamentary years. It would be too long, and not very relevant to my present purpose. I do realise, however, that those fourteen years in national politics have shaped my life. From my earliest years, particularly after my journey to India, I had had a mission to help those who could not help themselves. To take on the indifference, the greed and the coldness of modern society. I demonstrated and argued against apartheid and a new generation of nuclear weapons. I fought for the rights of dissidents and of women, I got worked up about the benefits paid to the poorest and the disabled, and called upon the government to boycott South Africa and Indonesia because of their human rights violations.

I was certainly not alone in doing these things in the eighties. Many people demonstrated for human rights and the environment. But over the years I began to be assailed by a nagging doubt. I began to ask myself if all this was doing any good. Was the Indian girl better off because of what I had done in the Dutch parliament? Were the poor better off, had a war been prevented anywhere? All those hours we had spent analysing balances of power, the motions we had submitted, the protests we had made to the government about all the injustices in the world: was there actually any point in it?

Sometimes, I had the feeling that I was making a genuine, if small contribution. Like the time that Dutch MPs stood up for the Russian dissident physicist Andrei Sakharov, or the time when other women and I were able to give support to children from Chernobyl who had suffered radioactive contamination. More often, though, the wrongs of the world continued unchecked. Street children were murdered in Rio, orphans in Budapest sniffed glue in the sewers that were their home, and we could do little about it. People were slaughtered en masse in Rwanda in scenes that equalled the Second World War in brutality. Then came the war in former Yugoslavia, so close to home and so terrible. Once again we were powerless – or disinclined – to take action. The image of the explorer in her jeep with the doctor next to her became increasingly absurd. A nice theme for a children's cartoon, but no more than that.

During the many parliamentary sessions in which we debated with the government how the war in former Yugoslavia could be stopped, I kept hearing the echo of my own voice more and more. Was there any point in this? Was I actually doing anything more than giving vent to my own feelings of outrage? On the other hand, if politicians did not do this, who would? The age of romantic protests and secure ideologies, the product of the sixties, had gone for good. In this new era of CNN and satellites, the crystal clear distinction between the good, the bad and the ugly has become blurred, and the political leaders of the world are ruthlessly stripped of their charisma. The clash between good will and harsh reality is etched out more clearly than ever before. Who would be idealistic enough, nowadays, to sacrifice themselves for a good cause, either in politics or in the world of human rights? It seems a pointless enterprise. Let's concentrate on our own problems, at least we can take stock of those! Cynicism lies in wait, threatening the moral safety net that holds societies together and that has also been built up, albeit sometimes with blood, sweat and tears, between nations. The Universal Declaration of Human Rights is part of this safety net, but at the same time illustrative of its vulnerability.

It is as if, at the end of this century, we have reached a parting of the ways. We could choose to abandon the pretence that human rights will ever become universal or we could decide to blaze new trails in the context of a rapidly changing world. A changing world that is called the global village, but whose benefits are at present largely confined to the prosperous and successful. Never before have such unrestricted opportunities been open to so many – though still too few – and never before have those same freedoms and opportunities posed such a fundamental threat to the continued existence of humanity as they do now. Technically speaking, it is possible both to save the environment and to banish hunger from the world. With a bit more imagination and courage, education and care could radically enhance the quality of life of many children, both boys and girls. We are held back not by a lack of technical capacity, but by our inability to break free from fossilised thought patterns and institutions that are firmly rooted in an expiring century.

Now that the century is drawing to a close, the established framework of society seems to leave no room for growth. The traditional family, in which the man works as breadwinner and the woman as carer, is beginning to fall apart. Women's liberation has had fundamental consequences for their place in society and in private life. The organisation of labour and care has not yet adjusted to this state of affairs. Political parties, rooted in the nation state and operating from a fixed Welt-anschauung, are not really in a position to adapt to the increasing inter-nationalisation of the world. The United Nations, on the other hand, whose mandate is to do just that, is too poor, too bureaucratic and too restricted to channel the mushrooming free market with its huge flows of capital in the direction of universal human rights. The UN has no coercive measures, and even if it did, it lacks the authority to enforce compliance – though some still dream of a Utopian world government, backed by a global police force.

We need a new culture. The first step is to increase the number of organisations that champion human and environmental rights. Not from charitable motives, but simply because it is in our own interests. We can no longer afford to split the economy, private life and public accountability into separate compartments. Nor can we continue to tolerate serving the economy during the week and good causes during the weekend. We need to integrate these traditionally separate sectors. In other words, we need to develop ethical entrepreneurship and enterprising politics. New alliances must be formed, and a link established between professional groups that currently operate separately from one another. Artists, politicians, journalists, scientists and entrepreneurs must take the lead in partnership with the human rights and environmental movements. An international platform is needed in order to exchange knowledge and experience, inspiration and creativity. It is not enough simply to acknowledge the universal validity of the Universal Declaration of Human Rights; its implementation must be viewed as a universal responsibility. A responsibility that all who shape today's society must share.

Consequently, political culture will have to be receptive to new forms of debate, harmonisation and alliances. Again, this will not be an easy task. When I suggested in the Dutch parliament in 1993 that each political party symbolically adopt 1,000 street children from Rio because they have no real political representatives, the reaction was one of amazement. It can't be done, I was told. That's not how our system works. And they were right, of course, but if you look at the world of today you see the need for an unconventional approach. If the market shifts, making use of the international media, the same must apply to moral and political action. We just cannot accept the dichotomy between these main areas of life any longer.

Is the creation of an international platform of this kind a realistic way of implementing universal human rights in everyday life? My answer is simple: where there is a will there is a way. There is sufficient vision, money, talent, technology, international communication and expertise to launch a platform that would both inspire and be effective. Such a platform would moreover not replace national and international institutions, but would be a necessary link between influential, international spheres. In this essay I merely provide a rough sketch of this idea, based on my experience in politics and my knowledge of movements, markets and international institutions. I see scope for new links in at least two areas.

An event that took place in March 1997 serves as an example. While I was responsible for equal rights policy I attended the annual session of the UN Commission on the Status of Women as a follow-up to the Fourth World Women's Conference in Beijing. A small but militant group of African women from the Sahel countries refused to leave the UN session before they were granted equal inheritance rights. 'We will no longer put up with being treated as objects to barter', they said. 'We work the land and look after our children. We provide food and shelter, so we will no longer allow ourselves to be thrown off our land if we are widowed. We accept our responsibilities, now we want our rights!' Despite resistance from states such as Iran and the Vatican City, and despite unorthodox procedures, they won the day. The news spread like a bush fire among the many women's groups throughout the world. Via modern means of communication such as the Internet, women in Chile, Afghanistan, the former Soviet Union and South Africa were informed of the victory. The good news inspired the exchange of more 'good practices', for instance in ways of combating sexual violence against women. These 'good practices' were exchanged in the way that our grandmothers ex-changed recipes, the difference being that these women did not know one another – indeed, were separated by thousands of kilometres – but were acting in the knowledge that they were confronted by the same problems.

There are interesting developments in a second field, too. I refer to the cautious dawnings of ethical entrepreneurship among large concerns such as Shell. Their international position – and undoubtedly the pressure of human rights and environmental movements – have led to a reorientation. Plans are afoot to rethink entrepreneurial practices and to ensure that they take account of human rights and environmental concerns in future. It is beginning to be understood that economic growth and the interests of mankind and the environment can no longer be diametrically opposed, but must go hand in hand.

I hope that these are signs of the emergence of a new link between the concepts of freedom and global accountability. An indication of a surprising symbiosis between the call of adventure and care for the community as I envisaged it, in my childish imagination, in the form of partnership between doctor and explorer. If we succeed in going down this road, perhaps we can give that child with the fearful gaze confidence that somewhere on the horizon a farm can be found that will offer warmth, security and food. As if it were the most natural thing in the world.

Article 7

All are equal before the law and are entitled without any discrimination to equal protection of the law. All are entitled to equal protection against any discrimination in violation of this Declaration and against any incitement to such discrimination.

THOMAS BUERGENTHAL

Centerpiece of the Human Rights Revolution

A Symbol of Hope

The Universal Declaration of Human Rights has over the years evolved into the centerpiece of the international human rights revolution. Whereas the Charter of the United Nations internationalized human rights as a legal concept, the Universal Declaration gave the concept the moral force that captured the imagination of mankind and transformed it into a powerful political manifesto.

The great irony here is that the Universal Declaration was drafted in hortatory language designed to emphasize its non-binding character because many member states of the United Nations did not want a binding legal document. Their governments no doubt believed that 'mere words' could do no harm, provided they did not impose legal obligations. How wrong they were! It is precisely the Declaration's language – at once eloquent, expansive and simple – that allowed it to express universal truths in words human beings all over the world could understand and wanted to hear. No formal legal instrument could have achieved that result and had quite the same inspirational impact on the human rights movement.

Its Place in History

The Universal Declaration is the first comprehensive international proclamation of the basic rights of the individual. It ranks with the Magna Carta, the French Declaration of the Rights of Man and of the Citizen, and the American Declaration of Independence as a milestone in mankind's struggle for freedom and human dignity. Its debt to these great historic documents is unmistakable: 'All human beings are born free and equal in dignity and rights', proclaims Article 1 of the Universal Declaration. Adds Article 28, '[e]veryone is entitled to a social and international order in which the rights and freedoms set forth in this Declaration can be fully realized'.

The Declaration is an historic milestone in yet another respect: it was the first international instrument to recognize that, in addition to civil and political rights, individuals also have economic, social and cultural rights. It thus articulated the basis for and foreshadowed the acceptance by the international community of the proposition that these two categories of human rights are interrelated and interdependent, something the United Nations was not able to proclaim formally until many years later.

Together with the UN Charter, the Universal Declaration laid the foundation of modern international human rights law. In one way or another, most of its provisions spawned binding international and regional instruments guaranteeing these rights as well as those adopted within the framework of the specialized agencies of the United Nations. Together with the two International Covenants on Human Rights, it comprises the International Bill of Human Rights. The International Convention on the Elimination of All Forms of Racial Discrimination, the Convention on the Elimination of All Forms of Discrimination against Women, and the Convention against Torture and Other Cruel, Inhuman or Degrading Treatment and Punishment, to mention only some major instruments, trace their origins to the rights the Universal Declaration proclaims.

The same is true of the treaties that established the three existing regional human rights systems in Europe, the Americas and Africa. The Universal Declaration also inspired the contents of various human rights instruments adopted within the framework of the specialized agencies, in particular UNESCO and ILO. In short, the Universal Declaration has provided and continues to provide the basic building blocks of the normative edifice upon which the contemporary code of human rights rests. No other instrument has had the same impact and lasting influence.

ITS NORMATIVE EFFECT

Ever since the Universal Declaration was adopted, international lawyers have argued about its legal character or effect. On one level, the debate is irrelevant given the Universal Declaration's status as a political and philosophical manifesto which expresses the hopes and aspirations of the human family and derives its moral force from those hopes and aspirations. It is like asking 'what is the legal effect of the Bible?' On another level, the debate derives its relevance from the mere fact that lawyers seeking to rely on the Universal Declaration in national and international tribunals may have to address the question of its normative character in a formal juridical setting. It may be useful, therefore, to say a word on this subject.

The starting point for such a discussion is that the Universal Declaration is not a treaty and that it was not adopted in the form of a legally binding resolution or instrument. When proclaimed, it was not intended to be legally binding. Instead, the Universal Declaration was to serve, as its preamble declares, 'as a common standard of achievement for all peoples and nations' by providing 'a common understanding' of the rights and freedoms that the member states of the United Nations pledged themselves to promote by ratifying the UN Charter.

Over time and in large part because it took the United Nations many years to adopt the International Covenants on Human Rights, the Universal Declaration came increasingly to be relied upon by the United Nations and cited in the diplomatic practice of states as a standard by which to judge their conduct in the human rights field. These developments gave rise to various legal theories seeking to establish the binding character of the Universal Declaration. One such theory proposes that the Universal Declaration has evolved into an authoritative interpretation or definition of the human rights which the member states of the United Nations have an obligation to promote under the UN Charter. As such, it derives its legal force from the Charter itself and is circumscribed by the scope of that obligation, which is conventional in character. Other legal scholars argue that some or all provisions of the Universal Declaration have crystallized into rules of customary international law. A third theory, recently propounded, claims that the Universal Declaration is an expression of general principles of law which, together with customary and conventional international law, create binding international obligations.

This is not the place to assess the respective soundness of these theories, although in one way or another all three, taken together, may well describe the true status of the Universal Declaration. Be that as it may, here it is probably more important to note that few international lawyers would deny today that the Universal Declaration is a normative instrument and that as such it is a source of legal obligations. Instead, the focus of whatever disagreement there may be among them is on the question whether the Universal Declaration as a whole or only some of its provisions are binding and in what context.

Not irrelevant to this debate are two other developments. One is that few, if any, governments would today claim that they have a right to violate the Universal Declaration. When charged with a breach of the Universal Declaration, they will as a rule deny the accusation or otherwise seek to explain their behavior. While clearly politically motivated, these denials have normative consequences given how international law evolves. The other development is that over the past few years some states have conferred constitutional law status on the Universal Declaration under their domestic law. These factors reflect the ever growing legal importance and political significance of the Universal Declaration – two realities that cannot really be separated in the international arena, where the confluence of law and politics is blurred more often than not, and for good practical reasons.

ITS LASTING IMPACT

By universalizing and legitimating mankind's yearning for human rights and human dignity, the Universal Declaration has also shaped the manner in which people around the world personalize their right to have rights. Never before have so many people in so many countries believed that they have human rights and that it is the purpose and duty of government to respect and protect these rights. This is not to suggest that at other times in history human beings did not wish to be treated with dignity or to have their rights respected. Of course they did. What has changed though is that in the past the vast majority of humankind accepted its suffering as preordained or unavoidable; today more and more people believe that those who cause their suffering are acting illegally.

This perceived illegality has a tendency over time to rob governments of the legitimacy they need to govern and forces them to pay attention to human rights concerns on the domestic and international plane. It also creates an international climate that is every day more sensitive to human rights violations, less and less willing to tolerate them and increasingly more responsive to public and private efforts to prevent them.

The Universal Declaration has started us on this road 50 years ago, and that is its great achievement. How long it will take to fully realize mankind's yearning for human rights and human dignity no one knows. One can only hope that it will be sooner rather than later.

Everyone has the right to an effective remedy by the competent national tribunals for acts violating the fundamental rights granted him by the constitution or by law.

JIMMY CARTER

The Universal Declaration of Human Rights:
The Next Fifty Years

The Challenge of Leadership

Out of the ashes of of World War II, leaders rose to the enormous challenge of articulating and implementing a new commitment to expose and prevent oppression. The result was the Universal Declaration of Human Rights. Half a century later, while there is a lot to celebrate, much work remains. We must not focus only on our accomplishments, but also chart the challenges for the current generation of leaders.

Since 1948, we have witnessed the birth and maturation of the human rights movement, which has swept through every corner of the .globe, calling into its ranks people from the world's great capitals to the most remote villages. Because of their courage and visionary leadership, human rights organizations have become effective and permanent voices that governments and leaders cannot ignore. The work of these organizations has forced the release of prisoners of conscience, corrected abusive practices, and integrated human rights into governance.

The world community also has created global systems and institutions designed to address human rights violations through international cooperation. These include the UN human rights system, now headed by the High Commissioner for Human Rights. This year, an International Criminal Court will be established as well.

These bodies are important because they foster common human rights principles and hold them up as standards for all countries. They also can prevent human rights violations by alerting the international community to emerging crises, or by acting quickly to hold accountable individuals who commit crimes against humanity, war crimes, or genocide.

But the most important factor in determining how successful we are in protecting all human rights is leadership. During the next 50 years, leaders in all fields of endeavor must provide the necessary vision and direction the world awaits.

For nearly a decade in the recent post-Cold War world, opportunities to improve the human condition have been missed by many leaders with the greatest influence and access to resources.

Instead, the moment often has been seized by oppressors who exploited the shift in the power balance, pursuing nationalist aims through ethnic cleansing and other forms of violence. In the wake of genocide in Rwanda and the former Yugoslavia, the international community was without a plan or adequate response. This was, in large part, due to the lack of leadership and mutual commitment among nations to increase respect for human rights in this new world order.

In contrast, leadership on matters such as strengthening trade ties and economic partnerships has been abundant. For example, the World Trade Organization was established because world leaders realized that global trade would be enhanced if everyone played by the same rules and if the implementation of those rules was monitored worldwide.

There was no shortage of leadership when the Allied Forces assembled to expel Saddam Hussein's army from Kuwait. The significant economic interests of powerful countries was combined with the specter of an unchecked aggressor, sounding a clarion call to the highest levels of leadership. But when Hussein's government was reported by human rights organizations as one of the world's worst violators throughout the 1980s, political and economic interests were given more weight by the same influential nations, preventing them from taking meaningful action to address these atrocities.

The American initiative in Somalia initially was an example of visionary leadership. The idea that the most advanced military force in the world would be deployed to save many lives was a snapshot of the civilized world for which we hope. But the opportunity to set a new course was overshadowed by a diversion of objectives and the pictures of American servicemen being dragged through the streets. The loss was tremendous and the nations' resolve dissipated. Our leaders failed to understand and explain the larger purpose of the effort that had been undertaken.

These trying moments are when leadership is most needed. Influential individuals in government, religious, and business communities have the obligation to lead. Each citizen must also lead in his or her own way.

Government leaders have the ability to ensure that police and armed forces respect human rights while maintaining peace and security and that judicial systems are independent and effective in providing access to justice for all citizens. They can permit civil society organizations to operate freely so social problems can be debated openly and solutions devised by the community as a whole, a process reinforced by free and open media. And only government leaders can determine how their nations will function within the international community. Will they support global human rights initiatives, such as the UN human rights bodies, or refuse to cooperate with them? Perhaps most important, governments can strive to resolve conflicts in which they are involved, directly or indirectly. No stone should be unturned in seeking peaceful solutions to the world's remaining conflicts because war is the greatest source of human rights violations.

Religious leaders can mobilize the hearts and minds of their adherents. Imagine how history might have been altered had the religious figures of the time affirmed the essential dignity and humanity of all people when Europeans first encountered America's native peoples or when the slave trade was first begun. In all regions of the world, some religious leaders use their influence to advocate and commit gross human rights violations – acts that in any religious tradition are essentially contrary to the expressed purpose of religion itself. It is instructive to contrast these examples with conscientious religious communities that have actively defended human rights in recent decades, as in Central America and South Africa. Today's religious leaders should spare no effort to promote tolerance and respect for others within and outside their communities.

Business leaders have a tremendous responsibility because they have, in many cases, more influence than governments on the quality of life enjoyed by their employees and others in countries where they operate. For this reason, corporations should be held to the same standards of human rights protection as are governments. Also, those who achieve great wealth have a moral obligation to give back to the communities that have enabled their success. The extreme disparities between the rich and the poor should be a great concern for all of us.

Individually, each of us can become a leader for human rights in our own communities by showing respect not only for our friends and families but also for those who are different from us. For those of us who live in nations where we have the right to choose our leaders, our commitment can be gauged by whether those we elect are effective in advancing human rights.

Ultimately, our humanity as citizens and leaders will be measured by the degree to which we help advance the rights of individuals, in our neighborhoods and throughout the world. My hope is that, 50 years from now, adherence to the Universal Declaration of Human Rights will be the norm for every community and country on earth.

BASIL FERNANDO

Fiftieth Year Get-Together

My little country - Pearl of the Indian Ocean
Paradise isle, Portuguese, Dutch, British knew
Feasted in, drank tea - Lanka, Sri Lanka

Illiterate women making love
To illiterate men
Made this land - my land - flowing with honey

For 50 years, my land, my lungs full
Of fresh air
Rice, smiles, kisses

Tears too, tens of thousands
Disappearances, bombs
Bullets, child prostitutes and soldiers

I wonder about
Reading histories, seeing
Photographs, other people's

Stalin - Koba - SoSo - Joseph
Bloodied humans like millions of flies
Hitler, European, Jewish blood encounters

Pol Pot not unequal
Asian blood rivers
Indonesian, Indian corpses

I try to pray - I am Christian
I try to meditate - my heritage is Buddhist
Each day is All Souls' Day

No gold medals for Stalin
Yet imitators everywhere
Fear, they believe, necessary for peace

Berlin Wall fell
Now they shoot only migrants
Higher white wall - you know

Hail Mary, my 7-year-old girl
Says, Father, say with me Hail Mary
Why disappoint a child - I join her

Why, I was like her too
I pleaded to the whole white heaven
Hail Mary, do hear our people's cry

Fifty years of prayers
How can I tell my child they do not care
No, I have joined in her prayers

Hail Mary, stop my land's bleeding
Jesus join us for tea in Buddha's land
Me and my child will join you anywhere; do stop the killers

Maybe we can play games when we meet
Put on masks: we become white
You brown

We know your crucifixion
Feel for you very much
Take a turn if you like and get to know ours

My little girl is funny
She may ask questions
We can laugh together - OK?

Sometimes she asks me
Father, can't we abolish hell - funny, no?
Lot of people will oppose us I told her

You may like our games - really
Very innocent, childlike
No tricks, no cheating

HIS HOLINESS THE DALAI LAMA

Humanity's Concern for Human Rights

The widespread concern about violations of human rights is very encouraging. Not only does it offer the prospect of relief to many suffering individuals, but it is also an indication of humanity's progress and development. Concern for human rights violations and the effort to protect human rights represent a great service to people of both the present and future generations. With the Universal Declaration of Human Rights, fifty years ago, people everywhere have come to realise the great importance and value of human rights.

A Buddhist Monk's View

I am not an expert in the field of human rights. However, for a Buddhist monk, like myself, the rights of every human being are very precious and important. According to Buddhist belief, every sentient being has a mind whose fundamental nature is essentially pure, unpolluted by mental distortions. We refer to that nature as the seed of enlightenment. From that point of view every being can eventually achieve perfection. And also because the nature of the mind is pure, we believe that all negative aspects can ultimately be removed from it. When our mental attitude is positive, the negative actions of body and speech automatically cease.

Because every sentient being has such potential, all are equal. Everyone has the right to be happy and to overcome suffering. The Buddha himself said that in his order neither race nor social class is important. What is important is the actual practice of living your life in an ethical way.

As Buddhist practitioners, we try to improve our day to day conduct first of all. Only on the basis of that can we begin to develop the practices of mental training and wisdom. In my daily practice as a Buddhist monk I have to observe many rules, but the fundamental theme of them all is a deep concern and respect for the rights of others. The principal vows observed by fully-ordained monks and nuns include not taking the life of other beings, not stealing their possessions and so on. These rules are explicitly concerned with a deep respect for the rights of others. This is why I often describe the essence of Buddhism as being something like this: If you can, help other sentient beings; if you cannot, at least refrain from harming them. This reveals a deep respect for others, for life itself, and concern for others' welfare.

Although it is important to respect others' natural rights, we tend to lead our lives in the opposite way. This is because we lack love and compassion. Therefore, even

101

in relation to the question of human rights violations and concern for human rights, the key point is the practice of compassion, love and forgiveness. Very often, when people hear about love and compassion, they have a sense that these are related to religious practice. It is not necessarily so. It is very important to recognise instead that compassion and love are fundamental to relations between sentient beings in general and human beings in particular.

At the beginning of our lives and again when we become old we appreciate others' help and affection. Unfortunately, between these two periods of our lives, when we are strong and able and can look after ourselves, we neglect the value of affection and compassion. As our very lives begin and end with a need for affection, would it not be better to practise compassion and love towards others when we are strong and capable?

We gather genuine friends only when we express sincere human feeling, when we express respect for others and concern for their rights. This is what we clearly experience in our daily life. There is no need to read some difficult philosophical meaning into it. In our daily life these things are a reality. Therefore, the practice of compassion, the practice of sincerity and love, are essential sources of our own happiness and satisfaction. Once we develop such an altruistic attitude, we will automatically develop concern for others' suffering. We will simultaneously develop a determination to do something to protect the rights of others and to be concerned with their fate.

The Universality of Human Rights

Human rights are of universal interest because it is the inherent nature of all human beings to yearn for freedom, equality and dignity and they have a right to achieve them. Whether we like it or not, we have all been born into this world as part of one great human family. Rich or poor, educated or uneducated, belonging to one nation or another, to one religion or another, adhering to this ideology or that, ultimately each of us is just a human being like everyone else. We all desire happiness and do not want suffering.

If we accept that others have an equal right to peace and happiness as ourselves, do we not have responsibility to help those in need? The aspiration for democracy and respect for fundamental human rights is as important to the people of Africa and Asia as it is to those in Europe or the Americas. But often it is just those people who are deprived of their human rights who are least able to speak up for themselves. The responsibility rests with those of us who do enjoy such freedoms.

Human rights abuses are often targeted on the most gifted, dedicated and creative members of society. As a result, the political, social, cultural and economic developments of a society are obstructed by violations of human rights. Therefore, the protection of these rights and freedoms are of immense importance both for the individuals affected and for the development of society as a whole.

Some governments have contended that the standards of human rights laid down in the Universal Declaration of Human Rights are those advocated by the West and do not apply to Asia and other parts of the Third World because of differences in culture and social and economic development. I do not share this view and I am convinced that the majority of ordinary people do not support it either. I believe that the principles laid down in the Universal Declaration of Human Rights constitute something like a natural law which ought to be followed by all peoples and governments.

Moreover, I do not see any contradiction between the need for economic development and the need to respect human rights. The right to free speech and association are vital in promoting a country's economic development. In Tibet, for example, there have been countless instances where unsuitable economic policies have been implemented and continued long after they have failed to produce benefits, because citizens and government officials could not speak out against them.

Internationally, our rich diversity of cultures and religions should help to strengthen fundamental human rights in all communities. Underlying this diversity are basic human principles that bind us all together as members of the same human family. However, mere maintenance of traditions should never justify the violations of human rights. Thus, discrimination against persons of different races, against women, and against weaker sections of society may be traditional in some places, but if they are inconsistent with universally recognised human rights, these forms of behaviour should change. The universal principle of the equality of all human beings must take precedence.

Tibetan Experience

As a Tibetan I have direct experience of the pain caused by the violation of human rights. This gives me a special feeling of sympathy for others whose human rights are violated. On the other hand, although there is no explicit mention of human rights in the Buddha's teachings, which we Tibetans follow, the whole Buddhist way of life is based upon principles of deep respect for the welfare of all our fellow beings. It is a system based on the practice of compassion, so there is a strong implicit emphasis on respect for the rights of others.

Today, the struggle of the Tibetan people to regain their rights is at a crucial stage. In recent times the Chinese government has hardened its policies, increased repression in Tibet and resorted to bullying tactics in addressing the issue of Tibet. Observance of human rights in Tibet has sadly, not improved. On the contrary repression and political persecution have lately reached a new peak in Tibet.

Violations of human rights in Tibet have a distinct character. Such abuses are aimed at preventing Tibetans as a people from asserting their own identity and their wish to preserve it. Thus, human rights violations in Tibet are often the result of institutionalised racial and cultural discrimination. In Tibet our people are being marginalised and discriminated against in the face of creeping Sinicisation. The undermining and destruction of cultural and religious institutions and traditions coupled with the mass influx of Chinese into Tibet poses a serious threat for the survival of the Tibetans as a distinct people. Whether intentionally or unintentionally, cultural genocide is taking place in Tibet. Nevertheless, the growing concern and support for the Tibetan cause from the international community, in particular from human rights organisations and non-governmental organisations, are a source of great encouragement. They not only create awareness for the need to respect the rights of all human beings but also give victims of oppression and human rights violations hope for the future.

China is also at a critical juncture: its society is undergoing profound changes. A transformation from totalitarian regime into one which is more open, responsive and liberal is inevitable. China needs human rights, democracy and the rule of law. These values are the foundation of a free and dynamic society. They are also the source of true peace and stability. A society upholding such values will offer far greater potential and security for trade and investment. A more democratic China is thus also in the interest of the international community in general and of Asia in particular. Therefore, every effort should be made not only to integrate China into world economy, but also to encourage her to enter the mainstream of global democracy.

Nevertheless, human rights, freedom and democracy in China can be brought about only by the Chinese themselves and not by anyone else. This is why the brave and dedicated members of the Chinese democracy movement deserve our encouragement and support.

For centuries the Tibetan and the Chinese people have lived side by side. In the future, too, we will have no alternative but to live as neighbours. I have, therefore, always attached great importance to our relationship. In this spirit I have sought to reach out to our Chinese brothers and sisters. What I find extremely inspiring is that with better understanding of the history and current situation of Tibet more and more Chinese, especially intellectuals and writers are showing their concern and sympathy for the Tibetan struggle for human rights and freedoms.

Tibet's spiritual and cultural traditions have long contributed to peace in Asia. Buddhism not only turned Tibetans into a peace-loving nation, but spread from Tibet throughout Central Asia, from the Himalayas to Mongolia. Over centuries people from these regions would also come to Tibet to train and study. Therefore, it is part of my vision for the future of Tibet that it should once more become a zone of peace, a neutral, demilitarised sanctuary where weapons are forbidden and people live in harmony with nature. This is not merely a dream – it is precisely the way Tibetans tried to live for over a thousand years before Tibet lost its freedom.

Need for Universal Responsibility

The world is becoming increasingly interdependent and that is why I firmly believe in the need to develop a sense of universal responsibility. We need to think in global terms, because the effects of one nation's actions are felt far beyond its borders. The acceptance of universally binding standards of human rights as laid down in the Universal Declaration of Human Rights and in the International Covenants of Human Rights is essential in today's shrinking world. Respect for fundamental human rights should not remain an ideal to be achieved but a requisite foundation for every human society.

Artificial barriers that have divided nations and peoples have fallen in recent times. The success of the popular peoples' movements in dismantling the East – West division which has polarised the whole world for decades has been a source of great hope and expectations. Yet there still remains a major gulf at the heart of the human family. By this I am referring to the North – South divide. This is not only morally wrong but also a potential source of problem. If we are serious in our commitment to the fundamental principles of equality, principles which, I believe, lie at the heart of the concept of human rights, today's economic disparity can no longer be ignored. It is not enough to merely state that all human beings must enjoy equal dignity. This must be translated into action. We have a responsibility to find ways to achieve a more equitable distribution of world's resources.

We are witnessing a tremendous popular movement for the advancement of human rights and democratic freedom in the world. This movement must become an even more powerful moral force, so that even the most obstructive governments and armies are incapable of suppressing it. It is natural and just for nations, peoples and individuals to demand respect for their rights and freedoms and to struggle to end repression, racism, economic exploitation, military occupation, and various forms of colonialism and alien domination. Governments should actively support such demands instead of only paying lip service to them.

It is my belief that the lack of understanding of the true cause of happiness is the principal reason why people inflict suffering on others. Some people think that causing pain to others may lead to their own happiness or that their own happiness is of such importance that the pain of others is of no significance. But this is clearly short-sighted. No one truly benefits from causing harm to another being. Whatever immediate advantage is gained at the expense of someone else is short-lived. In the long run causing others misery and infringing upon their peace and happiness creates anxiety, fear and suspicion for oneself. The development of love and compassion for others is essential for creating a better and more peaceful world. This naturally means we must develop concern for our fellow brothers and sisters who are less fortunate than we are. Therefore, we have a moral duty to help and support all those who are presently prevented from exercising the rights and freedoms that many of us take for granted.

As we approach the end of the twentieth century, we find that the world is becoming one community. We are being drawn together by the grave problems of overpopulation, dwindling natural resources, and an environmental crisis that threaten the very foundation of our existence on this planet. Human rights, environmental protection and great social and economic equality, are all inter-related. I believe that to meet the challenges of our times, human beings will have to develop a greater sense of universal responsibility. Each of us must learn to work not just for one self, one's own family or one's nation, but for the benefit of all humankind. Universal responsibility is the key to human survival. It is the best guarantee for human rights and for world peace.

Article 9

No one shall be subjected to arbitrary arrest, detention or exile.

PIETER VAN DIJK

The Universal Declaration is Legally Non-Binding; So what?

Ever since the adoption of the Universal Declaration of Human Rights in 1948, there has been a lively debate about its legal character; so much so that this debate has at times threatened to overshadow the evaluation of the Universal Declaration's normative character and influence. Even lawyers have to admit that this legalistic and positivist approach has become redundant and in certain respects even counter-productive. At its fiftieth anniversary, the Universal Declaration should be appreciated for what it is and what it has achieved, rather than for what it is not and was never intended to be.

The normative values that the Universal Declaration embodies and the normative effects it generates do not depend solely – nor even primarily – on its legal status, but rather on its authority within the international community and within the countries of the world. This authority, in turn, does not depend solely – nor even primarily – on legal institutions and legal procedures but rather on people's shared expectations that its norms will be respected and enforced, and on the willingness of the authorities to respect them, and to enforce them where breaches occur. Schachter rightly emphasizes that one should proceed from the assumption that legally non-binding agreements 'contain undertakings taken seriously by the States Parties to them'. In this context he refers to Henry Kissinger who, when Secretary of State, defended the view, before the Foreign Relations Committee of the Senate, that the fact that certain agreements are legally non-binding 'does not mean, of course, that the United States is morally or politically free to act as if they do not exist' (Oscar Schachter, 'The Twilight Existence of Nonbinding International Agreements', *American Journal of International Law*, 1977, p. 303).

The Universal Declaration of Human Rights was adopted by the General Assembly of the United Nations in 1948. Almost all the states of the then world community voted in favour of its adoption. The Universal Declaration was subsequently endorsed by other states, including states that emerged later, in other international instruments and at international conferences. Such a consensus justifies the expectation that this international expression of the political will to accept the Universal Declaration as a 'common standard of achievement' would be translated domestically into legislative and administrative measures and practical instructions to achieve the common standard. This undoubtedly 'constitutes an obligation for the members of the international community' as acknowledged in the 1968

Proclamation of Teheran and elaborated in the Vienna Declaration and Programme of Action of 1993.

The binding character of this commitment has been recognized at both national and international level, by political and legal institutions alike. Legally non-binding though the Universal Declaration may be, this has never proved a hindrance to its being considered binding, or impaired its scope of application or effectiveness. This applies both to courts (whether national or international) and non-legal authorities, as well as to non-governmental organizations. Where a national or international authority or institution has invoked the legally non-binding character of the Universal Declaration, it has done so merely as a pretext for not pronouncing on an alleged violation, or in an attempt to evade responsibility for it. The legally non-binding character of the Universal Declaration does also not prevent the international community or individual states from monitoring its universal and effective implementation. As the Universal Declaration constitutes an authoritative and commonly endorsed interpretation of the concept of human rights as referred to in the Charter of United Nations, international interference is not a form of intervention prohibited by Article 2, paragraph 7, of the Charter. All members of the world community are responsible and accountable for the way in which they implement this 'common standard'.

To the extent that, and in situations in which the issue of the Declaration's legally binding character is relevant, the existence of international human rights treaties and their ratification by a large majority of states will in most cases supplement and compensate for any lack that the Universal Declaration may have in this respect. This inevitably raises the question of the intrinsic and complementary value of the Universal Declaration, now that it has been followed by legally binding treaties, in accordance with the original plan for an International Bill of Human Rights.

First of all, it should be pointed out that where human rights treaties have not been ratified by certain states or ratification has been qualified by reservations and where they are less comprehensive or wide-ranging than the Universal Declaration in their formulation of rights and freedoms, or allow for derogations or limitations, the Declaration retains its full significance as a 'common standard of achievement' and as a source of customary law and *jus cogens* in the field of human rights. At the same time, this 'common standard' with its minimal but progressive commitment, offers a guarantee against a state's withdrawal from its treaty obligations, and against amendments or restrictive interpretations which would attenuate the hard core of the treaty standard. Moreover, it should be emphasized that it is these very human rights treaties that enable the Universal Declaration to play its authentic and original role. The Universal Declaration symbolises *par excellence* the fundamental character and universal value of human rights and their international recognition as part of the normative foundation on which the social order of the world community is based. The human rights embodied in the Universal Declaration set standards for the actions of governments and embody universally cherished expectations and aspirations. As such it has been – and still is – a beacon to countless people who seek to be treated with human dignity as individuals and seek protection of their collective entity as members of certain groups. The Universal Declaration is frequently cited as the epitomization of human rights standards and obligations in public debates on human rights and in the media, in cases where it would have been more appropriate, legally speaking, to refer to a specific human rights treaty.

I seem inadvertently almost to be speaking in biblical terms. And, indeed, the passage in the preamble which states that 'the advent of a world in which human beings shall enjoy freedom of speech and belief and freedom from fear and want has been proclaimed as the highest aspiration of the common people' sounds almost biblical. There are clear similarities, in fact, in normative values and influence, between the holy scriptures of certain religions and the Universal Declaration. In both cases their values and influence stem from outside the strictly legal domain. In both cases any attempt to redraft them, for instance in response to current realities, would misconstrue their timeless value and disrupt their inspirational tradition. In both cases their normative values and influence will endure only if their source is recognized and interpreted as a living instrument, attuned to the needs and realities of present-day life. Finally, in both cases their effectiveness depends primarily not on their preachers' zeal but on the faithful practice of the congregation.

Would – and should – the binding features of the Universal Declaration be enhanced by a specific supervisory mechanism? In my opinion, setting up such a mechanism would not contribute to the Declaration's normative effects but rather detract from them. First, the human rights domain is already saturated with supervisory procedures. Indeed, their number, complexity and overlap, added to the burden they place on national administrations, threaten to weaken their effectiveness. Second and more importantly, the introduction of a specific mechanism would reveal an underestimation of the fact that the Universal Declaration may be invoked universally in any international or national procedure as an accepted 'common standard of achievement', and derives its main effectiveness from that fact. The existence of a specific procedure might allow states and their institutions to argue that alleged violations could henceforth be raised exclusively in that procedure. The Universal Declaration should remain universal, not only in its acceptance and applicability, but also in the procedures in which it can be invoked.

A necessary and puissant tool to enhance the Universal Declaration's normative influence is education in human rights. Article 26, paragraph 2, states that education shall be directed to the full development of the human personality and to the strengthening of respect for human rights and fundamental freedoms. The crucial role of education in furthering human rights has constantly been stressed, in particular by UNESCO. Human rights education and information should aim to heighten awareness both of one's own rights and entitlement to equal treatment and tolerance, and of the rights and entitlement of others. Children should learn at a very early age – when they are most receptive – that human dignity requires and implies equality and tolerance. In the words of UN rapporteur Odio Benito, 'Attitudes learned in childhood from parents, teachers, churches or assemblies have a lasting and profound influence upon their whole approach to life, and it is almost impossible to set them aside, to be convinced that they are in error, and to adopt new ones' (Elizabeth Odio Benito, 'Study of the Current Dimensions of the Problems of Intolerance and of Discrimination on Grounds of Religion or Belief', UN Doc. E/CN.4/Sub.2/1987/26).

Beginning with young children, this education should be an ongoing process in which the subject-matter and messages to be conveyed are geared towards the age and educational background of the target group. It must include training people to become aware of the human rights issues in their daily private and professional lives and of their own scope for problem-solving and affirmative action. Both in formal schooling and in other kinds of training, people must have free access to adequate information that is tailored to their age and education. They must be taught about the availability of legal remedies at both national and international level. This applies not only to potential victims, but equally to law-enforcing authorities, whose actions can remove the need for international proceedings and who are indispensable to the implementation of the outcome of any such proceedings at national level.

The 1993 World Conference on Human Rights in Vienna emphasized the importance of incorporating the subject of human rights into educational programmes at all levels and recommended that states should develop specific programmes and strategies to ensure the widest possible human rights education and dissemination of public information. And the Parliamentary Assembly of the Council of Europe, in Recommendation 1346 of 1997, urges that member states be called upon to include human rights education in all school curricula, starting with teacher training programmes, to include education in human rights and tolerance in the training of all officials dealing with the public, such as the police, prison staff and people dealing with refugees, and to encourage politicians and the media to commit themselves publicly to the protection of human rights.

If people's human rights are fully respected without their being aware of it, it may make their enjoyment of these rights less intense, but this is nothing to worry about. If people's human rights are violated, on the other hand, it is of vital importance that they are aware of it and are well-informed about the domestic and international remedies that may exist. Ultimately, the Universal Declaration depends for its continuous vitality and pertinence on general awareness, a vigilant public opinion, committed individuals in national and international public service, and supportive non-governmental organisations.

Article 10

Everyone is entitled in full equality to a fair and public hearing by an independent and impartial tribunal, in the determination of his rights and obligations and of any criminal charge against him.

SHARON DIJKSMA

Human Rights: A Generation to be Won

Young people make up much of humanity. A large part of the current world population is under thirty years of age. And each one of them has the same rights under
the Universal Declaration of Human Rights; every individual can invoke its provisions. So it may seem a strange interpretation of the Declaration's 'universality' to
suggest that it has a specific application to young people, who constitute such a vast
group.

And yet there are a number of reasons for treating young people as a special case,
for which human rights should have a specific meaning. Young people are often in
a position of dependency and are therefore not always in a position to stand up for
themselves. This makes them particularly vulnerable.

Children are the most vulnerable of all. They are partly or wholly entrusted to
adult carers for their upbringing and education, and although adults often serve
them well, many abuses persist. Girls are mutilated by clitoridectomy. Children are
exploited economically, in carpet factories for instance. They are exploited sexually,
in prostitution, or drawn into armed conflict, whether as child soldiers or as victims.
Ill-treatment, exploitation, military service and being made to work are part of too
many children's lives.

The entry into force, in 1990, of the Convention on the Rights of the Child,
which the Netherlands ratified in 1994, was a salutary development. The Convention imposes a number of obligations on governments in relation to children,
and can also be made binding on others, including local authorities and individual
members of the public. It is good that numerous governments have agreed to be
bound by international agreements on the protection of children.

Children do not automatically cease to be vulnerable when they reach 18 years of
age and no longer fall within the definition of a child under the terms of the
Convention. Most young people continue to rely on their carers; it will be years
before they have built up an independent position in society. In some cases this
situation is written into statutory provisions; in the Netherlands, for instance, young
people are not deemed financially independent until the age of 21. In many other
cases, dependency is a material effect of the rules of social interaction.

The dependency of many young people over 18 years of age justifies focusing on
the intentional and unintentional effects of government policy on their position in
society. Young people over 18 years of age cannot be fully equated with children,
nor should they be treated as such. Even so, the Convention could at least serve as a

source of inspiration for the way in which the legitimate interests of this age group can best be safeguarded.

But young people are not only a group requiring special care on the part of authorities. Authorities sell themselves short if they do not learn to listen to them. Young people have independent minds that have not yet become shackled by established traditions and customs and are hence often better able to assess their merits. In some cases this may lead them to rebel against such traditions or even throw them overboard. Alternatively, they may balk at innovations that undermine values they want to see preserved.

Young people's views of humanity and the world are not always confined to their own narrow interests. Young people have proved themselves eminently capable of formulating fresh ideas about global issues such as environmental pre-servation and development. While their ideas may not always be politically feasible, they are often well thought out and carefully elaborated.

Human rights are a case in point. Young people are often uncompromising about the universality of human rights. In some cases, governments that have undertaken to respect the universality of human rights by endorsing the Universal Declaration excuse violations in their own country as manifestations of their country's culture. Where their governments express reservations about the universality of human rights, it is often young people, who are less ambivalent, who take the courageous step of denouncing human rights violations and refusing to accept that such injustice is inherent to their culture.

This is what happened in the People's Republic of China a few years ago, when students acted as the driving force behind the demonstrations at Tiananmen Square. Many of their brave protests were permanently silenced by the state's ruthless response, which demonstrated that the authorities were little troubled by human rights. Nonetheless, the young people's arguments for improving the human rights situation have lost none of their validity.

What is it that makes young people willing to put themselves forward in this way? Possibly it relates to the fact that they do not yet have established positions in society. They are not yet entangled in a web of political and economical interests that make it tempting to qualify the universality of human rights. They have not yet ascended to positions of power that make it expedient to turn a blind eye to matters such as human rights. Their dependency in society would hence appear to have a converse in their open-mindedness in forming opinions.

Whatever the case may be, the more opportunities young people have, and grasp, to further the cause of human rights, the better the prospect of the human rights situation will be. For those who devote themselves actively to the cause of human rights in their youth will be less likely to violate them once in a position of power. Thus the relatively young membership of Amnesty International, to give one example, is a hopeful sign.

Many young people have a positive attitude to human rights. So the sceptical note they sometimes sound about the United Nations may appear out of tune. After all, was it not the UN General Assembly that adopted the Universal Declaration of Human Rights, in Paris on 10 December 1948?

A sense of disappointment is felt about the inability of the United Nations to take decisive action. Although the United Nations has succeeded in playing a certain moderating role in international conflicts, there have been many massacres since the Second World War that have been tempered scarcely, if at all, by United Nations intervention. The brutal crushing of the Hungarian uprising in 1956, Pol Pot's Killing Fields in Cambodia, and the genocide between Hutu and Tutsi groups in Rwanda, are all examples of this. People had high hopes of the United Nations in connection with these events, hopes that were dashed: at such critical moments the United Nations proved incapable of invoking the Universal Declaration to take a resolute stand against injustice.

Anyone who is familiar with the organisation of the United Nations and the way in which its powers are divided will appreciate its limitations. Given all the circumstances, the United Nations could not perhaps have done much more than it did, in each of these cases, to prevent the massacres. Perhaps it had to confine itself to acting as a platform for discussion to preserve a foundation, at least, on which bridges could be built. Where people do what they can, they deserve to be treated with understanding.

But to understand is not to justify. Whatever the difficulties, there is every reason to work towards improving the organisational structure of the United Nations, so that it is better equipped to uphold human rights.

You can design an organisational structure to be as rigid or as flexible as you want. In this respect, it is possible to end on a hopeful note. Some countries include a youth representative in their delegations to the UN General Assembly. Each youth representative attends the meetings and addresses one of the commissions in a speech and a personal message that they have largely prepared themselves.

Afterwards, the youth representatives visit large numbers of schools in their own country to report on the results of their trip and to relate their findings. In so doing, they do more to raise awareness of the role and scope of the United Nations, and to widen the support base for its activities, than any public information pamphlet.

The Netherlands, like Norway and Denmark, is one of the countries with a youth representative. In 1991 I was fortunate enough to be chosen for this position. I know, not only from my own experience, but also from my successors, that it is indeed possible to further substantive dialogue using the United Nations as a platform. The result is a fundamental improvement in the functioning of the organisation.

Young people constitute a large proportion of the world population and frequently have ideas of their own about human rights. The platform offered by the United Nations is one of the places in which these ideas can be aired. Partly for this reason, it would be of immense value if more countries were to adopt this mode of youth participation.

ANNA ENQUIST

The Red Jacket

She's not worried about her rights,
the daughter. Splashing sunlight,
gentle water, sad song.

Over the safe grass she crawls
toward me. Knees, arms, mouth.
She's entitled to a red jacket.

I won't mention how the colors
were devoured by a casual dusk.
Stark white

hits the eye like a fist.
Entitled to the scream, the last
boat, the taste of bread?

Look: in the evening, time
lies down over things like a thin blanket.
We've a right to it. We're not affected.

Kid, these are lies, this has to do
with the thick skin and closed eyes
that rule the lines of the poem.

My Story

When I grew up, in a nomadic family in Somalia, there was little or no talk about the outside world. We just lived, from day to day, surviving with our routine and our animals. This was how everyone lived, and how everyone had lived as far back as any of us could remember. There was just one right way to live and we were doing it.

Human rights were unheard of and something like the Universal Declaration of Human Rights was totally unimaginable.

I am highly unusual because I ran away. I left home. I had never heard of anyone doing that before. But I did it. Why? To escape being married off to an old man for some camels. This was also part of how we lived, but I just couldn't accept it. I guess I was just different.

I was also extraordinarily lucky. I not only discovered a very big world outside my Somalian home, but I also managed to succeed in it.

Now when I look at the Universal Declaration of Human Rights I see that whoever wrote it must have had people like me in mind. I especially agree that '[n]o one shall be subjected to ... cruel, inhuman or degrading treatment'. Because that is exactly what happened to me when I was forced to undergo female genital mutilation (FGM).

I want to tell the whole world that FGM goes on. I want the world to know FGM is a life and death matter for many women. I want the Universal Declaration of Human Rights to be enforced so that the practice will be banned forever and everywhere. Everything I am about as a woman and all that I do today is directed towards this end.

Let me tell you my story.

I was one of 12 children. When I was about 5 years old, I was 'cut'. I remember it as if it were yesterday. My mother told me to be a good girl and not move. The woman who did it used an old razor blade with the dried blood of another girl still on it. She cut off my clitoris and everything else including the labia and then sewed me up with a needle – all this without anaesthesia. The pain was beyond belief. They tied my legs together so I couldn't walk and rip myself open. I bled for three months and all I wanted to do was to die.

I survived, but FGM killed one of my sisters and two of my cousins. In my country, you can't escape it. They catch you and tie you down and do it. Why? Because it's part of the culture. My mother had it done to her, so did her mother, grandmothers, and great-grandmothers before her. It's the men that want FGM. They say religion demands it. But it has nothing to do with religion. Neither the Bible nor the Koran talks about female excision anywhere. Men just don't want women to have sexual pleasure. They think that women who have not been circumcised will have sex with anyone because they can't control themselves.

The pain of FGM doesn't end with the first cutting. Every time a woman has sex, the man has to force himself in, or cut her open with his knife. Every time a woman gives birth, she has to be cut open. After giving birth, she is sewn up again.

FGM exits because women are seen as less than men. Man can do what they want with them because they own them. I once heard a man justify FGM in this way: 'A woman is my property. I have to protect my property. When I leave my house, I don't leave the door unlocked so others can just walk in.'

That is why we can also be married off without any say in the matter. When I was 13, my father was getting ready to sell me for five camels to a 60-year-old man. That's when I decided to run away. My mother knew what I was planning and she cried, but she kept my secret until I left.

I fled to my aunt's house in Mogadishu. I had to travel through the desert stealing milk from other tribes' camels at night when their owners were asleep. I made it to the city and found my aunt who welcomed me. Through her, I learned an uncle of mine was the Somali Ambassador in England and I wrangled a job as a housekeeper in the Somali Embassy in London.

I was overwhelmed by England. I was just a girl from the desert. I didn't speak a word of English. I couldn't read or write. But I knew right from the start that I was different. I found out quickly that what had been done to me wasn't done to girls in England. I was angry. I wanted to be the same as the girls around me. I kept saying to myself, 'Why me? Why?'

When my uncle's term of office ended, I refused to go back to Somalia. I got a job at McDonald's and enrolled in night school. I had met a photographer who wanted to take photos of me. I had refused at first until a modeling agency convinced me to do it. My first pictures appeared on the cover of the Pirelli calendar. When it came out, I became famous overnight. I have been a model ever since.

After 15 years away from home, I got a chance to return to Somalia for a BBC television programme on my life. I saw my mother for the first time after so long and so many changes. We just embraced and cried. I begged her to come back with me to London, but she wouldn't leave her home. I also felt at home almost immediately, even after 15 years. I didn't want to leave. Africa is so beautiful but it needs help so people can live decently, so kids can go to school and have some hope that the future will get better.

I'm married now and have a child. But I will never be able to live like normal women, women who have not undergone FGM. I can have a physical relationship like everyone else; I didn't lose the ability to experience physical sensation. But FGM has given me a bunch of lasting health problems. My periods are heavy and last a long time. Because of the pain, I stay in seclusion for days. And, there is nothing that can be done to change this.

FGM is nothing more than torture; it is cruel, inhuman, degrading and above all unnecessary. The Universal Declaration of Human Rights states that no one shall be subjected to this type of practice. Female excision is mutilation. It must be prohibited. I'll tell you one thing – if this was done to men, it would be solved overnight. Why? Because men have power and women often don't have any at all.

I don't like talking about this because it's very private. Even though I have a lot of shame about my personal situation, I realize that my fame gives me an opportunity to speak out against this terrible mutilation that still affects women every day. It is estimated that 120 million women have undergone FGM and that 2 million girls each year are at risk. I know what it is like. I have experienced the pain and have a right to speak. So I decided that it would be a crime for me to keep silent.

So today, I am an ambassador for the United Nations Population Fund (UNFPA) and for my sisters in Africa who can't speak out. We want female excision stopped. We want to be treated as human beings with the same basic dignity guaranteed by the Universal Declaration of Human Rights. I won't be silent until this happens.

Article 11

1. Everyone charged with a penal offence has the right to be presumed innocent until proved guilty according to law in a public trial at which he has had all the guarantees necessary for his defence.
2. No one shall be held guilty of any penal offence on account of any act or omission which did not constitute a penal offence, under national or international law, at the time when it was committed. Nor shall a heavier penalty be imposed than the one that was applicable at the time the penal offence was committed.

ASBJØRN EIDE

Freedom from Want:
Taking Economic and Social Rights Seriously

THE CONTEXT AND HISTORICAL SIGNIFICANCE OF THE UNIVERSAL DECLARATION OF HUMAN RIGHTS

The Universal Declaration of Human Rights restored and consolidated a process of normative development which had emerged in some societies during the 17th and 18th century but which had since increasingly been confronted by illiberal collectivist ideologies. It did much more, however. It broadened and gave more substance to the twin concepts of freedom and equality, and their interrelationship. Even more importantly, it significantly expanded the content of human rights when compared to traditional notions, and thereby overcame some of the criticisms which in the past had been made to notions of 'civil' or 'natural' rights. It declared that the rights should be made universal in geographical scope and be enjoyed by everyone without discrimination. It also initiated a revolution in international law by making compliance with human rights a legitimate concern in international law and relations.

There was at least a threefold historical context to the adoption of the Universal Declaration: the revulsion against the brutality and authoritarianism which had infested many political systems before and during the Second World War, the constructive reaction to the economic and social dislocation associated with the Great Depression which had made possible the emergence of those authoritarian and repressive regimes, and a belated revolt against centuries of racial discrimination based on the assumption that Europeans, or white people, were somehow superior and therefore also entitled to rule vast territories where other peoples lived.

FREEDOM FROM WANT AND THE GREATEST INNOVATION: ECONOMIC AND SOCIAL RIGHTS

Much of the inspiration for the preparation of the United Nations Charter, and later of the Universal Declaration, was the famous 'Four Freedoms Address' of the President of the United States, Franklin D. Roosevelt, in 1941 which included the freedom from want, to which this essay is devoted.

Probably the greatest innovation made by the Universal Declaration is the inclusion of economic, social and cultural rights. They constitute three interrelated

121

components of a more comprehensive package with close links to civil and political rights.

Article 22 refers to the economic, social and cultural rights 'indispensable for [one's] dignity and the free development of [one's] personality' and to 'the right to social security'. It precedes the five subsequent articles which declare the rights to work (Article 23), to rest and leisure (Article 24), to an adequate standard of living (Article 25), to education (Article 26), and to participate freely in the cultural life of the community (Article 27).

At the core of *social* rights is the right to an adequate standard of living (Article 25). This right requires, as a minimum, that everyone shall enjoy the necessary subsistence rights – adequate food and nutrition, clothing, housing and the necessary conditions of care and health services. Closely related to this is the right of families to assistance, briefly mentioned in Article 25 and elaborated in greater detail in subsequent provisions such as Article 10 of the International Covenant on Economic, Social and Cultural Rights and Article 27 of the Convention on the Rights of the Child.

In order to enjoy these social rights, there is also a need for certain *economic* rights. These are the right to own property (Article 17), the right to work and work-related rights (Articles 23 and 24) and the right to social security (Articles 22 and 25).

Property in the traditional sense of the word cannot be enjoyed on an equal basis by all. The right to own property therefore has to be supplemented by at least two other rights: the right to work which can provide an income ensuring an adequate standard of living, and the right to social security which can supplement, and, where necessary, fully replace, insufficient income derived from property or from work – insufficient, that is, for the enjoyment of an adequate standard of living.

The right to work is also a basis of independence, provided the work is freely chosen by the person concerned, that sufficient income is obtained from it, and provided the workers can protect their interests through free trade unions.

The right to social security is essential, particularly when a person does not have the necessary property, or is not able to secure an adequate standard of living through work, due either to unemployment, old age or disability (Articles 22 and 25).

CREATING THE CONDITIONS: ARTICLE 28 OF THE UNIVERSAL DECLARATION

'Everyone is entitled to a social and international order in which the rights and freedoms set forth in this Declaration can be fully realized' (Article 28). This article requires that social and international conditions be structured in such a way as to make possible the equal enjoyment of all the rights listed throughout the world. This requires adjustments of political and economic relations, both within states ('social order') and between states ('international order'). Obviously this could not be done over a short period of time. Some might say that Article 28 is a utopian aspiration. It is preferable, however, to see it as a vision to be pursued with determination, while taking into account that it will only gradually and partially be achieved in practice. As a vision, it has indeed inspired considerable activity in terms of both standards and action. Over the years the United Nations membership has sought to relate human rights to major global issues in its efforts to find solutions to human rights issues affecting the millions of deprived, dispossessed, discriminated against, and marginalized. The approach, reflected in the Proclamation of Teheran (1968) and many subsequent documents, is also known as the *structural approach*. It seeks to link human rights to major worldwide patterns and issues, to identify the root causes of human rights violations and to assess human rights in the light of concrete contexts and situations.

Such efforts can be traced back to Article 28 of the Universal Declaration and they are further developed in the Declaration on Social Progress and Development (1969) and the Declaration on the Right to Development (1986), as well as in the Declarations and Programs of Action of various world conferences over the last decade.

THE REALITY, AS ASSESSED BY RECENT WORLD CONFERENCES

The World Summit for Social Development, convened by the United Nations and held in Copenhagen in March 1995, noted achievements and failures 47 years after the adoption of the Universal Declaration.

The Summit's final document pointed out that there has been progress in some areas of social and economic development: 'The global wealth of nations has multiplied sevenfold in the past 50 years and international trade has grown even more dramatically. Life expectancy, literacy and primary education, and access to basic health care, including family planning, have increased in the majority of countries and average infant mortality has been reduced, including in developing countries.'

The failures, however, are staggering, 'Yet ... far too many people, particularly women and children, are vulnerable to stress and deprivation. Poverty, unemployment and social disintegration too often result in isolation, marginalization and violence. The insecurity that many people, in particular vulnerable people, face about the future – their own and their children's – is intensifying: Within many societies, both in developed and developing countries, the gap between rich and poor has increased.... More than one billion people in the world live in abject poverty, most of whom go hungry every day. A large proportion, the majority of whom are women, have very limited access to income, resources, education, health care or nutrition....'

The Summit also noted that there is a gender difference involved: 'More women than men live in absolute poverty and the imbalance continues to grow, with serious consequences for women and their children. Women carry a disproportionate share of the problems of coping with poverty, social disintegration, unemployment, environmental degradation and the effects of war....'

People with disabilities, the elderly, refugees and displaced persons also face serious difficulties. One in ten people have disabilities and are too often forced into poverty, unemployment and social isolation. In addition, in all countries older persons may be particularly vulnerable to social exclusion, poverty and marginalization. Millions of people worldwide are refugees or internally displaced persons. The tragic social consequences have a critical effect on the social stability and development of their home countries, their host countries and their respective regions.

The Heads of State and Government represented at the Social Summit therefore made a series of commitments. The Summit's final document states that the goals and objectives of social development require continuous efforts to reduce and eliminate major sources of social distress and instability for the family and for society. 'We pledge to place particular focus on and give priority attention to the fight against the worldwide conditions that pose severe threats to the health, safety, peace, security and wellbeing of our people. Among these conditions are chronic hunger; malnutrition; illicit drug problems; organized crime; corruption; foreign occupation; armed conflicts; illicit arms trafficking, terrorism, intolerance and incitement to racial, ethnic, religious and other hatreds; xenophobia; and endemic, communicable and chronic diseases. To this end, coordination and co-operation at the national level and especially at the regional and international levels should be further strengthened.'

The gender aspect of poverty was further highlighted at the Fourth World Conference on Women held in Beijing in September 1995.

The Human Development Report, published annually by the United Nations Development Program (UNDP), noted in its 1996 edition that economic and social conditions have declined at unprecedented rates for large numbers of people, possibly as many as 1.6 billion, while they have advanced at a dramatic pace for more than a quarter of the world's population (1996 Human Development Report, paragraph 29). The gap between rich and poor has doubled in the last three decades, with the poorest fifth of the world's population receiving 1.4 percent of global income and the richest fifth 85 percent.

In June 1996, the second United Nations Conference on Human Settlements (Habitat II) met in Istanbul to examine the present situation regarding housing and to develop commitments for the future. The conference noted in its final document that a large segment of the world's population, particularly in developing countries, still lacks shelter and sanitation. Since access to safe and healthy shelter and basic services is essential to a person's physical, psychological, social and economic wellbeing it should be a fundamental part of our urgent actions for the more than one billion people who do not enjoy decent living conditions. The objective is to achieve adequate shelter for all, especially the deprived urban and rural poor, through an enabling approach to the development and improvement of shelter that is environmentally sound.

The Habitat II conference noted that lack of development and the existence of widespread absolute poverty can inhibit the full and effective enjoyment of human rights and undermine fragile democracy and popular participation. Neither, however, can be invoked to justify violations of human rights and fundamental freedoms.

The conference noted that over the past twenty years world population has increased from about 4.2 billion to about 5.7 billion, with an increasing number of people living in cities. By the year 2000, over 50 percent of the population will live in urban areas. In developing countries, in particular, rapid urbanization and the growth of towns, cities and megacities, where public and private resources tend to concentrate, represent new challenges and at the same time new opportunities: there is a need to address the root causes of these phenomena, including rural to urban migration. The increasing globalization of the economy has contributed to an increase in the level of economic development of many countries, but the gap between poor and rich – countries as well as people – has widened.

Hunger and malnutrition were again in focus at the World Food Summit held in Rome in November 1996.

Together, these and other world conferences convened by the United Nations and its agencies during the last decade provide the basis for a vast agenda for the future. To implement that agenda, systematic implementation of the right for everyone to an adequate standard of living is essential.

SUMMARY OF PROBLEMS AND ISSUES

In sum, the world conferences have drawn our attention to the fact that while there has been significant growth over the last decades and many people have seen their conditions significantly improved, the economic and social rights of those who really need them have been increasingly undermined by the following factors:

(a) a steadily widening economic gap between rich and poor, within and among countries;

(b) increasing disemployment;

(c) decreasing attention for the fulfillment of basic needs;

(d) continued gender discrimination;

(e) population growth combined with a process of urbanization which is out of hand;

(f) serious environmental destruction.

THE RESPONSE MECHANISMS: THE STATE SYSTEM AND ITS ARCHITECTURE

A fundamental principle underlies contemporary international human rights law: primary responsibility for the implementation of human rights rests with the state. Not much was said in the Universal Declaration about state responsibilities, but these are spelled out in the international covenants. Under Article 2 of the International Covenant on Civil and Political Rights (ICCPR), states parties undertake to respect and to ensure to all individuals within their territory and subject to their jurisdiction the rights recognized in the ICCPR. Under Article 2 of the International Covenant on Economic, Social and Cultural Rights (ICESCR), states parties undertake to take steps, individually and through international assistance and co-operation, especially economic and technical, to the maximum of their available resources, with a view to achieving progressively the full realization of the rights recognized in the ICESCR by all appropriate means, including particularly the adoption of legislative measures.

Important contributions to the analysis of the content of the rights contained in the ICESCR, and on the nature of violations of that Covenant, were made by a group of experts who met twice at the University of Limburg (Maastricht), first in 1986 to define the content of the rights and second in January 1997 to clarify what constitutes violations thereof.

At the end of this millennium, however, we see an unmistakable decline and change in the role of the state. If we take the West European states as example, it can clearly be argued that two major concerns dominated conceptions of their role for most of this century, and particularly in the first three or four decades after the Second World War. One was the role of protecting national security, mainly understood in military terms, and the other was to develop and maintain a welfare state based on social integration and distribution of benefits.

For a number of reasons, both these roles seem to be in decline. The concern with military security against external enemies is significantly reduced after the end of the Cold War, and the maintenance of the welfare state at the level it had reached at its highest point has become impossible due to the impact of the global market and global economy. The commitments made under the World Trade Organization, the European Union and other arrangements reduce significantly the scope available to the state to regulate welfare.

On the threshold of the next century, a thorough review of approaches may be necessary because the world is now experiencing its greatest economic and social upheavals since the Industrial Revolution. Trends towards globalization, driven by economics and technology, are transforming trade, finance, currency, employment, the environment and social systems communications. This also affects deep-rooted structures of national societies.

All states and their societies are now intertwined in a complex system of global interdependencies. The nature of sovereignty is undergoing a profound change. It is in part transferred upwards and in part downwards. It goes upward – or rather outward – due to the emergence of a system of reciprocal dependencies and vulnerabilities which require decisions to be made jointly with other states, through informal networks such as the G7 (the group of the seven most industrialized states: the USA, Japan, Germany, France, Italy, the UK and Canada) or through the more formal intergovernmental institutions. It has been argued that the complexity of problems and the wide dispersion of the resources through which control is exerted are leading *de facto* to the emergence of a system of 'shared sovereignties'.

But sovereignty is also shifting downwards. Local politics appear to be increasing in importance. Decentralization and federal organizational structures are emerging, possibly because they help to overcome bureaucratic overload, but also because the central authority is unable to prevent this from happening.

The Future: The Role of the State in Global Governance and the Importance of Human Rights including Economic and Social Rights

For the foreseeable future, however, the state will at least nominally remain the foundation of international order. For it to be able to function properly, it will have to comply with the rule of law and will need to be considered legitimate by all parts of its population, in a setting where communications and contacts are increasingly open and where legitimacy can therefore only be based on the ability of the state to deliver what is expected of it. Since, however, it will by itself be less and less able to deliver, it can manage only through very extensive international co-operation.

This necessity is complicated by the fact that states, and groups of states, differ greatly in terms of power. In the years to come, power will be less determined by military than by economic indicators. The capacity to influence the decision-making of the International Monetary Fund and the World Bank is becoming much more important than the size of standing armies. In the 1980s the G7, which has met annually since 1975, started to rival other international organizations and in the 1990s it is seen by some as a possible super-network which will overpower other international organizations, such as the United Nations. So far, this has not happened due to the divergence of interests within the G7, but the prospects are there.

Towards Global Governance?

Since the United Nations was established, there has been tremendous growth in inter-governmental organizations (IGOs) and non-governmental ones (NGOs) worldwide.

A network for global governance is therefore in existence, consisting both of intergovernmental networks and international civil society. About 2,000 NGOs now have observer status with various parts of the United Nations system. They are

127

active participants at international conferences and play a significant role in the preparation of the global agenda.

The establishment of a social and international order in which the human rights contained in the Universal Declaration can be enjoyed by everyone will require increasing collaboration between international civil society and the evolving inter-governmental system. The bureaucracies of both are increasingly recruited from the same set of persons with an international spirit who draw their inspiration from international standards.

Efforts will be required to make the rule of law more effective within the international framework, to move towards greater justice along the lines of the Declaration on the Right to Development (1986), and based on the ethics of human rights.

The joint solution of problems in networks calls for trust between the partici-pants. This can be obtained only by relying on explicit, universally recognized values and principles. Human rights, as set out in the Universal Declaration, can play the integrating role of normative systems in the emerging global society.

The state will remain an important actor in this system. It is and remains the main repository for the application of the rule of law, but that task will increasingly be based not on national legislation but on standards adopted collectively by states in consultation with representatives of the emerging global civil society. This is of particular importance in the fulfillment of what is now the most important of the purposes set for the United Nations in Article 1 of its Charter:

> 3. To achieve international co-operation in solving international problems of an economic, social, cultural, or humanitarian character, and in promoting and encouraging respect for human rights and for fundamental freedoms for all without distinction as to race, sex, language, or religion; and
> 4. To be a center for harmonizing the actions of nations in the attainment of these common ends.

There are many unknowns in this scenario, however, and prediction alone will not suffice. What will be required is a continuous application of three tasks: assessment, analysis and action. The first is to assess the present situation in order to identify where, in particular, improvements have to be made. Having assessed the situation, there is a need for a proper analysis of the causes and the underlying problems, in order to have the best possible understanding of the obstacles to be overcome in order to move forward constructively. Then comes the most important task, which is to take action in order to remedy the situation. And then again, the effect of the action must be assessed. In this way the agenda unfolds. Article 28 of the Universal Declaration envisages that the guidance for the agenda shall be the rights contained therein.

The impact of the disparities discussed above on the lives of people – especially the poor – is dramatic and renders the enjoyment of economic, social and cultural rights illusory for most people. Poverty makes the right to an adequate standard of living illusory for vast numbers of people. To rectify this tragic situation is in quantitative terms the most important part of the human rights agenda.

Sustainable development of human settlements combines economic development, social development and environmental protection, with full respect for all human rights and fundamental freedoms, including the right to development, and offers a means of achieving a world of greater stability and peace, built on ethical and spiritual vision. Democracy, respect for human rights, transparent, representative and accountable government and administration in all sectors of society, as well as effective participation by civil society, are indispensable foundations for the realization of sustainable development. There is a strong need for worldwide partnerships to create a more favorable international economic environment.

AGNES GERGELY

From the Years of Barbarism

Because we are always stepping into the same river
Graham Swift

AROUND THE COMPASS

The east front is forgotten.
The copper mine shut down.
The last train was derailed
off the damaged track.
At one side of the treeless space,
where five Dutchmen fell down,
there are red stains on the steps:
whether from blood or red lead,
no one will ever tell.
And the pastor who said:
'This is no lard but cheese,
you may eat it' – he is now
an anecdote. The archives are empty.
The remembering one kneels down,
ontological force makes him
throw his pebbles in water,
the desert jackal flees in fright,
long rivers have stopped running.
We are born to be faithless
and cannibals.

BARCAROLA

A whole decade will slowly founder soon
desire drifts off on a raft below the house
in belfries Monteverdi's tunes arise
Canal Grande's lit by a yellow moon

the yellow moon that trembling yellow stain

a belfry with one bell-rope hanging low
the raft is like a wick of lamp aglow
   the continent a huge lamp on the main

the continent will slowly founder soon
rafts belfries Canal Grande and Gulag
three heart attacks pulped books and Petrograd
the mental home's lit by a yellow moon

the yellow stain that trembling yellow stain
but on canals there's life in a well-curb's range
a water-town for another in exchange
   with Akhmatova bending o'er his pain

FROM THE YEARS OF BARBARISM

Guard Captain Golyev killed Lieutenant Ilyin
in a duel. Then the Captain gave orders
to shell the noteworthy buildings of the town,
including the Byelchev palace, built in the
eighteenth century, with its stucco ornaments
and baroque stalls.
   I assure you, Sire, that
stucco ornaments were of no use. Why should we
dazzle barbarians? It's the proportions
that keep the town alive; destruction's draw.
What you deign to fly over is no chasm.
Fall is the only measure. That horseman
on the hilltop is no horseman unless caught up,
or else he's an equestrian statue.
   Listen, Sire,
the bells toll for Lieutenant Ilyin.
I recall him sitting before me at the college
with hands sweating in classes on fire-arms.
Now let him sweat, for ever if he likes. Here
history is to measure on my scale.
'The one who killed him. Who gave orders to shell.'
Ilyin will enter legends. And time's gaping depth –
just wait, Sire – will send up, as a landslide
sends up lava, the synthesis of the two of us.
'That death was not by him – it was for him'.

MIKHAIL GORBACHEV

A Landmark in the History of Moral, Legal and Political Culture

I firmly believe that the Universal Declaration of Human Rights, adopted by the General Assembly of the United Nations on 10 December 1948, is an outstanding landmark in the development of the moral, legal and political culture of mankind. In proclaiming respect for human rights and fundamental freedoms as a common standard of achievement for all peoples and all nations, the United Nations defined a new quality standard and new criteria for modern civilization.

In my view, the fact that this document reflects, in condensed form, the teachings of the great philosophers and moralists of the West and the East is of primary importance. In the Universal Declaration of Human Rights and in the human rights instruments adopted later one can discern the influence of the ideas embodied in the English Habeas Corpus Act, the French Declaration of the Rights of Man and of the Citizen, the Russian Declaration of the Rights of Workers and Exploited People and a whole range of other documents of this kind.

We must pay tribute to the wisdom, experience and skill of the people responsible for this document: the scholars who pored over the text, the diplomats who harmonised it, the statesmen who realised they must adopt it in spite of their many doubts and prejudices.

The appearance of this unique document was made possible by the upsurge of democratic feelings that followed the United Nations' victory over fascism and militarism, forces that had unleashed the bloodiest global war in the history of mankind.

People still had vivid memories of that terrible ordeal and were determined never to allow it to happen again.

The Allied nations that had defeated fascism still had a sense of collective responsibility for the development of international relations, for drawing lessons from this latest tragedy. The first signs of the 'Cold War' did not stop the adoption of the Universal Declaration.

Given the unique historical circumstances, the document had to be a compromise. And this compromise itself was unique, reflecting liberal, democratic and socialist positions at the same time.

Although adhering to their respective ideologies, the parties to the agreement recognised the absolute primacy of human rights, placing them higher than any political doctrine, dignifying them as a 'superideology'. And one should not forget that those who adopted this historic document included Communists and anti-

Communists, as well as supporters of literally all other social, political and religious trends. Having declared their determination to join forces to protect human rights they recognised the oneness of modern civilization and defined its supreme values.

To my enormous regret, this opportunity for constructive cooperation between states in the post-war era came to nothing. The historic chance was lost. Mutual suspicion, the desire to 'outwit' one's former allies at any price – including their destruction – the split into opposing military alignments, brought both the West and the East, and indeed the whole world, to the verge of complete self-annihilation in the inferno of nuclear war.

In these circumstances there was, as it were, no time for the observation of human rights. Declarations of commitment to human rights would frequently turn out to be nothing more than hypocrisy. Let us not forget the 'witch hunts' in both the West and the East, not to mention the so-called 'wars of liberation' in various regions of the world.

Fortunately, in the second half of the eighties it became possible to take some real steps towards averting the threat of a nuclear apocalypse and later towards ending the Cold War. The world once again has a historic chance to achieve the level of international civilization worthy of our modern times, the kind of civil and international relations that were so brilliantly outlined in the Universal Declaration of Human Rights and in the international conventions that followed it.

Will we be able to seize this opportunity? Or will we allow it to slip through our fingers again? Would we ever allow anyone to initiate a second 'cold war'?

No one has the right to close his eyes to the fact that it is mainly the citizens of countries with developed economies and stable democratic regimes who are able to enjoy universally recognized human rights in relatively full measure. Those who live in the vast regions plagued by hunger, poverty, illiteracy and mass unemployment can only dream of this. And between these two extremes – prosperity and disaster – in three quarters of all the countries of the world, people have very limited and, moreover, selective access to social rights and political freedoms.

Does this mean that we cannot talk seriously about human rights with reference to these nations? Are those who are inclined to apply different standards in talking about human rights in the West and in the East to be considered right? Can violence be justified on the grounds that a country does not respect human rights?

In my view, none of this is acceptable. While I admit the fact that the world is still far from perfect, I believe that we must not go to the extreme. What is most important is the direction in which social and political processes develop, the kind of future we can forecast on the basis of the prevailing trends. Given the fact that the half-century that has passed since the adoption of the Universal Declaration has been dominated by relentless opposition between the two political blocs, that vast quantities of resources have been thrown into the furnace of the arms race, that military conflicts are once again flaring up in several regions of the world and that a number of global problems – the environment, energy resources and population growth – are clearly worsening, even given all this we must nevertheless realize that the number of people for whom human rights are no longer just mere words has increased considerably since 1948.

In this respect there have been enormous changes in Russia and the other CIS states and in the countries of Eastern and Central Europe over the last decade. The political freedom *perestroika* offered to the peoples of this vast region gave them the chance to make their own choices and to enter into a process of democratization. But this process has its ups and downs. Democratic and authoritarian forces are clashing in a number of countries. We must not close our eyes to this either. This is a dangerous situation, especially in a country like, say, Russia. The democratic community at both the national and international level must be alert and active. And the main criterion for assessment must, without doubt, be the situation of the individual: whether and how much his life has improved, whether he is now better able to enjoy his natural and inherent rights.

There is one article in the Universal Declaration which, it seems to me, is undeservedly passed over by the commentators. It reads: 'Everyone is entitled to a social and international order in which the rights and freedoms set forth in this Declaration can be fully realized' (Article 28). This unequivocally connects the internal structure of individual societies to the international order and proclaims the well-being of the individual to be the main concern of both. It seems to me that philosophers and politicians might find it useful to contemplate this formula, which to a great extent is actually a warning.

Realistically speaking, it would be naive to say that everyone can realize the rights set forth in the above essay. It will not be possible in the near future. But in order to achieve this goal, we must persistently move towards it: every year, every day, including today. For only by taking a step at a time can we reach the end of this road.

No one shall be subjected to arbitrary interference with his privacy, family, home or correspondence, nor to attacks upon his honour and reputation. Everyone has the right to the protection of the law against such interference or attacks.

IAIN GUEST

The Universal Declaration and the Power of Shame

I have been covering human rights for over twenty years, as a journalist, UN official, and author. It has been a rocky road, with more than a few ignominious moments. Over the years I have watched, with a kerchief over my nose, as hundreds of bodies were dug up from the killing fields in Cambodia, found a frightened former Chilean air force officer in hiding in France and reintroduced him to a woman he tortured a decade earlier, shared my UN salary with frantic Haitians who were being hunted in Port au Prince by *Tontons Macoutes* and grieved with the brother of one of the American churchwomen who were murdered in 1980 in El Salvador at the graveside of his sister.

The Universal Declaration of Human Rights has been my companion throughout – steering me through roadblocks, jails and refugee camps, helping to make sense of arcane UN resolutions. I can think of no other document that was drafted with such clarity and common sense, and certainly none that involved so many contradictions.

The rights that are laid out in the Universal Declaration impose limits and obligations on government. But – and here is the contradiction – governments drafted these rules, governments monitor them, and governments sit in judgement on violations at the annual session of the UN Commission on Human Rights. This is rather like asking serial killers to act as judge and jury in a murder case. How can such a paradoxical formula possibly work?

I asked that question in the spring of 1976, after a tall, awkward-looking Argentinean general named Jorge Videla seized power from President Isabel Peron. Over the next six years, General Videla's troops kidnapped thousands of fellow Argentineans and whisked them into concentration camps to be tortured and killed. The operation ran like clockwork, even down to a plan which divided Greater Buenos Aires between the armed forces. By 1978 everyone knew that Navy death squads were killing people at the Navy's cadet training school in central Buenos Aires.

Argentina's dirty war was a spectacular violation of Article 3 of the Universal Declaration: 'Everyone has the right to life, liberty and security of person'. Strangely enough, however, it was also the first major human rights crisis to make sense of this 1948 formula. The disappearances changed the way the UN dealt with human rights. How and why helps to explain what it will take to keep the Universal Declaration relevant, as we look to the next fifty years.

The explanation begins with the fact that Argentina's military rulers and their opponents took the UN seriously. Until 1976, only three governments had been publicly condemned by the UN Commission on Human Rights. These were South Africa, Israel and Chile, and they accepted their pariah status with some resignation. But General Videla and his colleagues fought tooth and claw to keep their misdeeds from reaching the UN Commission on Human Rights. The task was entrusted to Argentina's ambassador to the UN, Gabriel Martinez, a smooth and eloquent diplomat. Martinez turned his skills against the relatives of the disappeared, who started coming to Geneva in the summer of 1976. To this day, I have never encountered such passion in a human rights campaign. Martinez must have feared it greatly, to judge from the way he denounced them as 'subversives' and 'terrorists'. If so, it was because he understood shame.

In 1977, the UN possessed no divisions, no police, and no court. (Governments had long ago dropped the idea of a permanent criminal court as being too intrusive.) Its only weapon was the power to shame. Martinez was never heard to dispute that Argentineans enjoyed the 'right to life'. The only issue was whether this right was being abused in Argentina. Gabriel Martinez said it was not, with a vehemence that was impossible to ignore. This made for good copy. We journalists had good reason to be grateful to this sinister man.

Martinez also managed to alienate UN officials who serviced the Commission meetings under the direction of Theo van Boven, a Dutchman. Van Boven sympathised with the relatives of the disappeared and felt strongly that UN officials could not remain neutral in defense of human rights even if it meant confronting governments. This earned him the undying hostility of Martinez, which caused Van Boven to further dig in his heels.

Until 1981 Van Boven was cushioned by support from the United States, which was finding – rather like the UN – that its own human rights policy was being defined by Argentina. President Jimmy Carter's Assistant Secretary of State for Human Rights, Patricia Derian, travelled to Argentina where she met with, and wept with, Mothers of the Plaza de Mayo. Back in Washington, she instructed American diplomats to push the UN into action on the disappearances. For this, she was vilified by many Americans, who felt she was antagonising an important trading partner. This may have been true. But by subordinating America's own narrow interests to human rights, Derian made the Universal Declaration more universal and greatly strengthened the credibility of the UN Commission on Human Rights. It was another crucial factor in making the 1948 formula function.

It must be said that at the time this alliance seemed to produce meagre results when Martinez succeeded in keeping Argentina off the UN's blacklist of gross violators. But this simply took the debate in a different direction, and in 1980 the Commission established a working group on disappearances. Initially, this was seen as a thinly-veiled and rather unsatisfactory attempt to punish Argentina. But it began to look like an inspired break-through, as it became clear that disappearances were being used by military regimes throughout Latin America and Asia. The pattern evidently existed in very different cultures and societies – further demonstrating the 'universality' of the human rights struggle.

In clarifying this, the new working group also made the UN more accessible. Normally, non-governmental organisations had to win a special bureaucratic status before they could address the UN Commission on Human Rights. But this did not apply to the new working group, and by 1982 it was hearing testimony from human rights advocates throughout the world. Not only was it taken seriously by relatives of the disappeared: it became the focus for their year-round lobbying.

This drew some remarkable people to Geneva. They included Emilio Mignone, a sad-eyed Argentinean lawyer whose daughter Monica had been seized in front of his eyes in Buenos Aires; Roberto Cuellar, who cradled the martyred Salvadorean Archbishop Oscar Romero in his arms and took up his work on behalf of El Salvador's poor and oppressed; Marianella Garcia Villas, another Salvadorean activist who was to be murdered in an army sweep; Miguel Angel Estrella, a world-famous pianist who was driven half-mad in Uruguay's infamous Liberty jail.

They made for a riveting story. I was not the only reporter to cut his teeth on human rights. And when I was at a loss for words, I could turn to Amnesty International. In yet another miscalculation, the Junta agreed to admit a delegation from Amnesty in 1976. Amnesty's subsequent report on the disappearances helped to win the Nobel Peace Prize. With this, human rights came of age. So, in a sense, did the Universal Declaration. And for this, we had to thank one of this century's most violent regimes.

Fast forward to the summer of 1992. In some respects the world seems a safer place. The dictators have gone. Communism has been swept away. Totalitarianism is in ruins. Every Latin American nation but one has elected its government. Dissidents of the 1980s have become the presidents of the 1990s in Czechoslovakia and Poland. The language of human rights has become *de rigeur* for campaigns of every persuasion – so much so that a major environment conference in Brazil has just concluded that communities have the right to be informed in advance about probable pollution. As well as disappearances, the UN Commission on Human Rights is now investigating summary executions, torture, and religious intolerance. Furthermore Amnesty International is campaigning to create the post of a UN High Commissioner for Human Rights.

As important as all this is, by 1992 human rights is no longer the sole preserve of a specialised corner of the UN system. The UN's Department of Peace-Keeping Operations (DPKO) has deployed human rights field monitors as part of peace-keeping missions in Cambodia and El Salvador. The monitors started work in El Salvador during the civil war and helped to convince both sides that the UN could be trusted as an intermediary. Here was an example of how human rights could indeed trigger peace (one of the goals of the UN Charter). In Cambodia, monitors have successfully negotiated the release of political prisoners and the removal of shackles in jails. These efforts were backed up by a Security Council that had never seemed more unified and committed in support of human rights. Security Councel Resolution 688 of 5 April 1991, which led to a safe haven in northern Iraq, has been interpreted as the first-ever to authorise the use of force in defense of human rights.

Ironically, it was at this moment of enormous promise that the UN suffered its greatest reverse. Early in April 1992, Bosnian Serb militia linked up with the Serbian army and attacked non-Serbs across a broad arc of Northern and Eastern Bosnia. Within weeks, Muslim women and children were being driven from their homes, placed in cattle trucks and 'ethnically cleansed'. Their husbands and sons were taken to concentration camps – Manjaca, Omarska, Trnoplje, Keraterm – to be starved, beaten and even killed. In December 1992, I visited some of these men in the Croatian town of Karlovac, shortly after their release. I remember how one Bosnian Muslim showed the orthodox cross that his captors had carved in his back and told me in a low voice how he had seen one of the inmates forced to castrate fellow prisoners in the centre at Omarska. (He knew his tale was grisly. But what really upset him was that he had to tell it through a female interpreter.) These abuses mocked the very concept of human rights. They had been supervised by the Deputy Interior Minister of the Bosnian 'Serb Republic', a man named Simo Drljaca.

Two years later the central African nation of Rwanda was visited by even greater evil, when Rwandan Hutu began to plan the elimination of the entire Tutsi minority. The trap was sprung in April 1994, after Hutu extremists shot down the plane carrying the Rwandan and Burundian presidents. Between 500,000 and a million Rwandans died. Four years on, the physical and psychological scars are still raw. I recently visited one site near the town of Gikongoro, where thousands of disinterred bodies await cleaning and burial. The smell and the shame of genocide still seem to cling to my clothes.

Two outbreaks of genocide within five years force us to ask whether the Universal Declaration of Human Rights is still valid. Pointing to Bosnia, some will say that the end of the Cold War has changed the face of human rights forever. In the former Yugoslavia, they will say, the retreat of Communism opened a Pandora's box of ethnic tensions and led to a war in Bosnia that produced abuses not seen in Europe since the Second World War. At least the Argentinean Junta had appeared to play by the rules, even while breaking them. The assailants in Bosnia (and Rwanda) ignored the fundamentals of human rights and humanitarian law, by targeting civilians. One communique of the UN High Commissioner for Refugees (UNHCR) had this to say about a young Bosnian who was evacuated from Sarajevo: 'The victim's left arm was chopped off by a machete, his right arm was slashed by a knife, his right eye pierced by a nail, and a bullet smashed into his head'. It was sadly typical.

But did this mean that the fundamental nature of the human rights challenge had changed? Some will argue that it has. They will point out that the terror of Bosnia or Rwanda was directed against an entire ethnic group instead of singling out individuals (like the disappearances in Argentina). Group violations are much harder for the UN to handle, because the Universal Declaration was drafted to protect individuals, not group rights.

The end of the Cold War has also forced us to reinterpret the right of 'self-determination'. During the 1980s this came to mean the right not to be invaded (as in Afghanistan and Cambodia). In this sense it thus reinforced the integrity of the state boundaries. The disintegration of Yugoslavia changed this. 'Self-determination' became the rallying cry of Croats who wanted to secede from Yugoslavia in 1991, and Bosnian Serbs who wanted to carve out their own ethnically pure 'republic' from Bosnia in 1992. Asylum has undergone a similar change. Under Article 14 of the Universal Declaration, everyone has the right to seek asylum. The Cold War gave Western governments a strategic reason to respect this right during the 1980s because most of the world's refugees were fleeing Communist regimes. But the end of the Cold War has removed that incentive and resulted in a dramatic collapse in support for asylum-seekers in the West. European governments were even reluctant to take in those seriously damaged Bosnians who were released from the Serb concentration camps in 1992.

Students of human rights will no doubt continue to debate the effect of these geopolitical changes as we approach the twenty-first century. They may conclude that the next challenge to human rights will come from forces that cannot be easily regulated or controlled by government, such as private global capital, the internet, and other new technology. Yet in some key respects, the genocide in Bosnia and Rwanda is a throwback to the 1940s, and a reminder that the Universal Declaration remains valid. The massacres in Rwanda and Bosnia were sanctioned and organised by state officials. In this sense they reaffirm the importance of the 'right to life' and the need to hold governments accountable. They also show how massive human rights abuses can lead to war and threaten international security – another of the 1948 assumptions.

The key difference lies in shame. The Argentinean military fought its dirty war in the shadows, kidnapping by night and denying it by day. Even the German Nazis kept their mass murder out of the sight of ordinary Germans. But the *interahamwe* and Bosnian Serbs gloried in the excess and tried to spread responsibility as widely as possible. One of the most terrifying images of the Bosnian war is that of Ratko Mladic, the Bosnian Serb Army Commander, after the fall of Srebrenica in July 1995. Flushed with success at having bullied the small contingent of Dutch peace-keepers in Srebrenica, Mladic laughingly dismissed the fears of terrified Muslims as they went to their death.

Similar scenes had occurred halfway across the world in Kigali, Rwanda. Here UN peace-keepers had watched in horror as Tutsi women and children were taken out of the church of Saint-Famille where they had sought sanctuary, and marched across the main road to a roadblock where their throats were cut in full view of passing traffic. Human rights had lost the power to shame. With that the Universal Declaration had been deprived of its greatest weapon.

This cannot be blamed on the United Nations human rights machinery. Plenty of mistakes were made by the UN Commission on Human Rights and secretariat during the 1980s and early 1990s, but they moved with unaccustomed speed on Bosnia and Rwanda. The Commission met in special session in August 1992 and appointed a former Polish Prime Minister, Tadeusz Mazowiecki, to investigate the former Yugoslavia on its behalf. Mazowiecki was to produce a searing series of reports that arguably went beyond his mandate by recommending the establishment of 'safe havens' to protect civilians, criticizing the UN's peace-making efforts, and even the humanitarian aid of the UNHCR. This raised hackles, but brought credibility to the Commission. The Commission also moved fast after the Rwandan genocide. The new High Commissioner for Human Rights, José Ayala Lasso, visited Rwanda in person in late 1994 and threw himself into the task of fundraising for a field mission that would investigate the genocide and help the new Rwandan government emerge from the nightmare.

If anything, this burst of activity by the Geneva-based human rights bodies makes the wider failure in Rwanda and Bosnia more disturbing. The rot set in at the UN Security Council. For a short time in 1991, the Council's five permanent members were able to unite in defense of universal values, when they repulsed Iraqi forces from Kuwait and created a safe haven for Kurdish refugees in northern Iraq. But within a year, this consensus had collapsed over Bosnia. The United States favoured the Bosnian Muslims, but was unwilling to risk American troops on the ground. The Russians sided with their Slavic allies, the Serbs. Britain and France had deployed peace-keeping forces in Bosnia and were opposed to any action that might jeopardise them. China was anxious to curb UN intervention.

The result was paralysis. Unable to agree on any action to stop the killing, the Council decided to treat the war in Bosnia as a humanitarian crisis instead of an act of aggression and genocide. At a meeting in London in August 1992, the UN and European Community joined forces and decided to increase humanitarian aid under the office of the UNHCR. In addition to preventing famine, UNHCR officials and convoys were expected to prevent further abuses and 'ethnic cleansing' by their mere presence. No one was fooled, least of all the Bosnian Serbs, who stepped up their attacks on Muslim civilians and aid workers. In desperation, the Security Council declared several 'safe havens', but failed to provide the means to protect them. This, too, served to fortify the resolve of the Serbs and convince Mladic and Karadzic that they had nothing to fear. It led, inexorably, to more violence and abuse. It was the same story in Rwanda. The UN deployed a peace-keeping force of 2,500 (UNAMIR) to monitor the Arusha Accords in 1993. By early 1994, UNAMIR's commander, General Romeo Dollaire, was reporting back that the Hutu *interahamwe* were preparing genocide. His warnings were ignored. Instead, when the killing began the Security Council reduced this force to 500 troops and told them to evacuate foreigners.

The cowardice and disarray of the UN Security Council crippled its decision to establish a tribunal in The Hague to prosecute war criminals in the former Yugo-slavia and Rwanda. This is arguably the most important development in international law since the adoption of the Universal Declaration. By allowing the prosecutor to invoke genocide, war crimes, and crimes against humanity, the tribunal's statute acknowledges the complexity and scope of the abuses committed in the two regions. The inclusion of genocide – hitherto a remote and legalistic concept – is particularly significant.

But the Security Council very nearly killed its own offspring by an extraordinary show of disdain and arrogance. The British government argued against the prosecution of war criminals on the grounds that it would provoke the Serbs and undermine the peace discussions. Once the tribunal was set up, the Council members wrangled about the choice of prosecutor for over a year and failed to provide the tribunal with a workable budget. Worse still, none of the Council's five permanent members formally agreed to cooperate with the prosecutor or hand over suspects to The Hague. This was to ignore the all-important lesson from the disappearances in Argentina – that 'world powers' like the USA, the UK and Russia will only win other governments over to a human rights campaign if they are prepared to submit to the same discipline. They could hardly expect the Serbs to surrender war criminals to the Hague tribunal, if they were unwilling to cooperate with its prosecutor.

As of March 1998, the tribunal has indicted a total of 35 Rwandans and 75 individuals from the former Yugoslavia, 47 are in jail in Arusha and The Hague, seven have gone on trial and two have been convicted and sentenced. This is respectable, but still not enough and ambivalence on the part of the Security Council remains the single greatest obstacle to the credibility of the tribunal. Russia and China have yet to pass a law to cooperate with the prosecutor. In Bosnia, NATO troops remain unwilling to arrest indicted war criminals. The real advances on accountability have all been made at the national level, most notably by South Africa's Commission on Truth and Reconciliation.

The final, grim lesson from Bosnia and Rwanda may be that the UN's human rights work can no longer be divorced from its wider efforts on behalf of war and peace. In Bosnia, the UN's peacekeeping force (UNPROFOR) tried so hard to remain neutral that it ended up appearing to side with the Bosnian Serbs (who held all the cards) instead of with their victims. In Rwanda, the UNHCR found itself feeding the Hutu killers in refugee camps in Zaire and Tanzania. It was no use telling the Rwandan Tutsis that asylum is a 'universal right' and that even suspected war criminals are entitled to be presumed innocent until found guilty. It added to the Tutsis' burning sense of injustice.

The result has been to compound the genocide. In Bosnia, it produced the immense, grotesque crime of Srebrenica, where thousands of Muslim men and boys were slaughtered in July 1995. There could be no better demonstration of the UN's impotence. But at least Srebrenica triggered a reaction from NATO and led to the

Dayton agreement, bringing some semblance of a solution to Bosnia. In the Great Lakes of Africa, the cycle of revenge continues. In late 1996, vengeful Tutsis pursued the Hutu – refugees and former killers alike – into the jungles of Eastern Zaire. Two hundred thousand may have died. In Rwanda, between 130,000 and 150,0000 detainees languish in jails on a charge of genocide. In spite of the efforts of aid donors, the system cannot begin to cope. Prisoners starve to death and die from gangrene. Meanwhile, in Eastern Rwanda, the military has begun a campaign of disappearances and torture against the Hutu that is forcing a trickle of refugees back into Tanzania.

This is as mystifying as it is disturbing. The Rwandan Tutsis are currently in control. But they are in the minority, and time is not on their side in their long-running blood feud with the Hutu. Can they not see that this is the time for conciliation and mercy – a time to respect due legal process? That disappearances is no more the solution to their war against Hutu extremists than it was in Argentina in the late 1970s? That what goes around must eventually come around? The answer is no. When I put this recently to a moderate Rwandan Tutsi, he replied: 'We are not persuaded that human rights is to our advantage. But we have nothing to be ashamed of'. Here it was again, the lack of shame.

As we look to the next fifty years, there is much that could be done to make the UN's human rights machinery more relevant: it needs money, technical expertise, and a greater sense of priorities in countries that are emerging from war, like Rwanda. But in a sense, all this is tinkering. We also need to remember the single most important feature of the Universal Declaration – its power to shame. That is what threatened the Argentinean Junta and heartened the relatives of the disappeared. That is what was lacking in Bosnia between 1992 and 1995 and is still lacking in Rwanda today.

It will not be retrieved without a profound change of heart from the world's most powerful governments, particularly the United States. As the dominance of the USA has grown, so America's lapses and inconsistencies have become more damaging. The United States owes $1.4 billion to the United Nations – even while denouncing Iraq and Libya for violating international law. The USA supports the creation of a permanent criminal court – as long as the Security Council is allowed to determine what issues are taken up by the prosecutor. To judge from Rwanda and Bosnia, this would be the kiss of death. America simply must put aside its reservations and submit to the same rules it expects of others. But this is precisely the kind of gamble that would make a court credible and effective.

Ultimately, however, the future, of the Universal Declaration rests with non-governmental organisations more than governments. The real heroes of the UN's long struggle with Argentina were the relatives of the disappeared, and their successors are flourishing even in the barren soil of Bosnia. Take, for example Faruk Sabanovic, who was crippled by a sniper's bullet in Sarajevo. Instead of giving in to despair, Sabanovic has formed an organisation, the Center for Self Reliance, which is successfully pushing the Bosnian authorities and aid agencies to provide for the rights of disabled people. To Sabanovic that means wheelchairs, access, and better benefits. To legal scholars, it also happens to be Article 25 of the Universal Declaration. Sabanovic's spirit is less evident in the Great Lakes of Africa, but even there women's groups are helping Hutu and Tutsis to reach out across the ethnic divide.

When I visited Bosnia recently, it was like turning back the clock. There is the same impatience, the same boldness and the same determination to shame government that was so remarkable in the relatives of Argentina's disappeared. Meeting such people, the possibilities seem endless. All said and done, and the Universal Declaration seems in safe hands.

1. Everyone has the right to freedom of movement and residence within the borders of each State.
2. Everyone has the right to leave any country, including his own, and to return to his country.

Václav Havel ♡

Nikdy nekončícím úkolem
všech lidí je, aby všeobecnou
deklaraci lidských práv chápali
stále silněji jako závazek,
na jehož plnění závisí jejich
osud.

Václav Havel ♡

It is the never-ending task of all mankind to perceive the Universal Declaration of Human Rights ever more clearly as a covenant on which their fate depends.

VÁCLAV HAVEL

A Spiritual Covenant for Mankind

A number of texts have played a fundamental role in human history. The Universal Declaration of Human Rights differs from all the others primarily in one respect: its impact is not intended to remain confined to one culture or one civilization. From the very outset, it was envisaged as a universal, global, set of principles to govern human coexistence. Furthermore, it has gradually become the point of departure for countless successive guidelines defining how the people and nations on this Earth can live together with dignity. Texts of such fundamental importance are not born easily. The Universal Declaration was obviously the fruit of a very special climate right after the Second World War, when humanity realized that if the world wanted to prevent repetitions of such apocalyptic horrors it had to rise above particular interests and national prestige, and agree on a certain fundamental code.

The life of the Universal Declaration of Human Rights has been marked by contradictions.

On the one hand, the Universal Declaration has predetermined the direction of the United Nations in the fifty years that have followed. Its imprint is borne by many ensuing UN documents, as well as by hundreds of international treaties and the constitutional instruments of individual nations. It was also present in the background of the Final Act of the 1975 Helsinki conference. The emphasis that document placed on human rights helped to put an end to the bipolar division of the world. It added momentum to the opposition movements in the Communist countries, who took the accords signed by their governments seriously, and intensified their struggle for the observance of human rights, thus challenging the very essence of totalitarian systems.

On the other hand, it is also true that human rights have been violated, ignored or suppressed in many countries of the world – sometimes in milder forms, at other times very brutally – throughout the fifty years since the Universal Declaration was adopted. This is not surprising: the immensely complex world that we live in can hardly be changed overnight simply by adopting a declaration.

Nevertheless, I believe that the frequent breaches of its principles have been far outweighed by the historic importance of this global commitment. For the first time in history, there has been a valid, and globally respected, instrument holding up a mirror to the misery of this world: a universal standard with which we can constantly compare the actual state of affairs, to which we can point, and in whose name we can act, to combat injustices if need be. Since everyone has subscribed to this standard, few would venture to criticize it as such. This means that all those who commit substantial violations of its principles must face this historical novelty.

To put it simply: the life of all those who scorn human rights is much more difficult with the Universal Declaration in place than it was before.

For this reason we must not allow human rights and their consistent enforcement to be quietly relegated to second-class or third-class status as an inconvenient and politically inexpedient issue. Massive violations of fundamental human rights, which clearly include the right to life, are, in fact, often explained away as being in the national or state interest, and are, unfortunately, becoming an everyday reality which, in the past decade, we have been able to watch virtually as a live transmission. The genocide in Rwanda, the killings in Chechnya and Bosnia and Herzegovina, the situation in Tibet, North Korea, Burma, Cuba and Kosovo – these are but a few of the events we have to bear in mind. Backed by the provisions of the Universal Declaration of Human Rights, we should be able to confront these threats to human life, freedom and dignity, or at least to always clearly identify them.

Why should human beings have the prerogative to enjoy human rights? I often ask myself this question, and I have considered it in many speeches. Time and again, I come to the conclusion that this is something essentially different, and much more profound, than a mere contract between people who have found it practical to have their rights articulated and guaranteed in some way or other in order to have an instrument that automatically restricts the rights of those who could, or who would wish to, deny others their rights. In formal terms the Universal Declaration does indeed take the form of a contract or covenant, like the hundreds of thousands of laws or regulations governing human coexistence. This covenant, however, derives from certain paradigms, established notions and preconditions that need no further explanation. Let us take, for example, the concept of human dignity. In one way or another, it permeates all the fundamental human rights and human rights documents. We find this so natural that we see no point in asking what human dignity actually means, or why humanity possesses it; nor do we inquire why it is practical for us all to recognize it.

I am convinced that the deepest roots of what we now call human rights lie somewhere beyond us, and above us; somewhere deeper than the world of human covenants – in a realm that I would, for simplicity's sake, describe as metaphysical. Although they may fail to realize this, human beings – the only creatures who are fully aware of their own being and of their mortality, and who perceive their surroundings as a world and have an inner relationship with that world – derive their dignity, as well as their responsibility, from the world as a whole: that is, from that in which they see the world's central theme, its backbone, its order, its direction, its essence, its soul – call it what you will. Christians put this quite simply: man is here in the image of God.

The world has changed markedly in the past fifty years. There are many more of us on this planet now; the colonial system has fallen apart; the bipolar division is gone; globalization is advancing at a dizzying pace. The Euro-American culture that largely moulded the character of our present civilization is no longer predominant. We are entering an era of multiculturalism. While the world is now enveloped by one single global civilization, this civilization is based on coexistence of many cultures, religions or spheres of civilization that are equal, and equally powerful.

These different cultures naturally all have their own historical, spiritual, political and moral traditions. More and more often, we have witnessed clashes between these traditions and the notion of human rights embodied in the Universal Declaration of Human Rights. Often, an alleged contrast has served as an ignoble pretext for autocrats who have sought to legitimate their evil actions by pointing to the 'otherness' of their cultures. On other occasions, however, the incongruity is real, and the various standards developed by the Euro-American world are perceived in all sincerity as an alien creation that can perhaps be respected, but not inwardly embraced. Moreover, some find this creation much too secular, much too mundane, much too material, claiming that it fails to show respect to the higher authority that is the only source of all moral imperatives and all the rights that are derived from these imperatives, or safeguarded by them. This is not quite correct: the Western human rights standards are, in fact, a modern application of Christian principles. Seen from the outside, however, this might well be regarded as religious imperialism under a civil cloak.

What can be done in this situation?

Certainly there are a thousand avenues. One viable course might be to place emphasis on the spiritual source of human rights. This will not make these rights an alien phenomenon for the non-European or non-American worlds. On the contrary: it might bring them closer to these realms. First and foremost, however, it might bring them closer to those of us who come from the Euro-American environment, who are the ones most inclined to lose sight of the spiritual dimension of the values we believe in, and of the metaphysical origin of the rights we claim; and who regard documents like the Universal Declaration of Human Rights as some kind of 'good business'.

Most importantly, the foundations of all the main religious systems of the world include the same basic principles and the same moral imperatives, albeit in different forms. The various religions differ tremendously in emphasis, in spirit, in character and in liturgy, but somewhere deep down we always find the same fundamentals – the same call for humility before that which is around us and above us, for decency and for solidarity; the same reference to the memory of the universe where all our actions are proven for their true worth; the same emphasis on our responsibility for the whole world.

I do not think that the United Nations today could draft a document whose significance would match that of the Universal Declaration of Human Rights. I could see that for myself during the preparations for the Anniversary Summit, when attempts were being made behind the scenes to adopt a concise declaration that would respond, in a fundamental way, to the changes in the world in the past fifty years. Taking part in the preparations, I soon realized how difficult it was to reach agreement on anything. Not that nobody agreed to the proposed texts, but many were concerned about who had written them, and whether the authors were people whom they should oppose. Others wanted to have something added or deleted for reasons of sheer prestige. As a result of this – not surprisingly – no document was produced in the end. Nevertheless, I still believe that those of us who want to could make an effort to highlight the spiritual dimension and origin of the values guarded by the United Nations, and to ensure they are reflected in the organization's activities. If a better future for this world lies in the realm of spirit, of moral order, and of a renewed sense of responsibility for this world, who but the United Nations should be the one to restate this again and again?

I believe the United Nations should become the scene of a quest for a common denominator of the spiritual values that unite the different cultures of our modern world. The UN should look for ways in which the entire system that is designed to foster human rights, and all the other rights and responsibilities shared by humanity today, can be more deeply embedded in this spiritual foundation.

Furthermore, I think that the United Nations and the various UN agencies, committees and commissions should increasingly incorporate into their efforts a systematic concern for human rights. All their actions should be rooted in, related to, or derived from, the concept of human rights. This might, perhaps, create a climate in which there would be less particularism, less indifference, less tolerance of obvious evil, motivated by egoism or by economic or geopolitical interest. To my mind, the biggest problem of today's multipolar world – a world which has witnessed a reawakening of hundreds of atavistic national interests – does not lie in evil as such, but in tolerance of evil. To give just one example: let us not forget how long it took before Europe was able to stop the war in Bosnia and Herzegovina! And who knows whether that war would not have continued to this day had the United States not intervened!

It is my hope that the Universal Declaration of Human Rights, whose birth we are commemorating, will not be just a dream about what humanity's position in this world should be. May it gradually turn, in all countries, into a living reality.★

★ The text is an edited version of the speech by President Václav Havel at the event commemorating the 50th anniversary of the Universal Declaration of Human Rights in Geneva, Switzerland, on 16 March 1998.

JIMMY CARTER

Hollow Eyes, Bellies, Hearts

We chosen people, rich and blessed,
rarely come to ask ourselves
if we should share our voice or power,
or a portion of our wealth.

We deal with problems of our own,
and claim we have no prejudice
against the people, different, strange
whose images we would dismiss:

Hollow eyes in tiny faces,
hollow bellies, gaunt limbs, there
so far away. Why grieve here
for such vague, remote despair?

Human debris tries to reach
a friendly port, however far.
We can't pay them mind forever,
wretched dregs from an ugly war.

With apartheid's constant shame
Black miners slave for gems and gold.
The wealth and freedom are not theirs;
White masters always keep control.

Bulldozed houses, olive trees axed;
terrorist bombs, funeral wails;
no courts or trials, prison still.
The land is holy, hate prevails.

One alone in a Chinese square
confronted tanks, while others fled.
He stood for freedom for us all,
but few care now if he's jailed or dead.

Visits in the dark of night
by lawful thugs – indrawn breaths
of fear, and then the last farewells.
The death squads won't admit the deaths.

Torture, murder … bitter loss
of liberty and life. But they
are friendly tyrants! What would all
our cautious questioning convey?

Why think of slaves, nameless deaths?
Best be still, as in other days.
Response was bland to Hitler's deeds -
Should we condemn our fathers' ways?

We chosen few are truly blessed.
It's clear God does not want us pained
by those who suffer far away.
Are we to doubt what He ordained?

COR HERKSTRÖTER

Respecting and Supporting Human Rights

The Scottish-born American industrialist, Andrew Carnegie, who funded the construction of the Peace Palace in The Hague, said that settling international disputes by arbitration instead of war was: 'The greatest one step forward ever taken by man, in his long and checkered march upward from barbarism'.

Carnegie's words reflected a growing belief that respect for the rule of law could help protect individuals – and corporate entities – from the vagaries of dictators and despots. From the 18th-century Enlightenment on recognition had been emerging that there were such things as universal rights; principles that applied to all individuals no matter what their race, creed or colour.

Nearly a century has passed since he spoke in 1913 and, despite the extraordinary economic, scientific and technological progress we have made, sadly our tumultuous and violent century has not lived up to the hopes of the jurists and diplomats who gathered in The Hague on that day.

We have witnessed unspeakable wars and savage crimes against humanity, brutality on a hitherto unimagined scale and regimes which have practised un-precedented cruelties on their own peoples. Yet, despite this dismal record there is growing hope and optimism. As the century ends, respect for human rights and the rule of democratically determined law is spreading across the globe. More and more countries are, at least verbally, committing themselves to respect the fundamental human rights of their peoples. The formation of the United Nations, the adoption of the Universal Declaration of Human Rights and the proliferation of non-governmental organisations campaigning for human rights are all positive signs of a broadly based recognition of human rights principles.

This recognition of human rights has been matched in recent decades by an even more widespread recognition that market-based economies are the best and most efficient way to provide goods and services. They offer freedom and hope and allow people to develop in the way that they see fit, rather than in the way that they are told. Our century has conclusively demonstrated that large economies are so complex and interconnected that no centrally planned system can possibly control them. This realisation has taken a long time to dawn – and is still not shared by all. Furthermore, there are some who still believe that a nation can have a market-based economy without respecting individual human rights.

In fact the opposite is the case; a market economy cannot work truly efficiently unless all the fundamental freedoms and rights are respected. The free flow of both information and goods is essential for the proper functioning of markets of all types. Markets can operate under systems which limit freedoms but they cannot operate truly efficiently.

Given today's global economy and virtually instant communications, business inevitably tends to flow to the most efficient markets where, by definition, the best deals are to be had. Markets operating under limitations, such as censorship of information, are automatically disadvantaged. Market-based systems are therefore major drivers of the move toward more widespread recognition of fundamental human rights.

THE ROYAL DUTCH/SHELL GROUP'S POSITION ON HUMAN RIGHTS

The Royal Dutch/Shell Group of companies takes as its benchmark the Universal Declaration of Human Rights and we recognise that human rights are, as the Universal Declaration says, 'indivisible'. However we think that we, as a business, must make important practical distinctions between various personal, civil and political rights and freedoms and economic, social and cultural rights. We see a clear distinction between the roles of Shell companies as employers and their relationships with the communities in which they work, and society in general.

The Group's Statement of General Business Principles calls for respect for the human rights of employees and also calls on Shell companies to express support for fundamental human rights – in line with the legitimate role of business. What we regarded as implicit is now explicitly stated.

The Principles are, in effect, the constitution of the Royal Dutch/Shell Group, a critical part of its identity. Recognition of and support for human rights is now a fundamental part of the way the Group does its business.

All the geographically diverse companies in the Group must abide by these principles and regularly demonstrate, to the satisfaction of internal management and external interest groups, that they are doing so.

Shell companies have the capacity to be good or bad employers. As good employers – we would hope among the best – they can do a lot to protect and promote the personal rights and, within appropriate limits, the economic, social and cultural interests of those who work for them.

The Royal Dutch/Shell Group is amongst the largest and most complex business organisations in the world: Shell companies do business in or with almost every country and it is inevitable that some do business in nations which may be controlled by oppressive or corrupt governments. This does not mean that they collude with those governments, quite the reverse. Shell companies aim to set an example by the way they do business, by doing this they are a force for good.

However it is not their function and they do not have, nor do they seek, the capacity to determine how the countries in which they operate are run. That function and capacity belongs to the people and the governments of those countries. Shell companies are not in the business of overthrowing governments. They are businesses and their duty is to conform with local laws. Furthermore they must respect local customs and cultural diversity without compromising global standards. A challenging dilemma!

In recent decades, like many other major multinational companies, Shell companies have been criticised for operating in areas where there have been human rights abuses. In the 1970s there was an organised campaign to get the Group to leave South Africa and more recently there has been repeated strident criticism of Shell's operations and investments in Nigeria. Given that the Group is very proud of its standards and of the way it takes care of its employees and considers itself to be a force for good in the world, these criticisms have never been lightly dismissed and have caused much serious soul-searching and self-examination by generations of managers and employees alike.

In practice, over the long term, Shell's policy has been remarkably consistent. We have not dis-invested – removed our investments from criticised nations or regions. I can think of no country that the Group has withdrawn from voluntarily for non-commercial reasons. Rather, we have sought to increase our contribution to those societies by fostering economic stability in order to help them move toward a broader recognition of the rights of all citizens. While we have not left these areas, it would be fair to say that such considerations have probably had some influence on decisions as to whether businesses should be expanded or new markets entered.

This policy of staying and contributing is grounded in the Group's identity, in the belief that it is doing the right thing and in the broad range of responsibilities we have to many interested parties. Critically, that is based in the fundamental belief of Shell employees that, through their activities and the companies they work for, they can help build a better future for all.

THE ROLE OF A COMMERCIAL ENTERPRISE

In the last few decades there has been a sea change in the public perception of how a commercial enterprise should behave and what it should contribute to society. Where once companies were expected to take a very restricted role and limited responsibilities, there are now new broader expectations and demands. In the 1970s campaigners wanted to limit the activities of multinational companies; today they want them to take on more responsibilities and deliver more goods and services.

These new priorities reflect evolving cultures and changing societal values across the globe. The question for those of us in business, especially in multinational business, is how to adapt appropriately to those changes, many of which may vary or even conflict. All economic activity, all business and trade, is after all a part of the overall society, reflecting the values and aspirations of the population. Which of these new and expanded expectations can be met and what role should a private company legitimately take? There are certainly no simple answers, and versions of these questions confront Shell managers virtually daily. To give them guidance we had to come up with a core definition of what we should, and what we should not, undertake.

About two years ago we began work on this definition. It became a wide-ranging process as we consulted numerous internal and external groups in order to determine exactly how societal expectations of companies such as Shell are changing and developing. Perhaps unsurprisingly, the picture that emerged was extremely complex and showed marked variations within individual societies and across geographic regions. However, within that complexity there are some common trends including rising demands for transparency and accountability. We characterise this as a 'show me' world where, in the absence or diminution of trust, greater transparency is demanded.

So, we developed a broad definition aimed at giving managers a sound basis for their decisions. It covers:

- What we *must* do – be true to our values and principles.
- What we *should* do – further enhance shareholder value.
- What we *cannot* do – act in a way that is outside the legitimate role of business.

This framework for any definition of our roles and responsibilities is fundamental, both for us and for those who have expectations of us. It allows us to determine which expectations we accept as legitimate and which we reject. So we accept that we have a fiduciary duty to our shareholders and we accept that we have a range of obligations to our employees. We accept that each stakeholder has certain legitimate demands, rights and responsibilities. This provides a basis for decision-making and assessment of opportunities. Furthermore, by defining what we consider to be the legitimate role of business, we can set universal standards for relationships both with stakeholders and with external individuals, governments, businesses and other organisations.

So, for example, the Group's decision that it cannot take part in party political activities sets the stage for the principle, included in the Statement of General Business Principles, that there is an absolute ban on political donations. A similar motivation lies behind the absolute ban on the taking or offering of bribes.

In the human rights area this clear definition of roles allows the Group to accept the obligations mentioned earlier – the duty to respect the human rights of our employees and, within the legitimate role of business, the duty to express support for fundamental human rights.

WHAT DOES THIS MEAN IN PRACTICE?

A man may be very sincere in good principles without having good practice.
Dr Samuel Johnson (1709-1784)

Carefully formulated policies mean little unless put into practice. This is a challenge in areas where respect for human rights is limited or non-existent, complicated by the fluid nature of political developments. While there is a clearly discernible tendency for more and more countries to abide by global human rights standards, there are also instances where nations abandon standards they previously held.

Furthermore, although there is widespread consensus on some issues there is less on others. For example, in some countries providing jobs for relatives is a virtue. In others it is regarded as nepotism. In some countries using gifts to facilitate business relationships is the norm. In others such actions are regarded as bribes.

The challenge for business is further complicated by the way societal expectations are changing. Earlier this century national governments were considered to be the most competent authorities on questions such as human rights. Today many of those expectations have been shifted to commercial enterprises. Increasingly, consumers not only want a good product, they also want to know that it was produced in a morally acceptable way.

Typically, energy projects – the main business activity of Shell companies – are long-term investments, lasting from a quarter to half a century. In that time, many governments can come and go even in the most stable of countries. Particular challenges arise for multinationals like the Royal Dutch/Shell Group when a new government which restricts freedoms takes power in a country in which we have invested much time and money.

Nigeria has posed challenges of this type for many years now. When the Group first went to that country it was a British colony. Since independence it has experienced civil war and a succession of civilian and military governments, few of which have won accolades from human rights activists. The issues here are complex: should multinational companies use their influence more widely with governments in relation to human rights, or to other social and political problems? Do they have a responsibility to do so, or would it be an illustration of power without accountability?

The Royal Dutch/Shell Group has clearly marked out its position in support of fundamental human rights; it has put its stake in the ground. However this does not mean that it in any way tells other companies what they should do. In the business community as a whole the debate about the appropriate role of companies in relation to human rights questions is far from resolved.

In practical day-to-day terms, for the company that works in such a country the questions are even more specific. Can Shell Nigeria speak up for all those whose rights are not being respected? Should it do so? Does it have the competence to do so? The answer clearly is that the company's rights and competences are limited. Shell Nigeria is a commercial organisation with a certain range of skills and knowledge. It does not have the capacity, nor the competence to speak out on all such issues. But one issue on which it can and should speak out is on human rights within the communities in which it operates. So Shell Nigeria spoke out against the arrest and execution of Ken Saro-Wiwa and continues to speak out on the Ogonis still held in detention without trial. It has continued to do so publicly and privately, on appropriate occasions.

Critics have persistently said that the Group has not done enough to prevent abuses in Nigeria. I would challenge that view. Within the legitimate sphere of business, we have made a serious effort to uphold human rights. Tragically our actions, and those of other concerned individuals, organisations and governments, have only occasionally changed the path of events. But that will not deter us from continuing to express our support for human rights in that country, and continuing to make appropriate representations. However, we do not feel that, as a business, we can solve these issues on our own. Nevertheless, we recognise that we have a role to play in the countries in which we operate, whether in Nigeria, the Netherlands or elsewhere.

A different type of challenge is created in societies which adhere to traditional structures, many of which are not democratic by modern standards.

Many of the major resource-owning nations in the world have governments based on traditional rather than democratic structures. Moreover some of these have legal systems which impose penalties on convicted criminals that would be considered to be cruel and unusual by human rights standards. The existing social structures almost always limit the rights of some social groups.

A highly technological company such as Shell cannot help introducing new ideas when it enters such a traditional society. The scientific and technological basis of its activities makes that inevitable. Therefore the development of a major energy project will always create some form of disturbance in a traditional society leading to changes and possible dislocation. What is the responsibility of a company in such a situation? Should it seek to limit the impact on the traditional society? Or should it act as a moderniser, bringing in 20th-century standards – including human rights standards?

This dilemma is subtle but very real. Even the question of how much money to inject into the local economy becomes a difficult challenge. There is no surer way of influencing a traditional society than by providing young employees with cash. That immediately disrupts normal income patterns and disturbs traditional relationships.

Confronted with these very real dilemmas in many countries, Shell companies have tried to minimise their impact, working with national and local governments and interest groups to ensure that development takes place in the most acceptable way possible.

SIZE IS IMPORTANT – IT CREATES SPECIAL CHALLENGES AND OBLIGATIONS

As I mentioned earlier, the Shell Group is today one of the largest and most complex business undertakings in the world. Of course, in many countries we are just one of a number of large companies. But in others the operations of the local Shell company constitute a major part of the national economy. That size alone is an important factor. It means that our operations are very visible to the public and it creates certain obligations that a smaller company may not attract.

A Shell company in such a situation must aim to set an example by the way it conducts its business. It must contribute to the country both economically and socially, providing jobs, income and personal development for individuals, and royalties and income for the nation.

Shell companies operate from nearly 50,000 locations. Each day more than one hundred thousand employees and hundreds of thousands of contractors and indirect employees conduct tens, if not hundreds, of millions of transactions. Ensuring that each and every one of these separate transactions meets the same ethical standards is a serious management challenge. If an employee of a Shell company undertakes a dishonest or criminal transaction, he or she has, by definition, violated the rights of the other actor in the transaction.

The company, the corporate entity which employs that person, obviously has an interest in the transaction and a range of responsibilities and rights relating to it. The employee involved also has a direct interest and a range of responsibilities and rights. So do the customers, suppliers and contractors.

The interests, rights and obligations involved differ from region to region and from nation to nation. In polygamous societies it may be the practice for companies to pay pensions to all the partners after the employee dies. Such practices would be considered highly unusual, even illegal in other societies.

Regulations vary from nation to nation and may be contradictory. In some, prices must be set after consultation with other firms and the responsible government body. In others such consultations would be considered illegal anti-competitive behaviour. In each nation the laws are set to reflect the local understanding of what is correct and appropriate behaviour.

Another dilemma in the economic rights area is created by wage rates. Shell companies, which set themselves the goal of being amongst the leaders in whichever industry they are participating, typically pay at or above the prevailing market rate. The aim is to get the very best available within that market. However market rates vary. While a technician in Aberdeen may feel adequately recompensed when he compares his income to the local market he may feel cheated when he compares his income to a technician in Singapore or Houston. Are equitable remuneration packages a human rights question? Some would say that they are, especially in the rapidly globalising markets of today.

None of these dilemmas are going to go away. To help Shell employees deal with them and to ensure that Shell companies set an example, we have developed the Group-wide standards and guidelines described earlier. I firmly believe that, while these management tools cannot provide any form of definitive solution, they can assist Shell people to deal with these problems in a consistent, thoughtful and effective way.

CONTRIBUTING TO PROGRESS IN A BROADER WAY – SUSTAINABLE DEVELOPMENT

Fundamentally our businesses exist to meet the needs and wants of the societies within which we operate. To a great extent our actions are a reflection of the wider community of which we are a part. Our primary contribution is necessarily economic, but we recognise that we have broader responsibilities.

Development which is sustainable, which respects human rights and helps contribute to the progress of society is, we believe, the greatest contribution we can make to the advancement of human rights.

From a Legal Point of View

The importance of the Universal Declaration of Human Rights is as an idea, rather than as a technical legal instrument. The impact of this idea has been extraordinary, both because of what it has led to and because of the continued perception that it has relevance in today's world, fifty years after it was drawn up.

In the 1940s the world was already beginning to face the deep divisions represented by the capitalist and communist systems. It was also a world in which states routinely insisted that what went on within their own borders was not a proper matter for international concern, being reserved to their own domestic jurisdiction. Nonetheless, the text of the Universal Declaration, which predicated an inherent entitlement to rights available to all regardless of the societies in which they lived, was agreed to by all states. These states included, incidentally, important states of the third world, such as India, who had made significant contribution to the drafting.

From the outset, therefore, the Universal Declaration represented certain basic truths. It represented acceptance that rights are inherent and universal and also that they consist of economic, social and cultural rights as well as political and civil rights. Indeed, it was thought at the time that the various rights there referred to were each of a comparable legal status.

Occasionally – very occasionally – non-binding resolutions of the UN General Assembly achieve a political significance beyond their initial legal status. The Universal Declaration is the prime example of such a phenomenon. International lawyers have noted that the Declaration has never been a mere recommendation of the General Assembly. Although in resolution form, it was the product of careful negotiation, drafting and revision. It had the support of the entirety of the UN membership. It represented more than a passing political moment, because it spoke to certain fundamental truths, expressed at a significant moment in history. It was included in the constitutions of many new countries, including countries of the third world. By this means, it became part of the domestic law of many nations, giving real and enforceable rights within the domestic system. Moreover, in national courts it became frequently invoked by counsel and rendered legally authoritative by the response of the judiciaries of the various national systems. There is now a vast comparative law jurisprudence on the invocation and application of the Universal Declaration of Human Rights, taking the legal effect of its provisions far beyond that of a mere General Assembly resolution.

That the Universal Declaration would achieve a special and unusual legal status, notwithstanding its non-binding form, was not clear at the outset. It is well known that prolonged and ultimately successful efforts were made to turn the Universal Declaration into legally binding form of a more usual sort. All students of human rights law know that the two United Nations Covenants on Human Rights, which were agreed only in 1966, represented the fruition of those efforts.

The ultimate decision to have two Covenants – one for economic, social and cultural rights (ICESCR), and one for civil and political rights (ICCPR) – represented the reality that there was a consensus to move to efficacious monitoring methods only in respect of the latter. In recent years, with the belated establishment of a Committee also under the ICESCR, there has been a return to the idea of the Universal Declaration that these rights too are indeed 'real' rights and not mere aspiration. The practice of the monitoring organs under the two Covenants has undoubtedly contributed to the original intention of the Universal Declaration in the following way: the Human Rights Committee under the ICCPR has emphasized that violation of the rights in that instrument can never be excused by reference to lack of development or economic hardship. The right to be free from torture, or to be able to speak without fear, is not dependent on an advanced economy. And the Committee under the ICESCR has shown that there are a variety of legal norms available to ensure compliance with rights and that it can well fashion appropriate ones for economic and social rights within diverse political and economic systems. That, in turn, has shown that rights are not dependent upon monolithic and uniform state and religious structures.

The Universal Declaration is rightly to be viewed as the originating post-war instrument that led not only to the two Covenants, but also to the great regional instruments. The European Convention on Human Rights, even though a partial reflection of the Declaration, was closely modelled on it. And the Inter-American Convention on Human Rights has the same provenance.

It is only in recent years that we have seen attempts to rewrite history: to suggest that the Universal Declaration, and the Covenants which sprang from it, represent a Western view of things, at odds with other political and cultural perceptions. But the truths of the Universal Declaration remain constant. Fundamental rights are inherent in the human being. The dignity of humankind is not dependent on political, regional or religious particularities. Indeed, it is governments, and not the afflicted, who emphasize what is different between us. International law generally, and human rights law specifically, emphasizes what we have in common – we, the peoples, and not those who govern us. Human rights represent the basic aspirations of peoples, not of their governments. A human being is not less worthy of protection from torture, arbitrary imprisonment, hunger or deprivation because he comes from one place rather than another.

I have sometimes been quite puzzled by the hold that the Universal Declaration of Human Rights continues to have on the minds not only of ordinary people but of government officials. Aggrieved citizens insist to newspapers that their treatment 'violates the Universal Declaration' (and not the International Covenants). As a former member of the Human Rights Committee, I remained perplexed (and, if I am honest, sometimes irritated) by the constant reference by governments during examination of their reports to the Universal Declaration, when the instrument under examination was a later instrument by which they were legally bound – the ICCPR. Indeed, some states seemed oblivious of the fact that the ICCPR (unlike the Universal Declaration) contains no provision on property rights, and they added in their periodic reports pages of information on this matter. Again, the constant reference to and invocation of the Universal Declaration not only ignores that it has in a sense been overtaken by subsequent instruments, but also that it was a rather crude statement of rights. In particular, the Universal Declaration contains none of the permitted limitations spelled out in the later instruments. The permitted limitations are not a reluctant acknowledgement of the realities of state power, but rather a balancing of rights of different persons within society. They represent a further and necessary legitimacy, without which the bare enunciation of rights in the Universal Declaration can only be a first step.

Our task, fifty years on, is thus to acknowledge the continuing truths represented by the Universal Declaration – truths concerning the indivisibility of rights and the universality of rights – while acknowledging the ever-continuing task of elaborating and implementing human rights through more contemporary modalities.

Article 14

1. Everyone has the right to seek and to enjoy in other countries asylum from persecution.
2. This right may not be invoked in the case of prosecutions genuinely arising from non-political crimes or from acts contrary to the purposes and principles of the United Nations.

HANS KÜNG

Human Responsibilities Reinforce Human Rights: The Global Ethic Project

Anyone who is interested in seeing human rights more fully respected and more effectively defended throughout the world must surely also be interested in achieving a change of consciousness concerning human obligations or responsibilities. These need to be seen in the context of global challenges and efforts to establish a global or world ethic, an ethic for humankind. By this I mean a minimum basic consensus as regards binding values, immutable standards and basic moral attitudes – a consensus which can be accepted by all religions as well as by non-believers.

Efforts to establish a global ethic (for which I laid the theoretical foundations in my book entitled *Global Responsibility: In Search of a New World Ethic*, published in German in 1990 and in English in 1991) have received widespread international backing in recent years. Two documents are of particular relevance:

- On 4 September 1993, for the first time in the history of religion, delegates to the Parliament of the World's Religions in Chicago adopted a 'Declaration Toward a Global Ethic'.
- On 1 September 1997, again for the first time, the InterAction Council of former presidents and prime ministers called for a global ethic and submitted to the United Nations a proposed 'Universal Declaration of Human Responsibilities', designed to underpin, reinforce and supplement human rights from an ethical angle.

In the remainder of this essay, I would like to make some fundamental comments on the relationship between human rights and human responsibilities.

The Declaration by the InterAction Council is not an isolated document. It is a response to the urgent calls of influential international bodies for global ethical standards, to which an entire chapter is devoted in the 1995 reports of both the Commission on Global Governance and the World Commission on Culture and Development. The same issues have been on the agenda for some time at the World Economic Forum in Davos and also in the new UNESCO Universal Ethics Project. They are also receiving increasing attention in Asia.

Within these international, interdenominational bodies, the contemporary backdrop to these issues is that globalisation of the economy, technology and the media has also meant globalisation of problems (from financial and labour markets to the environment and organised crime). What is therefore also needed is globalisation of ethics: not a uniform ethical system, but a necessary minimum of shared ethical values, basic attitudes and standards to which all regions, nations and interest groups can subscribe – in other words, a shared basic ethic for mankind. There can be no new world order without a world ethic!

The Universal Declaration of Human Responsibilities supports and underpins the Universal Declaration of Human Rights from an ethical angle, as announced in the preamble: 'We … thus renew and reinforce commitments already proclaimed in the Universal Declaration of Human Rights: namely, the full acceptance of the dignity of all people; their inalienable freedom and equality, and their solidarity with one another'. If human rights are not being asserted everywhere that they could be, this is usually for want of the necessary political and ethical will. Even the most fervent of human rights activists must acknowledge that 'the rule of law and the promotion of human rights depend on the readiness of men and women to act justly'.

Of course it would be wrong to suggest that the legal validity of human rights should be dependent on the actual fulfilment of human responsibilities. The idea of human rights as a reward for good behaviour is absurd – for this would mean that only those who had shown themselves worthy of the community by fulfilling their responsibilities towards it would be entitled to enjoy such rights. This would clearly conflict with the notion of the unconditional dignity of the individual, which in turn is a pre-condition for both rights and responsibilities. No one is suggesting that certain human responsibilities must be fulfilled, by the individual or by a community, before any claim can be laid to human rights. The latter are part and parcel of the individual, who is always, however, the bearer of responsibilities as well as rights: 'All human rights are by definition directly bound up with the duty to respect them' (V. Deile). While rights and responsibilities can be clearly distinguished, they cannot be separated. The relationship between them must be described in differentiated terms. They are not quantities to be superficially added or subtracted, but two interrelated dimensions of humanity in both the individual and the social sphere.

No rights without responsibilities. As such, this issue is by no means a new one – it goes back to the days when human rights were first 'invented'. During the debate on human rights in France's revolutionary assembly in 1789, the following demand was already being made: any declaration of human rights must be accompanied by a declaration of human responsibilities. If not, everyone would eventually have rights and play them off against one another, but no one would be aware any longer of the responsibilities without which such rights cannot operate. Today, two centuries after the French Revolution, we essentially find ourselves living in a society in which individual groups all too often invoke rights against other people without acknowledging that they themselves have responsibilities of any kind. This must not be attributed to codified human rights as such, but to certain erroneous developments which have a great deal to do with them and which, in the minds of many people, have led to a predominance of rights over responsibilities. Instead of the hoped-for culture of human rights, what we frequently see is a perverse culture based on exaggerated claims, in which the original purpose of human rights is forgotten. Equilibrium between 'freedom, equality and participation' does not simply 'happen', but must be re-established again and again. There can be no denying that we live in a society based on rights, which often also presents itself as a 'society based on legal rights' or even a 'litigious society', and turns the state – the term has been applied to the Federal Republic of Germany – into a 'judicial state' (in the words of the legal historian S. Simon). Perhaps it is time, particularly in our society with its overemphasis on the law, that the legitimate insistence on rights should make room for a new focus on responsibilities.

The worldwide occurrence of serious human rights violations should make it especially clear to professional human rights activists, who seek to defend human rights 'unconditionally', how empty any declaration and formulation of human rights is bound to be in situations where people – and above all rulers – ignore their human responsibilities ('It's got nothing to do with me!'), neglect them ('My job is to protect my company's interests!'), reject them ('That's for the churches and charities to deal with!') or dishonestly claim to be fulfilling them ('We in the government / on the board of directors are doing everything we can!'). The 'weakness' of human rights does not, in fact, lie in the concept as such, but in the lack of political and moral will shown by the responsible players. In other words, effective assertion of human rights depends on an ethical impulse and normative motivation! This is fully understood by the many front-line human rights activists who have expressed their advocacy of a global ethic in a separate publication of their own. Anyone who wishes to defend human rights effectively should therefore welcome a new moral impulse and ethical frame of reference rather than reject them (to the detriment of his or her own cause).

In many respects, the ethical frame of reference of the Universal Declaration of Human Responsibilities goes beyond that of human rights, which only indicate what is right and wrong in certain specific areas. Indeed, the Universal Declaration of Human Rights does not even make such a comprehensive moral claim. This is why any Universal Declaration of Human Responsibilities must extend much further and aim much higher. The two basic principles of the Universal Declaration of Human Responsibilities alone provide a comprehensive yet specific ethical framework for everyday practice, namely the basic requirement that every person be treated in a humane way and the Golden Rule 'What you do not wish to be done to yourself, do not do to others', not to mention the specific requirements in the Declaration of Responsibilities concerning truthfulness, non-violence, fairness, solidarity, partnership, etc. Where the Universal Declaration of Human Rights must leave open what is and is not morally permitted, the Universal Declaration of Human Responsibilities tells us – not as a law, but as a moral imperative.

Whereas the Universal Declaration of Human Rights is mostly phrased in 'anonymous' terms, since it is aimed less at the individual (who needs protection) than at the state (whose power must be curtailed), the Universal Declaration of Human Responsibilities, though also aimed at the state and at institutions, is aimed primarily and specifically at the people responsible. Again and again it refers to 'all people' or 'every person', and appeals specifically to particular occupational groups which bear a special responsibility in our society (politicians, public servants, business leaders, writers, artists, physicians, lawyers, journalists, religious leaders, etc.). In this age of suit-yourself, take-it-or-leave-it pluralism, such a declaration of responsibilities undeniably throws down a challenge — at least to all those whose sole standard of 'morality' is 'as long as it's fun' or 'as long as it helps me to fulfil myself'. Yet the Declaration of Responsibilities is not a new 'community ideology' — something the communitarians inspired by Amitai Etzioni are wrongly accused of promoting, whereas they are certainly not out to establish a 'tyranny of consensus' and to entirely relieve people of their individual responsibility. The latter can more properly be levelled at those who in this day and age, fatally misjudging the current crisis, persist in claiming that a 'belief in the value of selfishness' or 'the virtues of non-orientation and non-attachment' should be our guide in tomorrow's world.

Like the Universal Declaration of Human Rights, the Universal Declaration of Human Responsibilities is thus a moral appeal, which of course is also intended to have a legal and political impact, but not to 'codify' morality. The Universal Declaration of Responsibilities is not, as has been claimed, a 'blueprint for a legally binding canon of responsibilities with a claim to global validity'. People should refrain from conjuring up such spectres at a time when even the Pope and the Curia are no longer able to impose their codified authoritarian moral views even in their own immediate sphere (let alone in the outside world); neither the declaration of the Parliament of the World's Religions nor that of the InterAction Council says anything about such controversial moral issues as contraception, abortion or euthanasia. The aim of the Universal Declaration of Human Responsibilities is thus emphatically not legal codification, which is simply not possible with regard to moral attitudes such as truthfulness or fairness. Its aim is voluntary self-obligation. In individual cases this can, of course, lead to legal regulation, but a Universal Declaration of Human Responsibilities does not in principle imply legal obligations. What it does imply are moral obligations.

My concluding wish for the ensuing debate is this: that there should be no false fronts, no artificially constructed antithesis between rights and duties, between the ethic of freedom and the ethic of responsibility. Rather, we should seize the opportunities which may lie in such a potentially historic declaration, should it ever be promulgated. For it is not every day that statesmen from every continent agree on such a text and advocate such a cause. Above all, we should not be afraid of a global ethic, which, if properly understood, can liberate us rather than enslave us — can help us to be, and to remain, truly human.

LES MURRAY

One Kneeling, One Looking Down

Half-buried timbers chained corduroy
lead out into the sand
which bare feet wincing Crutch and Crotch
spurn for the summer surf's embroidery
and insects stay up on the land.

A storm engrossing half the sky
in broccoli and seething drab
and standing on one foot over the country
burrs like lit torch. Lightning
turns air to elixir at every grab

but the ocean sky is untroubled blue
everywhere. Its storm rolls below:
sand clouds raining on sacred country
drowned a hundred lifetimes under sea.
In the ruins of a hill, channels flow,

and people, like a scant palisade
driven in the surf, jump or sway
or drag its white netting to the tide line
where a big man lies with his limbs splayed,
fingers and toes and a forehead-shine

as if he'd fallen off the flag.
Only two women seem aware of him.
One says *But this frees us. I'd be a fool –*
Say it with me, says the other. *For him to revive
we must both say it. Say Be alive. –*

But it was our own friends who got
him with a brave shot, a clever shot. -
Those are our equals: we scorn them
for being no more than ourselves.
Say it with me. Say Be alive. —

Elder sister, it is impossible. —
Life was once impossible. And flight. And speech.
It was impossible to visit the moon.
The impossible's our summoning dimension.
Say it with me. Say Be alive again. —

The younger wavers. She won't leave
nor stop being furious. The sea's vast
catchment of light sends ashore a roughcast
that melts off every swimmer who can stand.
Glaring through slits, the storm moves inland.

The younger sister, wavering, shouts *Stay dead!*
She knows how impossibility
is the only door that opens.
She pities his fall, leg under one knee
but her power is his death, and can't be dignified.

CATHARINE MACKINNON

Are Women Human?

Fifty years ago the Universal Declaration of Human Rights defined what a human being is. It told the world what a person, as a person, is entitled to. Are women human yet?

If women were human, would we be a cash crop shipped from Thailand in containers into New York's brothels? Would we have our genitals sliced out to purify us (of what?) and to bind and define our cultures? Would we be used as breeders, made to work without pay our whole lives, burned when our dowry money wasn't enough or when men tired of us, starved as widows when our husbands died if we survived his funeral pyre, forced to sell ourselves sexually because men won't value us for anything else? Would we be sold into marriage to priests to atone for our family's sins or to improve our family's earthly prospects? Would we be sexually and reproductively enslaved? Would we, when allowed to work for pay, be made to work at the most menial jobs and exploited at barely starvation level? Would we be trafficked for sexual use and entertainment worldwide in whatever form current technology makes possible? Would we be kept from learning to read and write?

If women were human, would we have little to no voice in public deliberations and in government? Would we be hidden behind veils and imprisoned in houses and stoned and shot for refusing? Would we be beaten nearly to death, and to death, by men with whom we are close? Would we be sexually molested in our families? Would we be raped in genocide to terrorize and destroy our ethnic communities, and raped again in that undeclared war that goes on every day in every country in the world in what is called peacetime? If women were human, would our violation be *enjoyed* by our violators? And, if we were human, when these things happened, would virtually nothing be done about it?

It takes a lot of imagination – and a determinedly blinkered focus on exceptions at the privileged margins – to envision a real woman in the Universal Declaration's majestic guarantees of what 'everyone is entitled to'. After fifty years, just what part of 'everyone' doesn't mean us?

The ringing language in Article 1 encourages us to 'act towards one another in a spirit of brotherhood'. Must we be men before its spirit includes us? Lest this be seen as too literal: if we were all enjoined to 'act towards one another in a spirit of sisterhood', would men know it meant them, too? Article 23 encouragingly provides for just pay to '[e]veryone who works.' It goes on to say that this ensures a life of human dignity for 'himself and his family'. Are women nowhere paid for the work we do in our own families because we are not 'everyone', or because what we do there is not 'work'? Don't women have families, or is what women have not a family without a 'himself'? If the someone who is not paid at all, far less the 'just and favorable remuneration' guaranteed, is also the same someone who in real life is often responsible for her family's sustenance, when she is deprived of providing for her family 'an existence worthy of human dignity', is she not human? And now that 'everyone' has had a right 'to take part in the government of his country' for the past fifty years, why are most governments still run by men? Are women silent in the halls of state because we do not have a human voice?

A document that could provide specifically for the formation of trade unions and 'periodic holiday with pay' might have mustered the specificity to mention women sometime, other than through 'motherhood', which is more bowed to than provided for. If women were human in this document, would domestic violence, sexual violation from birth to death including in prostitution and pornography, and systematic sexual objectification and denigration of women and girls simply be left out of the explicit language?

Granted, sex discrimination is prohibited. But how can it have been prohibited for fifty years, even aspirationally, and the end of these conditions still not be concretely imagined as part of what a human being, as human, is entitled to? Why is women's entitlement to an end of these conditions still openly debated based on cultural rights, speech rights, religious rights, sexual freedom, free markets – as if women are social signifiers, pimps' speech, sacred or sexual fetishes, natural resources, chattel, everything but human beings?

The omissions in the Universal Declaration are not merely semantic. To be a woman is not yet a name for a way of being human, not even in this most visionary of human rights documents. If we measure the reality of women's situation in all its variety against the guarantees of the Universal Declaration, not only do women not have the rights it guarantees – most of the world's men don't either – it is hard to see, in its vision of humanity, a woman's face.

The world needs to see women as human. For this, the Universal Declaration of Human Rights must see the ways women distinctively are deprived of human rights as a deprivation of humanity. For the glorious dream of the Universal Declaration to come true, for human rights to be universal, both the reality it challenges and the standard it sets need to change.

When will women be human? When?

1. Everyone has the right to a nationality.
2. No one shall be arbitrarily deprived of his nationality nor denied the right to change his nationality.

JONATHAN MANN †

Health and Human Rights

The Universal Declaration of Human Rights only mentions the word 'health' once, yet to a health professional, the entire document is full of health-related messages and meaning. So much so that a new health and human rights movement is now under way, exploring the many vital consequences which flow from recognizing that health and human rights are inextricably connected. To appreciate this viewpoint, and to understand why it took so long for the health and human rights linkage to be discovered, it is important to consider the recent history of public health.

The World Health Organization has defined health as a state of physical, mental and social well-being; public health has been defined as the task of ensuring the conditions in which people can be healthy. The key question then becomes: 'What are these essential conditions which people need to achieve optimal physical, mental and social well-being?'

First, we know that medical care, despite its importance, is not the crux of the matter. Probably about ten to twenty percent of population health status can be explained by the availability and quality of medical care. The major conclusion from decades of research is that 'societal factors' are the major determinants of health status.

Curiously, however, public health has not developed a sufficiently deep analytic framework to understand what it is about a society which weighs so heavily on health status. As a result, despite knowing that for many, if not most people, the social context is a powerful determinant of health, public health has avoided addressing directly the societal-level conditions which strongly influence the burden of preventable disease, disability and premature death. Instead, confronting an issue like family planning, public health has tended to focus on individuals, seeking to provide information, education and specific health-related services, like assuring access to safe and effective contraceptives. While these activities are responsible and humane, they do not deal with the underlying, societal-level sources of vulnerability to unwanted pregnancies.

The public health dilemma can be summarized in a syllogism: if public health means ensuring the conditions in which people can be healthy, and if those conditions are predominantly societal, then public health must work for societal transformation. Yet public health needs three tools to proceed: a conceptual framework to analyze society and identify the societal-level factors which determine vulnerability; a vocabulary to permit identifying commonalities among health problems as experienced by different communities; and clarity about the direction of necessary societal change to address the vital health conditions.

The remarkable insight linking health and human rights stems from recognition that the modern human rights movement, exemplified by the powerful Universal Declaration of Human Rights, can provide health with a more useful framework, vocabulary and guidance for analysis and response to the societal determinants of health than any framework from the biomedical tradition. Human rights has this capacity because it, like public health, seeks to identify the societal-level pre-conditions for human well-being.

I first learned about this linkage between health and human rights in the context of HIV/AIDS. From 1986-90, I was director of the World Health Organization's Global Program on AIDS. At that time, we learned that married, monogamous women were increasingly becoming infected with HIV in Uganda. At first we thought that the women did not know enough about AIDS; this was not the case. Then, we thought that perhaps condoms were not adequately available; yet although there were recognizable deficiencies, condoms were often on sale in the marketplaces. Then, by speaking to the women, we discovered the underlying cause of their vulnerability to HIV. Wives could not refuse unwanted or un-protected intercourse with their husbands, even if they knew they were HIV-in-fected, for two major reasons. First, the woman could be beaten, with no civil or criminal protection or recourse. Second, she could be divorced, leading to a situation equivalent to civil and economic death for the woman. Under these circumstances, the availability of condoms, or the content of AIDS informational brochures, was not the key issue; rather, it was the status and rights of women which created vulnerability to becoming HIV-infected.

The 1994 United Nations Conference on Population and Development (held in Cairo, Egypt) demonstrated and built upon this same basic understanding. At this meeting, the goal of population policies was changed to become ensuring that women can make and put into practice free and informed choices about their reproduction. Traditional public health would contribute to this goal, as suggested above, by providing information, counselling and contraceptive services. The Cairo meeting called for public health to go further, and act directly to improve the societal conditions which strongly condition women's ability to actually make and effectuate free and informed choices. For only and to the extent that women's human rights – to information, to bodily integrity, equal rights in marriage and political participation, among others – are realized, can reproductive health and population policies truly help women. That human rights need to be strengthened as an integral part of population policies does not devalue more traditional public health approaches; rather it emphasizes that without attention to underlying, societal-level conditions (human rights), such programs will remain inherently limited and inadequate.

This is one example from among many, for the major health challenges in the modern world – including cancer, heart disease, injuries, infectious diseases, maternal mortality, child abuse and neglect, and domestic violence – are all amenable to the same kind of human rights-based analysis. This is the basis of the new health and human rights movement, which considers that promoting and protecting human rights is inextricably connected with promoting public health.

Dignity is also essential for health – that is, for physical, mental and social well-being. In this regard, it is highly meaningful that in the Universal Declaration, dignity comes first, 'All human beings are born free and equal in dignity and rights' (Article 1).

When dignity is violated, people suffer. Situations in which personal dignity is violated evoke strong emotions – of shame, humiliation, disgust, anger, power-lessness and sadness – which persist. Clearly, some of the lifelong and even transgenerational impact of torture is related to dignity, for injuries to dignity last far longer than the physical injuries which have been inflicted; similarly, with rape, the true injury is far greater, and persists much longer than the physical damage involved. Consider also the enormous personal and societal energies invested in protecting and promoting individual and collective dignity.

For these reasons, it seems evident that violations of dignity have such significant, pervasive and long-lasting effects that injuries to individual and collective dignity may represent a hitherto unrecognized pathogenic force, of destructive capacity towards human well-being at least equal to that of viruses or bacteria. In future years, I believe that health professionals will look back and wonder how we could have failed to recognize a pathogenic force of such importance. Clearly, much needs to be learned and discovered in the realm of human suffering and its alleviation.

For all these reasons, the discovery of the connection between health and human rights and dignity ranks among the major steps forward in the collective effort to struggle against the weight of human suffering. In teaching about health and human rights, I came to realize that some people reject or refuse the concept of human rights, and I have often wondered why. After several more years of teaching at undergraduate, graduate and postgraduate levels, I now wonder if the major difference between those who accept and those who reject human rights thinking has to do with people's belief in whether the world can change! Those who do not believe that the world can change can find abundant evidence of the failure of human rights to change the world; yet those who believe that the past does not have to determine the future, and that the chains of human suffering can be broken, also find evidence, in the brief history of modern human rights, for optimism and confidence.

Since 1990, all graduates of the Harvard School of Public Health receive two scrolls. The first is their academic diploma, which each has earned; the second is a copy of the Universal Declaration of Human Rights, which is the birthright of all.

The Dean of the School reminds graduates that the Universal Declaration of Human Rights is as important to their future work as public health professionals as a Hippocratic Oath or similar document would be to a medical doctor.

In this 50th-anniversary year of the adoption of the Universal Declaration of Human Rights, I believe we can be both humble and bold. Humble in that we have to realize that fifty years in the course of human history is short, and that enormous work lies ahead in promoting and protecting human rights. Yet also bold, because the modern human rights movement is a unique civilizational achievement. Therefore we in health can see, that when the history of our time is written, the understanding of an inextricable linkage between health and human rights and dignity may have been our most important contribution.

Article 16

1. Men and women of full age, without any limitation due to race, nationality or religion, have the right to marry and to found a family. They are entitled to equal rights as to marriage, during marriage and at its dissolution.
2. Marriage shall be entered into only with the free and full consent of the intending spouses.
3. The family is the natural and fundamental group unit of society and is entitled to protection by society and the State.

GABRIELLE KIRK MCDONALD

The Universal Declaration of Human Rights: The International and the American Dream

What happens to a dream deferred?

Does it dry up
like a raisin in the sun?
Or fester like a sore
And then run?
Does it stink like rotten meat?
Or crust and sugar over–
like a syrupy sweet?

Maybe it just sags
like a heavy load.

Or does it explode?

Langston Hughes

… being furnished with like Faculties, sharing all in one Community of Nature, there cannot be supposed any *Subordination* among us, that may Authorize us to destroy one another, as if we were made for one anothers [*sic*] uses, as if the inferior ranks of Creatures are for ours [*sic*]. Every one as he is bound to preserve himself … by the like reason … ought he, as much as he can, to preserve the rest of Mankind…..

John Locke

Fifty years after its adoption, the Universal Declaration of Human Rights remains one of the defining achievements in the history of humanity. That it retains such status half a century later is testament to the conceptual achievement its adoption signified. Notwithstanding its comprehensive declaration of existing rights, however, it failed to establish explicit mechanisms for observing, enforcing or protecting those rights. Its strength lies in its purpose: to serve as a common standard for all peoples and nations. It is the first formal recognition by the community of nations that there exist rights that are enjoyed by all people, in all places, at all times. The signatories thereby confirmed that such rights are an inherent part of humankind.

Many aspects of the Universal Declaration have a special significance for me as an African-American. Indeed, the same principle of right was proclaimed by the framers of the American Declaration of Independence one hundred and seventy years before the adoption of the Universal Declaration. In this essay, I will discuss the actualisation of the rights proclaimed on the international level by the Universal Declaration by analogy to the enforcement of such rights within the United States domestic context.

AN EVOLUTION OF PRINCIPLE

Whereas the establishment of the United Nations signalled wide recognition and acceptance of the common interests of states, the adoption of the Universal Declaration expressed the inherent value of all men and women by recognising their rights as individuals. The savagery of the war of two generations ago presaged the very real destruction of humanity. With thirty articles, the world community responded by establishing the foundations of an international law based on the rights of individuals and their communities. That process entailed an evolutionary development in states' perceptions: a recognition that individuals shared a *human status*.

The Universal Declaration is thus founded on the principle that it is upon individual human beings, not states or governments, that humankind's survival is dependent. When one person's rights are violated, the human species itself is violated. Only by recognising its interest in upholding and protecting the rights of every individual would states be able to create appropriate conditions to enable all individuals to enjoy those rights.

In proclaiming a panoply of rights that included equality of the person and equality of access to liberty, the law, property, work and education, the Universal Declaration represented the international analogue to a series of national instruments adopted as post-revolutionary means of preventing the return of tyranny and oppression.

Following my own country's war of independence, the Declaration of Independence of 1776 proclaimed, out of 'Respect to the Opinions of Mankind', as self-evident that all men are created equal and that they are endowed with inalienable rights, including life, liberty and the pursuit of happiness. The universal nature of these values was highlighted again when, in the midst of the Second World War, President Roosevelt explained his vision of a secure world founded on freedom of speech and expression, freedom of religion, freedom from want and freedom from fear. The four fundamental freedoms, were not, he said, the prize 'of a distant millennium. [They are] a very definite basis for a kind of world attainable in our time and generation.' A generation later, as groups within the USA campaigned for their civil rights, Dr Martin Luther King, Jr alluded to the principle espoused by the Universal Declaration, writing that 'injustice anywhere is a threat to justice everywhere'.

AN EVOLUTION IN PRINCIPLE ONLY

Eleven years after the Declaration of Independence, the US Constitution established a government to ensure the enjoyment of those rights. However, that Constitution reinforced the inequality of certain groups within society: African-Americans and women. All men were free and equal but until the passage of the Thirteenth and Fourteenth Amendments, former slaves were perceived more as human commodities than human beings. For the purposes of government re-presentation, they were considered to be three fifths of free men. Until the adoption of the Fifteenth and the Nineteenth Amendments, neither African-Americans nor women were entitled to vote.

Yet, even with these Amendments, in 1948 many of the rights proclaimed in the Universal Declaration continued to be denied. The constitutional proclamation of equality under law and in the political process did not prevent the institutionalisation of racial discrimination, made possible through the existence of legally sanctioned impediments to full and equal treatment for all. For many millions of African-Americans, equality was an idea grounded in hope rather than realism.

Similarly, the Universal Declaration, together with the other components of what is often referred to as the International Bill of Rights, was and, regretfully, to a great extent remains, a reflection of aspirations rather than intentions. The rights of many were neither observed nor enforced in 1948. The political polarisation and the prevalence of traditionalist notions of state sovereignty since then have ensured not the enjoyment of rights but the repeated violations of them. To paraphrase the preamble of the Universal Declaration, the numbers of those killed, raped, tortured or disappeared stand in stark contrast to the recognition of the inherent dignity and of the equal and inalienable rights of all members of the human family. The continued commission of barbarous acts that outrage the conscience of mankind symbolises a continuing disregard and contempt for human life. Today, the world that in 1948 was to be founded on justice, freedom and peace is instead constructed on an edifice of impunity and justice denied.

As with my own country, the failure to create and to implement legal obligations that would regulate and uphold the application of equal treatment principles facilitated the continuation of institutionalised discrimination, whether as an end in itself or as a means to further brutality, throughout the world.

An instructive example, and one that demonstrates the relevance of domestic human rights efforts to those undertaken on a more global scale, is provided by the case of Edward H. Lawson, former Deputy Director of the UN Center for Human Rights. As an employee of the US Federal Government, Mr Lawson worked to end discrimination against minorities, particularly in employment practices. Subsequently, while acting as Secretary to the Commission on Human Rights, he assisted Eleanor Roosevelt in the drafting and negotiation of the Universal Declaration. He was later involved in the preparation of many other international instruments proclaiming and protecting human rights, including the two International Covenants of 1966. Until his retirement from the United Nations in 1975, he organised and directed efforts to promote the acceptance and implementation of various aspects of human rights.

Yet, in 1947, while an employee of the United Nations, indeed while involved with the project to draft the Universal Declaration, Mr Lawson himself encountered the reality of odious discrimination. While attempting to obtain accommodation, he was informed that a housing project in the heart of Manhattan, where other United Nations employees lived, was reserved for white people. The ironic injustice of the situation is tempered only by the tangible effects that such actions had on Mr Lawson's life and work.

ENFORCING RIGHTS

In the USA, effective enforcement mechanisms did not exist until passage of the Civil Rights Act of 1964, the Voting Rights Act of 1965 and the Fair Housing Act of 1968. These statutes together prohibited discrimination in public accommodations, in employment, in federally funded facilities, in the administration of the voting system and in the sale or rental of housing. Thus, it was not until two centuries after their proclamation, that *all* men and women could look to the law to safeguard their rights.

That such legislative action did not occur until twenty years after the adoption of the Universal Declaration affords a further insight into the problems of enforcement and the similarities between national and international systems. In the same manner as several of the fifty states of the USA argued that their prerogative enabled them to legislate *against* equality, states of the international community have consistently cited considerations of sovereignty as a bar to the domestic enforcement of internationally codified standards of human rights.

The reasoning advanced by both domestic and international sovereign bodies denies the fundamental character of the concept at issue: rights that are inherent in all people are universal rights. The duty to uphold them is an incontrovertible one and is, therefore, a matter that concerns all forms of government. Governments are nothing more than the representatives of their constituents, on whom they depend for their continued existence. Where they breach the duty and thereby cease to be representative, it is within the prerogative of a higher order, as the final guarantor of the rights of members of a broader constituency, to compel the remedy for the breach. Thus, the US Federal Government enacted the civil rights legislation referred to above, and used military force to uphold the right to desegregated education.

Just as the enforcement of rights within domestic systems requires practical measures that operate within the framework of the rule of law, it is in an analogous context that the United Nations may operate. As a supranational representative, it is endowed with an implicit residual power to perform or to mandate the performance of obligations on which states have defaulted. As noted above, a great many defaults have occurred since the adoption of the Universal Declaration. Through its silence, the world community has facilitated impunity for the perpetrators of those crimes.

There have, however, been two notable exceptions: the establishment, pursuant to Chapter Seven of the Charter of the United Nations, of *ad hoc* international tribunals to prosecute human rights violations that rank in infamy among the most barbaric acts of this century. The International Tribunals for the former Yugoslavia and for Rwanda were established by the Security Council in, respectively, 1993 and 1994, to judge individuals charged with responsibility for the crimes committed in the recent conflicts in South-Eastern Europe and in Rwanda. By this adjudication, the Tribunals are relevant to the Universal Declaration in four ways.

First, as a means of affording redress, the Tribunals are a specific measure implementing Article 8 of the Universal Declaration, curing the defects of national systems. Second, the Tribunals reaffirm the rights of the victims of abuses – to life, to security of person, to legal status, to free movement, to nationality and religion, to be free from humiliation, arbitrary arrest and detention. Third, through due process of law, including the presumption of innocence and the right to a full defence, the Tribunals uphold the equally fundamental rights of accused persons, as stated in the Universal Declaration. Finally, the very existence and operation of the Tribunals vindicate the Universal Declaration's principles: both were established under the mandatory provisions of Chapter Seven of the Charter of the United Nations, as measures to contribute to the restoration and maintenance of international peace and security. The international community acting in concert, employing the rule of law to challenge the notion of impunity as the norm, reaffirms the universal character of the rights violated.

These first exceptions to the rule of injustice – the Tribunals – have exposed the sophistry of that rule, which was founded on a false notion of sovereignty. The Tribunals' continuing existence and development, notwithstanding its extraneous limitations, negates the arguments of those who deny the utility of international enforcement. Although the Tribunals' early months and years have been characterised by uncertainty, this was a necessary consequence of the creation of representative international criminal courts, whose subject-matter jurisdictional basis had rarely, if ever, been subject to judicial consideration. However, further uncertainty, borne of a lack of political support, was entirely avoidable. Lacking an enforcement agency, both Tribunals rely on the assistance of relevant states and international organisations to enforce its orders. To establish such a criminal jurisdiction without facilitating its operation is to paralyse it, thereby negating its creation and ultimately damaging the very ideals that such creation sought to preserve.

Referring now only to the Tribunal of which I am President, the International Criminal Tribunal for the former Yugoslavia (ICTY) has successfully carried out its mandate to the extent that it is independently able to do so. In developing substantive jurisprudence on international humanitarian law, the ICTY has considered and elucidated norms that have evolved, many since the adoption of the Universal Declaration, without the benefit of judicial application. Complementing this, the Tribunal has established the normative structure necessary to the execution of its mandate. In addition to a set of Rules of Procedure and Evidence and hundreds of procedural decisions, various codes govern myriad matters, including the assignment of counsel to indigent accused, the conduct of counsel and the rights of detainees, all drawn from relevant international norms, while a detention unit was constructed to United Nations specifications to house indictees in the Tribunal's custody, under the supervision of the International Committee of the Red Cross.

Nevertheless, although the ICTY is functioning, it remains dependent on the co-operation of entities over which it has no effective control, notwithstanding its status as a Chapter Seven mechanism. Although state co-operation improved significantly through 1997, at the time of writing, the great majority of indicted persons remain at liberty, more than four and a half years after the establishment of the Tribunal. Moreover, the overwhelming majority of states have eschewed the enactment of legislation to facilitate such co-operation, have failed to express a willingness to accept convicted persons for detention and have declined to afford assistance in relocating the witnesses who bravely appear before the Tribunal. The provision of such co-operation is the single factor that will determine whether the Tribunal will have the capability to fulfil its mandate, and whether the values of the Universal Declaration will have at last emerged from the realm of aspiration into reality.

In that respect, the success of the Tribunals is of crucial import to the proposed permanent International Criminal Court. Such a court will benefit from the institutional practice of the Tribunals, which have melded theory with practice to create a functioning and effective international judicial institution. Of particular value will be the procedural code, combining aspects of the common and civil law systems, and the experience gained conducting trials in multiple languages, with witnesses who are located throughout the world.

Two other factors will be instrumental in determining the effectiveness of the Court, with a consequent effect on its role as a mechanism for upholding human rights. First, the prevalence of state involvement in mass human rights violations indicates that an objective and impartial forum of adjudication is the only means to enforce the canons of the Universal Declaration. The vagueness of the principle of complementarity may permit the continuation of immunity and therefore of impunity because of the lack of certainty regarding what constitutes an effective national court system. Again, the experience of the United States system proves instructive: the existence of state legislation permitting racial discrimination negated the possibility that such states could enforce rights to equality and redress discriminatory conduct. In response, federal courts conferred upon themselves jurisdiction over all matters arising under the Constitution and the laws of the United States.

Second, the record of state co-operation with the Tribunals, in particular with the ICTY, will dictate whether the permanent International Criminal Court is to be impotent or efficacious. Irrespective of the nature of the Court's relationship to national courts, it is imperative that it be vested with the power to issue binding orders, including *subpoenae* and arrest warrants, and that there is a means of ensuring that such orders will be enforced. Without such certainty, the Court will likely face the same obstacles to effectiveness as have been encountered by the Tribunals.

CONCLUSION

It is said that in the conduct of their affairs, states' actions are cyclical, comparable to the motion of a pendulum. Fifty years ago, the pendulum swung briefly, too briefly, towards its peak: justice and humanity. As we approach the twenty-first century, the pendulum is once again swinging to its apex. There is now an opportunity to create a permanent institution that will serve as the keeper of the spirit of the Universal Declaration, promoting human rights through the redress of violations and the affirmation of the universal character of the rights. The process was initiated with the two *ad hoc* Tribunals, limited in competence, and has been proven to be viable and effective if adequately supported.

Yet, the interregnum was one of horrific suffering and destruction that constituted an affront to the principles of the Universal Declaration. This alone is cause enough to guard against optimism. The continuing prevalence of systematic abuses of human rights renders such caution imperative. Domestically, the American Dream is confronting the legacy of the inconsistent enforcement of civil rights initiatives, evinced through a potential resurgence in institutionalised racial discrimination. Internationally, the Tribunals' continued success in redressing and deterring human rights violations depends wholly on the continuing and increased co-operation of states. The value of the permanent Court is in its potential to ensure that justice will not be selective. Its realisation – and the assurance that the pendulum will attain its zenith – requires the vigilance of every person who desires to retain their liberty.

The dream has been deferred too long. We must seize the day, lest failure extinguish this opportunity and postpone again the realisation of our human right to live in a world of more justice and less violence.

Article 17

1. Everyone has the right to own property alone as well as in association with others.
2. No one shall be arbitrarily deprived of his property.

CECILIA MEDINA QUIROGA

Some Thoughts to Mark the 50th Anniversary of the Universal Declaration of Human Rights

When I was invited to write about the 50th anniversary of the Universal Declaration of Human Rights, I felt very honoured. It was like being invited to a gathering to pay tribute to some distinguished person's work and career. And, in a way, that is what we are doing here: remembering all those who helped to create this Declaration, directly or indirectly, through their wisdom and commitment, through their example and their devotion. We are remembering not only its official authors, those whose names and work we can identify, but also its unofficial authors – the hundreds of thousands of men and women who have fought and are fighting for human dignity all over the planet.

Much has been written about the Universal Declaration, and from all kinds of different perspectives: its legal value, its impact on international relations, its ethical dimension, and many other aspects. I would certainly not deny that new contributions can be made in such areas, even if derived, to a greater or lesser degree, from the extensive literature that already exists. However, I feel that this occasion should be used to take a closer look at what the Universal Declaration means today.

As a formal document, the Universal Declaration has acquired a privileged position in the international community. From an ideal to be fought for, it has become an international obligation (at least as far as the greater part of its provisions are concerned). At the same time, its authority as a frame of reference for countries' behaviour is unquestioned. No government today would dare tell its counterparts that it rejects the principles of the Universal Declaration or that it challenges the legitimacy of the rights enshrined in it.

A second relevant fact is that, for fifty years, the Universal Declaration has continued to be an extraordinarily comprehensive expression of the standards which enable human beings to live together with dignity. While there are those who point out its shortcomings with regard to issues which it failed to cover adequately or at all, it clearly remains a colossal testament to faith in the individual and in human dignity. It should not be forgotten that the Universal Declaration wisely conceives of human beings in their entirety, enshrining both their civil and political rights and their economic, social and cultural rights, and delivering the clear message that all human rights are interdependent.

A third noteworthy aspect is the extent of its dissemination throughout the world. If the frequency with which the Universal Declaration is reproduced and invoked could somehow be recorded, there can be no doubt that it would have a leading place among international instruments. Moreover, it is often invoked as a mandatory basic standard from which the fundamental rights enshrined in many of the world's constitutions are derived.

A fourth aspect is the complex system for the protection of human rights which has been built up on the basis of the Universal Declaration (from international conventions to regional treaties). Yet formal compliance with the Universal Declaration, the breadth and aptness of its provisions, the extent of its dissemination, and the system of protection which has grown up under its influence seem hard to reconcile with the experience of those of us who are endeavouring to ensure that human rights are upheld more effectively. The Universal Declaration, though acknowledged as universal and acclaimed as an expression of humanity's conscience, sadly continues to be betrayed with shameful frequency by the realities of power in many parts of the world.

This brings me back to my original question about what the Universal Declaration means today. There are two aspects that strike me as relevant here. First, we should beware of thinking that universal acknowledgement of the Universal Declaration has turned it into a document of purely historical value, to be referred to when talking of how things used to be; things have not yet changed that much. Secondly, the Universal Declaration can – and must – play a leading role in the struggle against other types of assault upon human dignity which, although they were not invented in our era, have certainly acquired greater notoriety in the course of it.

As regards the first of these, the circumstances in which societies develop regularly remind us that the task of enforcing the rights set out in the Universal Declaration is an unending one. Injustice, oppression, helplessness in the face of arbitrary authority are all part of day-to-day reality. At the same time, it is increasingly apparent that there are sectors of society which are able to enjoy their rights only with the greatest of difficulty: women and indigenous peoples are cases in point. We have made a good deal of progress in relative terms, but there are many crossroads along the way and our only road map is the Universal Declaration.

Turning to the second aspect mentioned above, it seems almost idle to recall that the Universal Declaration was born out of a sense of revulsion at the barbarity which had so recently ravaged the world. It was drawn up in response to the denial of people's most basic rights – through genocide, torture, summary execution, and political oppression. For all its breadth, it was seen by the public as being restricted to individual life and security and resistance to tyranny. However, the scope of the Universal Declaration has had to be widened and enhanced over the past fifty years to take account of other forms of injustice which are prevalent in so many countries. The fact that this was at all possible is one more praiseworthy feature of the Universal Declaration, which was worded in such terms that it can have meaning and achieve its aims irrespective of time or place.

We are currently witnessing the emergence of societies in which fear of the future is treated as a virtue because it helps boost production; in which competitors are increasingly seen as enemies against whom any weapon may fairly be used; and in which the weak are not comforted but are contemptuously cast aside. All this serves as a forceful reminder that the Universal Declaration is as relevant as ever. Our own experience enables us to discover in it ideas which we may not have noticed before. Faced with the unemployment which is now such a tragically constant feature of our lives, how can we forget that the Universal Declaration was drawn up to help create a world in which human beings would enjoy freedom from want? Faced with the headlong rush of progress – whose proponents forget that its only possible aim is the well-being of each individual, and are undaunted by the fact that they are putting much of the world's population at risk – how can we forget that the Universal Declaration calls for a world in which human beings will enjoy freedom from fear?

Oppression and injustice, social exclusion and gross inequality challenge us to look afresh at the Universal Declaration and invoke it in response to the demands of those whose rights have been infringed. There are sceptics who claim that this is a pointless exercise or, at best, that its outcome is uncertain. Yet those of us who work in the field of human rights know that, as Leopoldo Marechal said, words can develop the power to bring to life the things that they touch. This is what we must try to achieve.

We must continue to proclaim the Universal Declaration and use it to give succour to those whose rights are violated. We must use its legitimacy to urge those who now only pay it lip service to put it into actual practice. We must remind powerful states of the commitments which they made at a time when they were overwhelmed by grief and anger. We must encourage those who abide by its provisions to devote themselves to the task of ensuring that others do so too. Above all, we must show individuals that the Universal Declaration is the most powerful argument that they can wield in their struggle for human dignity – because, even when it is ignored, invoking it exposes the iniquity of those who choose to disregard it.

We owe this debt to those who first gave shape to the Universal Declaration of Human Rights, and especially to those who, even today, see it as a far-off, distant ideal.

Article 18

Everyone has the right to freedom of thought, conscience and religion; this right includes freedom to change his religion or belief, and freedom, either alone or in community with others and in public or private, to manifest his religion or belief in teaching, practice, worship and observance.

HOSSEIN MEHRPOUR

Human Rights in the Universal Declaration and the Religious Perspective

The Universal Declaration of Human Rights was adopted fifty years ago by the United Nations General Assembly as the common aspiration of all nations. It was the first international document that reflected the fundamental rights and freedoms of the human person and it established the present international human rights order. At the time of its proclamation, the United Nations consisted of 56 member states and the 30 articles of the Universal Declaration were adopted by 48 member states. The fiftieth anniversary of the Universal Declaration avails us of the opportunity to examine its various aspects and its impact. In this essay, we will have a brief look at the standards and contents of the Universal Declaration of Human Rights, human rights from a religious perspective, and finally, the possibility of a reconciliation between the two.

AN OVERVIEW OF THE STANDARDS AND CONTENTS OF THE UNIVERSAL DECLARATION OF HUMAN RIGHTS

The Universal Declaration of Human Rights draws much of its inspiration from the standards and concepts of the French Declaration of the Rights of Man and of the Citizen. In the Universal Declaration, the inherent worth and dignity of the human person are emphasized and fundamental freedoms recognized without any reference to God and divine inspiration as the source of such rights. Unlike the American Declaration of Independence (1776) in which God is referred to as endowing men with certain inalienable rights, and the French Declaration of the Rights of Man which refers to the Almighty, in the Universal Declaration of Human Rights there is no mention of God whatsoever. During the debate on Article 1 of the Universal Declaration, the Brazilian representative proposed that the second sentence of Article 1 which reads: 'They are endowed with reason and conscience and should act towards one another in a spirit of brotherhood' be redrafted as: 'Created in the image and likeness of God, they are endowed with reason and conscience, and should act towards one another in a spirit of brotherhood'. The representatives of certain other countries, however, disagreed and stated that no mention of God and His commandments should be made in United Nations documents; the name of God was therefore, omitted from the said article. Human rights, as set forth in the Universal Declaration, do not derive their legitimacy from God's commandments; rather, their legitimacy arises from the meeting of minds of the members of the

United Nations General Assembly based on considerations of public interest. The goal of the drafters of the Universal Declaration was to bring about the necessary conditions for social life on an international level; respect for human rights has been recognized as a prerequisite for preventing a situation in which man is compelled to have recourse to force against tyranny and oppression. In the preamble to the Universal Declaration, we read: '... it is essential, if man is not to be compelled to have recourse, as a last resort, to rebellion against tyranny and oppression, that human rights should be protected by the rule of law....'

From a philosophical point of view, the Universal Declaration of Human Rights is based on individual freedom and the viewpoint that human beings are free to act how they wish as long as they do not infringe upon the rights of others; accordingly, the drafters of the Universal Declaration believed that bringing about proper social life on an international level would in practice require the observance of the rights set forth in the Universal Declaration. The Universal Declaration seeks to be practical and applicable in its goal and does not, in principle, deal with people's spiritual and moral progress or their lasting happiness.

The Universal Declaration basically falls into three parts. The first part, comprising Articles 1 through 21, sets forth the political and civil rights and freedoms of the human person. In this section, the rights and freedoms of human beings are stipulated in greater detail and in more explicit terms than in the French Declaration of the Rights of Man and of the Citizen. The most important of these include: the right to life, the right to liberty and not to be held in slavery under any circumstances, entitlement to equal protection of the law, equality before the law, prohibition of arbitrary arrest, prohibition of torture and cruel and inhuman punishment, the presumption of innocence, the right to freedom of residence, the right to have a nationality, the right to freedom of choice of a spouse, the requirement of free and full consent of both spouses, the right to freedom of thought, conscience, choice and change of religion, the right to freedom of expression, and the right to take part in the government of one's country.

The important point in the first part is that all human beings must be able to exercise such rights and freedoms and that differences in race, language, sex or religion must not provide grounds for discrimination regarding these rights. For example, a woman must have the same right to life and security, to recognition as a person before the law, to freedom of residence, nationality, choice of spouse, and to property as a man, and the fact of being a woman must not constitute a reason for limiting certain of these rights. Moreover, whether atheist or monotheist, Muslim or non-Muslim, God-worshipper or idolater, every human being has all the above-mentioned rights and in particular, the right to freedom of speech, the right to take part in governing the affairs of his country, to hold office and the like. If certain limitations are imposed of necessity, no one should be singled out.

The second part of the Universal Declaration, comprising Articles 22 through 27, sets forth the economic, social and cultural rights such as the right to education, work and welfare. These rights are defined in greater detail in the International Covenant on Economic, Social, and Cultural Rights adopted by the United Nations General Assembly in 1966.

The third part deals with the establishment of order and limitations on the exercise of the rights mentioned above. The Universal Declaration treats this subject with extreme care and circumspection. Article 29 permits the imposition of limitations on such rights only in connection with securing the rights and freedoms of others and meeting the just requirements of morality and public order. At the same time, the Universal Declaration recognizes that the imposition of such limitations must be subject to the rule of law in a democratic society.

The Universal Declaration of Human Rights formed the basis for many human rights declarations and treaties, was the subject of numerous commentaries and was a source of great hope. Mr René Cassin, one of the main drafters of the Universal Declaration stated that this is the most important document ever made accessible to man; it inaugurates a new era in the history of man and constitutes the charter of freedom for the dispossessed and the victims of tyranny and oppression.

HUMAN RIGHTS FROM A RELIGIOUS PERSPECTIVE

It may rightly be claimed that the main precursors and defenders of fundamental human rights concepts such as the inherent dignity of the human person, the right for every human being to be born free, equal rights, equality before the law and the eradication of discrimination, are the divinely-ordained religions and the prophets. The main difference between the religious and the philosophical perspective on human rights is that religion focuses on the human person and his or her individual destiny, piety and corruption regardless of the relationship with others. Religion does not abandon man to himself; its goal is the spiritual and moral progress of every single individual and it is not indifferent to individual wrongdoing and corrupt personal conduct. The purpose of religion is to bring lasting happiness to man and that is only possible through monotheism, obedience to God's commandments, performance of one's prayers and religious duties and naturally, through proper social conduct and observance of the rights of others.

However, the other important task which is entrusted to the prophets of God and monotheistic religions relates to the administration of the affairs of human beings in their social life. In this connection, the best standard bearer for the principles of freedom, equality of rights, eradication of discrimination and promotion of justice is the teachings of divinely-ordained religions. The holy Qur'an depicts the prophets as rational beings, supporters of freedom of thought, heralds of justice, opponents of oppression and discrimination; on the other hand, it depicts their adversaries as selfish, irrational, despotic, supporters of discrimination and class privilege. The latter group could even include official religious administrators. The reason why idolatry has, in principle, been fought so rigorously in all the divinely-ordained religions and particularly in the Qur'an is, to a great extent, that idols are the manifestations of ignorance, extreme bigotry, class privilege and tyranny. The *raison d'être* of the prophetic mission, notably the administration of justice, has been expounded in the Qur'an: 'Indeed, We sent Our Messengers with the clear signs, and We sent down with them the Book and the Balance so that men might uphold justice...' (Qur'an 57:25). Pharaoh is described in the holy Qur'an as the one who exalted himself in the land, divided its people into parties, promoted class discrimination and oppressed and tyrannized one party: 'Now Pharaoh had exalted himself in the land and had divided its inhabitants into sects, abasing one party of them, slaughtering their sons, and sparing their women...' (Qur'an 28:4). And Moses, the Messenger of God, has a divine mission to eradicate this oppression and rescue the oppressed and the dispossessed: 'Go to Pharaoh, for he has waxed insolent; yet speak gently to him, that haply he may be mindful, or perchance fear...' (Qur'an 20:43&44).

The mission of Jesus Christ, the son of Mary, consisted mainly of fighting against the corruption of Jewish clerics who used the religion of God as a means of amassing wealth and gratifying their greed; they concealed religious truth and ruled their subjects with hypocrisy. The Qur'an describes them thus: 'O believers, many of the rabbis and monks indeed consume the goods of the people in vanity and bar from God's way. Those who treasure up gold and silver, and do not expend them in the way of God – give them the good tidings of a painful chastisement...' (Qur'an 9:24). It is true to say that divine religions and Islam in particular claim to be global, aspire to be all-encompassing and to prevail over all doctrines: 'It is He who has sent His Messenger with the guidance and the religion of truth, that He may uplift it above every religion, though the unbelievers be averse' (Qur'an 9:23). However, the main social goal of Islam is to establish an order based on justice, to eradicate discrimination and oppression for all mankind. In no way does it intend to create a religious elite who, distinguishing themselves solely through religious affiliation, can behave in a discriminatory fashion towards others. In many of the verses of the Qur'an, man is enjoined to be fair, truthful, and to promote justice even if such an act proves to be detrimental to himself. The following two verses are examples in point: 'O believers, be you securers of justice, witnesses for God. Let not detestation for a people move you not to be equitable; be equitable – that is nearer to God-fearing...' (Qur'an 5:18) or : 'O believers, be you securers of justice, witnesses for God, even though it be against yourselves, or your parents and kinsmen...' (Qur'an 4:135).

Although in a religious form of government the leadership and the administration of the affairs of the community are entrusted to the Prophet, the Imam or to the pious and wise, and although it is desirable to respect and follow them, the most liberal and democratic government is a religious government which allows people to vote, comment and criticize freely and to participate in and control the affairs of the community. Indeed, the most conspicuous feature of the followers of

Islam in the Qur'an, which distinguishes them from the followers of other religions is the principle of bidding to honour and forbidding dishonour. Taken in broad terms, it means that people can and must subject even the government to the principle of bidding to honour and forbidding dishonour and voice their criticism: 'You are the best nation ever brought to men, bidding to honour, and forbidding dishonour...' (Qur'an 3:110).

When they came to power, instead of parading their piety or infallibility before their subjects and demanding absolute obedience from them, the pious rulers and even the Prophet (Peace Be Upon Him) and the Imam (Peace Be Upon Him) reminded their subjects that it was possible for them to err and asked the people to express any criticism they had. The prime example in this regard is the statement made by the Commander of the Faithful, Imam Ali (Peace be Upon Him), who in criticizing the panegyrics addressed to him by some of His companions said: 'Treat me not as a despot and a dictator nor adulate me; hesitate not to speak the truth and think not that such truth is difficult for me to hear; indeed, come forth with your reminders and criticisms for I am, nonetheless, a human being and humans are fallible'. The rule of the Prophet Mohammad (Peace be Upon Him) and the first four caliphs, notably that of Imam Ali (Peace be Upon Him), which was a wholly religious form of government, in fact constituted the most democratic form of government. Their subjects lived in complete and reasonable freedom and played a most effective role in the administration of the affairs of the country; they could freely express their views and criticisms. Despite the dominant power and the lofty spiritual status of the Prophet, Imam or caliph, people were not only free to express their opinions but in fact, as we read in Imam Ali's (Peace be Upon Him) statements, were actually reprimanded if they did not do so.

Unfortunately, the government of Islam soon fell into the hands of autocratic rulers. To secure their influence and power, they resorted to coercion, apotheosizing religious rule and the caliphate to such an extent that their Muslim followers could do nothing but display absolute obedience and dared not speak their minds. For this reason, it is said that the dictatorial form of religious government is the worst type of dictatorship since it enables the dictatorial spirit to permeate people's minds disguised as faith and belief. It is not, however, the religious form of government which is dictatorial; rather, it was and still is the dictatorial rulers who, with the aid of religion and the misinterpretation and misreading of certain of its concepts, endeavour to secure their rule. One need only look at Imam Ali's (Peace be Upon Him) governing policy and in particular, His administrative instructions issued in a letter addressed to Malik-i-Ashtar, the governor in Egypt, to see how highly human rights and freedoms were to be regarded and with what degree of respect a religious government should treat its subjects. In these instructions, the Imam (Peace be Upon Him) even upholds the rights of non-Muslims and reminds the governor of the necessity to avoid oppression. He entrusts the people to his governor's care and urges the governor to observe their rights, saying: 'Beware lest you threaten their lives like a rapacious wolf; beware lest you trample upon their rights for they are either your coreligionists or your fellow men', that is they are human beings, no matter how you regard them, and as such, their rights must be respected.

In conclusion, it may be stated that apart from that aspect of religion which consists of the important duty to spiritually guide and instruct, there are no serious differences or contradictions in their social aspects and application between religious teachings and what social thinkers came to believe at the end of the dark night of the Middle Ages and the dawn of the age of enlightenment. Indeed, the social goal embodied in the prophetic mission and the practice and governing methods of the Prophet Muhammad (Peace be Upon Him) and of Imam Ali (Peace be Upon Him) and the different verses of the Qur'an, notably the verse inviting all peoples to join the community, demonstrate that the principles of human rights as set forth in the Universal Declaration of Human Rights and its source document, the French Declaration of the Rights of Man and of the Citizen, are not alien to religious standards. Perhaps the principle of freedom of religion has been underscored not because of opposition to religion, but as a reaction to the sectarian and racial implications of religious affiliation that prevailed in Europe particularly during the Middle Ages.

It would seem that if education on the Universal Declaration of Human Rights takes place alongside the strengthening of religious belief and the teaching of moral standards, greater respect for and observance of the fundamental rights of human beings will open up a new and brighter horizon to humanity.

Everyone has the right to freedom of opinion and expression; this right includes freedom to hold opinions without interference and to seek, receive and impart information and ideas through any media and regardless of frontiers.

RIGOBERTA MENCHÚ TUM

The Universal Declaration and the Rights of Indigenous People

In the course of time, peoples, states, nations and the international community as a whole have devised, refined and perfected mechanisms and instruments to help humankind create better material, spiritual, legal, economic, political and social conditions in which women, men and children can live their lives. Often, however, what we have seen are models which are designed to help small ruling elites wield power more effectively, and economic systems which fail to benefit the vast majority of people.

Man, considered as an integrated concept, that is to say, the human race, is by nature a creator. Throughout history, the whole of humankind has experienced a constant process of developments, changes and transformations which most of the time are imperceptible but together have enabled humanity to make great advances.

The Universal Declaration of Human Rights, proclaimed by Resolution 217 (A) of the United Nations General Assembly in Paris on 10 December 1948, was a response to the numerous violations of human rights which continue to occur day after day throughout the world, as well as an acknowledgment of this regrettable state of affairs. For, despite mankind's ceaseless struggle to achieve better living conditions, to attain development under conditions of equality, freedom and security, and to banish racial, ethnic and cultural discrimination; despite the vast transformations which man has experienced over the past millenniums; despite major scientific and technological advances, continuing economic development and the emergence of economic systems which, without managing to eradicate poverty and inequality, have brought about at least some improvement in the living conditions of entire peoples; and despite the constant evolution of the law, man has so far failed to wipe out oppression, exploitation, discrimination, subjugation, tyranny and other practices which constitute an assault upon the lives, freedom, security and integrity of individuals and communities.

The Universal Declaration of Human Rights saw the light of day just three years after the defeat of the fascist powers which had unleashed the Second World War – the worst conflagration that the world has experienced this century. The Universal Declaration was proclaimed at a time when it was necessary to give capitalism a new face and rid it of its markedly inhuman features, so as to prevent and bring to an end the constant abuses and atrocities committed against entire peoples by ruling minorities, in their desire to impose economic, political and social models for their own exclusive benefit.

However, this was no easy matter. Many battles had to be fought by the supporters of a Universal Declaration, which would not merely be signed by the UN member states but would be respected and complied with in the smallest details, so as to ensure that peoples, societies and individuals could live and develop under better conditions.

The Universal Declaration of Human Rights undoubtedly represents an enormous advance in human rights, for a number of reasons. Firstly, it constitutes an international instrument which was proclaimed in order to be respected and complied with by the UN member states. Secondly, it represents a commitment by countries to ensure that human rights are respected and upheld within their territories. Thirdly, it represents a commitment by the international community to ensure that human rights are fully upheld in every country which belongs to it.

Nevertheless, the Universal Declaration has been used by various powers to intervene in other countries' internal affairs. We have seen military aggression, immoral and unethical economic blockades which are an affront to humanity and reason, and thousands or even millions of men, women and children throughout the world condemned to die of hunger and malnutrition – all in the name of human rights.

The Universal Declaration of Human Rights has been manipulated and used to further the interests of the dominant powers within the United Nations. Even when in countries such as Guatemala, El Salvador or Iran, the most basic human rights are being trampled underfoot by military juntas or dictatorships in pursuance of the interests of some military or economic power, the world appears to turn a blind eye, and the United Nations seems unconcerned.

Those of us who are fighting for human rights have had to struggle hard to open up a space within the United Nations in which the victims can finally be heard, and in which resolutions can be adopted, at least, deploring the appalling violations of human rights in our countries!

One would expect the United Nations to take an automatic interest in ensuring that human rights are fully upheld throughout the world. Instead, we, the victims of injustice and aggression, have had to go there ourselves and fight to make the United Nations turn its gaze towards countries where human rights are basically non-existent. This is a symptom of the crisis that besets the United Nations, a sign that things are deteriorating rather than getting better.

The United Nations has been playing an increasingly inappropriate role, not only in its commitment to human rights, but also in what is one of its most sacred functions, namely global peacekeeping. The role of the United Nations has gradually come to reflect the interests of certain economic and political powers. And hence the Universal Declaration of Human Rights, like so many other instruments, conventions and treaties emanating from this, the most important of international bodies, has been reduced to a set of rhetorical utterances, of principles which are not upheld and which no one observes or respects.

In the name of the Universal Declaration of Human Rights, the United Nations has sent the Blue Berets, peacekeeping missions, to various parts of the world – or rather, the Universal Declaration has been invoked in UN-backed efforts, which have proved largely fruitless, to prevent countries from fighting among themselves. War has continued unabated.

Yet the United Nations is the ultimate global authority, and millions of us throughout the world are confronted daily with the impact of its decisions. This is why we must take a critical view of what it does and must keep urging the UN member states to shoulder their responsibilities under the Universal Declaration. We must not allow the human rights tragedy to be lost in a welter of intergovernmental lobbying and bureaucratic red tape. The interests of authoritarian governments which systematically violate human rights must no longer be allowed to prevail within the United Nations, and human rights must cease to be treated with such apathy and indifference.

How can the United Nations be seen as the custodian of world peace if human rights are not fully upheld in every country? How can we believe in the commitment of the United Nations to human rights if it defers to the interests of certain powers which are bent on manipulating it for their own purposes?

The Universal Declaration of Human Rights has been adopted and proclaimed, but it has yet to be put into practice. Before it can be fully and unambiguously implemented, many parts of the world – countries in which human rights still seem a naive illusion – will continue to experience great suffering. Things are improving, but there is still much to be accomplished.

We are obliged to urge the United Nations to undertake a thorough review of its work, to launch a series of reforms in pursuance of its own Universal Declaration, and to ensure that the Declaration is complied with. Economic, civil, political, social and cultural rights need to be seen as part of the same basic issue. If the United Nations can enforce strict compliance with the Universal Declaration, social inequality may begin to make way for equality.

But more than this is needed. The United Nations needs to look at the issue of the autonomy and rights of indigenous and aboriginal peoples and of ethnic and cultural minorities, which are not mentioned in the Universal Declaration.

In this connection, the United Nations is under an obligation to adopt a Declaration on the Rights of Indigenous Peoples. For the past 15 years, a working group of the Sub-Commission on Prevention of Discrimination and Protection of Minorities has been working on a draft, with input from representatives of indigenous peoples. Now it is up to a working group of the Commission on Human Rights to approve this draft (and subsequently the Commission, ECOSOC and the General Assembly). If they do, the United Nations Declaration on the Rights of Indigenous Peoples – which we hope will develop into a binding international convention – could be a sort of supplement to the Universal Declaration of Human Rights and, if fully implemented, would form a solid basis for the individual and collective development of the peoples of the world.

The forthcoming 50th anniversary of the Universal Declaration of Human Rights is a suitable moment to reflect and to propose ways of solving the serious difficulties which beset human rights throughout the world. This is an opportune moment for us to make a resolute commitment to tackle the serious and systematic violations of human rights that still occur in every corner of the planet.

I trust that the 50th anniversary celebrations will not founder in rhetorical statements, verging on demagoguery, and hollow declarations of support, and that the UN organization and its member states can truly commit themselves to ensuring that human rights will one day be respected and upheld throughout the world. This is a goal which all of us – nations and states, societies and governments, indigenous and non-indigenous peoples, and the international community – should make every effort to achieve.

RENDRA

Song of the Sun

The sun rises from my heart
and touches the ocean.
The sun emerges from my mouth,
becoming a rainbow.

Your face emerges from my forehead,
you, poor woman,
with your feet planted in the mud,
working for a few pounds of grain.
The landlord comes out into the field
and plows you.

A million bare-headed men
leave the jungle,
their bodies covered in mud.
The sun is reflected
from their heads.
Their eyes glow.
Their bodies blaze.
They burn the world.

The sun is an orange disk
flung by Krishna.
It is your blessing and curse,
mankind.

DANIELLE MITTERRAND

Towards a New Era of Peace and Equitable Democracy?

In 1948, three years after the end of the Second World War, came an event of global significance: the proclamation of the Universal Declaration of Human Rights.

Faced with the spectacle of human suffering on a massive scale – involving millions of men, women and children and affecting people throughout the continent of Europe: British, German, Italian, French, Belgian, Dutch and Danish, as well as Japanese, Russian, African and American – many of the most brilliant minds of the time were eventually struck by the self-evident fact that it was peace treaties drafted by heads of state and military leaders that sowed the seeds of the next war. National interests, exacerbated by the ambitions of the great powers and by clever rhetoric, set peoples at each other's throats even where there was no natural animosity between them.

Whole populations would line up against each other, even though as individuals they had no personal reason to do so. They would obey the summons on behalf of interests in which they themselves had no part, and die for the honour of their country.

Rich or poor, country-dweller or townsman, shop-keeper or office-worker, handsome or ugly, morally indifferent or confirmed zealot, writer or illiterate, each would do his duty as a citizen: to slaughter his opposite number from the other side of the border.

Plants and animals display a universal life force which reacts instinctively – within the limits of their understanding – to protect them from the threat of bad weather or predatory species. Was humanity, then, to use the gift of its superior evolved intelligence to develop its brute force to engage in sterile aggression designed to eliminate all who crossed its path, including its fellow man? Was it the destiny of mankind to achieve sole dominion over the depleted resources of the Earth only to discover its own solitude? Was the attempt to respect difference not an essential part of life?

At the close of the Second World War, the people of London, Berlin, Moscow and a host of other cities stood amid the smoking ruins and stared disaster in the face. Victors or vanquished, they set to work to rebuild Europe conscious of the similarity of their lot; their elected representatives noted the absurdity of such confrontations ... who did they benefit? The warmongers, deranged by power and pride, had disappeared from the scene: miserably assassinated or executed by those same populations. People heard the lamentations of bereaved families on both sides;

they were revolted by the atomic annihilation of Hiroshima. Was this the only way to make the warring powers see reason and to bring them to their knees? Hiroshima would remain inscribed in the long list of human crimes against humanity. And hardly had the last despicable authors of hatred and bitterness been silenced and passed into oblivion than we began to witness the emergence during the cold war (the third world war) of the first signs of a new global conflict: the confrontation between tyrannical wealth and poverty.

Today, fifty years on, the question we must ask ourselves is whether the international solidarity that began to emerge in the aftermath of the Second World War has advanced sufficiently for us now genuinely to honour those who so successfully redrafted and universalised the Declaration of the Rights of Man and of the Citizen of 1789? There seems now to be a realisation of the chaos caused by the concept of the 'hereditary enemy', inculcated down the centuries, even as yesterday's enemy became today's ally. The only real victory has been that won by Europe over itself and over false doctrines.

These days the term 'hereditary enemy' – a despotic invader who lays down the law and periodically decimates all opposition – no longer suggests to us the armed forces of a neighbouring country, likely at any time to sweep in to kill, plunder and subjugate. It is used rather to describe a new type of conflict: that between the profits of the world's powerful and the losses of exploited local peoples.

So now, in 1998, how close are we to being able to win the trial of strength that we are experiencing as the twentieth century grinds to its close? Can the civilised philosophy of 'being', symbolised by the Universal Declaration and founded on respect for life and the pursuit of justice and equity, ultimately overcome the philosophy of 'having', which takes the doctrine of the profit motive to shameless extremes while ignoring the unacceptable consequences for those exploited and excluded from the 'good life'?

In the face of this universalisation of human rights, the world of power and of money has had to organise a worldwide system of finance and global financial institutions. How otherwise could it defend itself against claims legitimated by a document endorsed by the majority of states? But what did the money-men have to fear, given that *raison d'état*, founded as it is on the market mechanism, is anyway subject to the tyranny of unconstrained profit-seeking? And that our governments are losing all reason to protect their subjects or people elsewhere in the world when a crisis occurs.

For most people, the consumer society has had its day and there is a growing aspiration towards a life based on other criteria of success.

Ordinary people are crying out to stop being economic pawns and to become active and respected citizens. The most advanced technology is now dedicated to the service of information, knowledge, thought and judgement.

Since the dawn of time, man has sought to ease his lot by inventing tools to enhance his life. Now, in the age of computer science and digital technology, the human brain has built on the achievements of our ancestors to produce machines and robots which can replace people in the workplace: to be their servants (as they innocently believe). Maximum returns being guaranteed in the use of raw materials and in industrial processing, corporate earning capacity increases and profits mount.

If mankind sought to ease its lot, it has certainly succeeded. Free time is being created in which each individual can live as he or she wishes. Can the human brain have performed such feats solely on behalf of a tiny minority of already privileged members of humanity, while redundant manual workers are relegated to unemployment and driven to despair?

Can the stolen fruits of this success continue to be withheld from the majority? Modern communications technology encourages cooperation and the exchange of ideas and initiatives. Society's rejects are beginning to turn their intelligence and spirit of enterprise to the creation of a new solidarity, and the interest aroused by this movement is mobilising public opinion; it is gaining the support of national and international bodies. An organised alternative is undeniably emerging and attracting the attention of the rising generation, fearing as they do the precarious future predicted for them.

Those of us who were twenty in 1948, in a Europe experiencing the aftermath of a war which had set brother against brother, were offered the chance to create a zone of peace and security transcending our national frontiers. A few years earlier, a young German recruit caught up in the tide of the invasion had passed me a crumpled scrap of paper bearing the message 'Love knows no frontiers'. Alas for my young admirer, it was then too soon for such sentiments and I was simply offended by his message. But just a few years later, my outraged patriotism would have been a thing of the past. By armistice day 1995, François could declare: 'Right from the late forties I wanted to take part in the first European assembly because I had been a soldier and seen the hatred around me, and because I realised that this hatred had to take second place to the need for Europe and its people to survive. Our European brothers might be enemies, but they were brothers first and foremost, and that is what we must remember. I believe that one day this lesson will apply to people throughout the world.'

Having escaped a militarised Europe, unacceptable to the spirit of peace then prevailing, we witnessed the inevitable emergence of a trading, economic and monetary Europe in line with the dominant capitalist politics. It has taken two generations for the citizens of Europe finally to express their aspiration to develop a social and political Europe. How much longer will it take to accomplish the psychological change required to move towards a new era of peace and equitable democracy?

It is for today's twenty-year-olds to take up this new historical challenge: to persuade their representatives to draw their inspiration from the seeds of change now being sown by those rebelling and demonstrating against the present order and imagining, dreaming and organising themselves to bring about a new one; those who, as Marcos says, take up arms for long enough to be heard but not long enough to go to war.

Today, the Universal Declaration of Human Rights underlies all our thinking, whether we are aware of it or not, but we still have a long way to go before it becomes a practical reality for all mankind. A commemoration confined to speeches would fail in its purpose. It is up to all of us to pursue and to ensure the application of its universal principles in this anniversary year.

Article 20

1. Everyone has the right to freedom of peaceful assembly and association.
2. No one may be compelled to belong to an association.

BISHOP MARTINUS MUSKENS

Cultural Rights

The Universal Declaration of Human Rights, proclaimed by the General Assembly of the United Nations on 10 December 1948, lists the basic rights long accepted in the national constitutions of the then member nations, the victors of the Second World War. Among these were 'habeas corpus', the right to property and freedom of expression, the right to hold meetings and form associations, the right to work and the right to education. To these Article 22 added the economic, social and cultural rights indispensable for human dignity and the free development of human personality. Through the strength of their economies and their political power, countries in Europe and North America can defend their economic rights and their own social and cultural rights. Their political structures and economies are interwoven with their culture. In wealthy Western countries, economic, social and cultural relations are experienced as one, indivisible whole. Here everyone has what is needed for the 'free development of his personality'.

One implication of this is that disastrous results can occur when an economic system that is interwoven in Western culture is imposed on people of another culture. Sooner or later this 'foreign' economy is doomed to collapse because it has no indigenous socio-cultural foundation. The economic crisis in many Asian countries and in Africa can be explained by the scant attention given to their native cultures. People do not *have* a culture, they *are* a culture.

I would like, first of all, to use Indonesia as a case study to delineate the problem. Indonesia implicitly recognised the Universal Declaration of Human Rights in 1950, when it became a member of the United Nations, shortly after the Dutch recognised its independence on 27 December 1949. After this I will draw on several other examples and then present a general conclusion.

More than a thousand years ago, the inhabitants of the islands now known as Indonesia adopted, through their trade contacts, much of the culture of India. This is the origin of the name Indonesia, a contraction of 'India' and the suffix '-nesia', which means archipelago (compare this to Melanesia, Micronesia, Polynesia).

In the primeval religion of these islanders, with their original socio-cultural system, everyone and everything had its place. The macrosociety encompassed moon and sun, day and night, and wet and dry seasons and so on. The microsociety included the communal planting and harvesting of rice and co-operation in building a house (called *gotong-royong*). This microsociety had its own form of democracy. Power was not a question of 50%+1. Everyone had a right to a say in the discussions, the *musyawarah*, that sought a consensus acceptable to everyone, a *mufakat*. In this way, everyone in a village had both rights and duties.

This same harmony was expressed on higher levels: the village, the principality and the cosmos. In modern times, this has become the village, Indonesia, the world and the cosmos. During the centuries of Indian influence on the islands of Indonesia, the two best known Indian mythological stories, the *Mahabharata* and the *Ramayana*, were given a place in the local culture, especially on the island of Java. At present half of the two hundred million Indonesians live on this island. Buddhism, Hinduism, Christianity and Islam (in this historical order) have never completely displaced the old cultural attitudes. V.S. Naipaul has demonstrated this again in his recent book (*Beyond Belief*, 1998).

The notions of conqueror and conquered do not fit in the indigenous culture of Indonesia. For this reason, a fundamental change was made to the translation of the *Mahabharata*. In the Indian version, one of the two competing ruling families (the *Kurawa*) dies, while the Pandawa gains supremacy. But in the performance of the Indonesian version, the ancient Javanese divinity *Semar* intervenes to raise the dead to life. The *Kurawa* are needed to maintain a balance in society and in the cosmos.

After the failed Communist coup attempt in October 1965, hundreds of thousands of members and sympathisers of the *Partai Kommunis Indonesia* were killed. The military units that led these killings bore names borrowed from the *Mahabharata*. The document with which general Suharto took over executive power from the first president of Indonesia on 11 March 1966 bears the name *Super Semar*. Everyone who was familiar with the *wayang* stories knew from this what to expect from the new president: the restoration of balance in society. A few years later, large sculptures of the fiery chariot and eight horses from the *Mahabharata* were added to the square that contains the national monument. The heroic charioteer from the epic was intended to symbolise the new president of Indonesia (This landmark can be seen almost daily on TV as the background behind the reporters of BBC World).

When the USA launched a satellite in 1972 to facilitate communication within Indonesia, the satellite was given the name *palapa*, fruit of the coconut tree. This name is borrowed from a famous saying from the period of the Javanese 14th-century kingdom *Majapahit*, which united all the archipelago's coastal areas, including Malaysia and South Vietnam. General *Gaja Mada* gave the order at the start of the conquest that no one in the archipelago was to drink *palapa* until the whole archipelago was united. Not long ago Suharto invited the ministers of his cabinet to his house to surprise them with a puppet performance. He told the ministers he had to make an important decision. Afterwards the president said he hoped his message had become clear. These are but a few examples to show how deeply the old traditions still permeate twentieth-century Indonesia.

According to the first generation of nationalists, Indonesian identity is still grounded in the centuries-old village structure. 'The heart of Indonesian life is still to be found in those socio-religious microsocieties which are called desa, 47,000 in number. They still determine to a large extent the cultural, legal, and economic infrastructure of the nation. The fundamental aim of the desa inhabitants is to live in peace and harmony among themselves, with the supradesa authorities, and the surrounding world; this last is supposed to be crowded by good and evil spirits whom one has to appease. The various events of the life cycle of man (birth, initiation, marriage, and burial) have to be integrated in a cosmic and social totality. The rites-of-passage celebration inserts particular happenings in a redemptive totality, which bestows God's blessing and protection against harm. Worship is indispensable for maintaining cosmic and social order. The desa community is a salvation community that encompasses the present and the hereafter. Gods, ghosts, and ancestors are the guardians of the established order, reflected in a sacrosanct customary law' ('Religion and Revolution', *Herder Correspondence,* volume 3, 1966, p. 55).

To use the words of Koentjaraningrat, the greatest Indonesian anthropologist, 'a man has to cultivate and improve his spiritual environment, which is usually visualised in terms of the customs, mores, and common ideals and values of the community rather than of his own ideals and values' (*Javanese Culture*, 1990).

This sacrosanct customary law is called adat. The Dutch only gradually discovered adat, especially its legal implications for the population, and then recognised it as the official law of the indigenous population. On the island of Java as many as 600 adat villages were recognised in the year 1942 alone. On the island of Bali and elsewhere we still see today at the entrance to certain villages the notice: 'recognised adat village'.

Clifford Geertz describes as follows the religion of the *abangan*, the Javanese who never really converted to Islam. It is, he says, 'a balanced syncretism of myth and ritual in which Hindu gods and goddesses, Moslem prophets and saints, and local place spirits and demons all found a proper place ... The village religious system commonly consists of a balanced integration of animistic, Hinduistic and Islamic elements, a basic Javanese syncretism which is the island's true folk tradition, the basic substratum of its civilisation ... A little native curing, a little Tantric magic, a little Islamic chanting, all clustered about a simple communal ritual, served to define and order the basic social interrelationships in which the work they did, the lives they led, and the values they held all made cosmic sense' (*The Religion of Java*, 1964).

Indonesian culture is in essence communal, anti-individualistic. Terms such as 'good' and 'bad' do not have the same moral meaning as they do in cultures based on Jewish, Greek and Christian traditions. Rather, they refer to fitting or not fitting into a salvation community. This keeps people from being excluded; everything must ultimately be shared with the family, the village, etc. But it also hinders the progress of an individual with greater opportunities and talents than others. Individualism is foreign to the Indonesian's basic attitude. Koentjaraningrat quotes an often heard saying, 'Even if there is not much to eat, it is important that we are together'.

More than anyone else, the supernationalist Sukarno fascinated Indonesians for forty years with his defence of national identity, from his rise in 1926 to his fall from power in 1966. He exalted national culture. He compared himself to the famous heroes in the Hindu-Javanese stories. He explained certain decisions as being inspired by characters from the *wayang*. He said, 'I must see to it that Indonesians are proud of themselves'. He often praised the communal character of society as the *suasana keluarga*, the spirit of belonging to one family, or as *nikmatanya kebersamaan*, the pleasure of being together. Sukarno saw the national identity of Indonesia in that magic-cosmic awareness that everything and everyone has a right to his or her place.

The hardcore nationalists always opposed the introduction of a Western model of democracy. Despite all the pressure to give Islam a privileged position, the nationalists' desires were enshrined in the constitution accepted on 18 August 1945, the day after the declaration of independence. This constitution adopted the administrative form of the Indonesian village for the administration of the independent republic. The president is the nation's village chief. The preamble to the Constitution reflects Sukarno's philosophy, the *Pancasila*, the five principles or pillars: faith in God, national unity, consultation leading to consensus (*musyawarah – mufakat*), humanism or internationalism, and social justice. Ultimately, under pressure from the Netherlands and the USA, Western democracy was introduced. Once everyone saw that this was not working, the 1945 constitution was readopted on 5 July 1959. The former colonial power had to travel a long way before Queen Beatrix of the Netherlands declared, during her state visit at the end of August 1995, that she appreciated the specifically Indonesian form of democracy, *musyawarah* and *mufakat*.

Khruschev, weary of all the cultural events offered to him in Jakarta, complained and pointed out that the only thing Indonesians needed were machines to increase production. Sukarno replied that he did not want to make robots of his people. Sukarno did indeed neglect the economy.

After Sukarno, Indonesia changed dramatically. The New Order, *Orde Baru* (a term not without a cosmic connotation), as the present system is called, is oriented expressly toward economic progress. In this context, Islam is 'protected' in the hope of using it as an instrument of progress. The only choice that foreigners offered the government was to accept the Western capitalist free market system.

For twenty-five years this system has operated in a society that is essentially anti-individualistic. The individualism of the imported neo-liberal, capitalist system contrasts with the communal character of the indigenous socio-cultural system. The free-market mentality puts pressure on the traditional sense of togetherness. The result is that the economy in the *Orde Baru* is dominated by the cooperation of a few feudal families, the Chinese in Indonesia and the foreign capitalists. The Chinese make up 3 percent of the Indonesian population, but they dominate 75 percent of the economy. Tens of millions of Indonesians, called *pribumi* (to distinguish them from the Chinese) relied on and profited from the economy, but were not its social foundation.

When I visited Rama Mangunwijaya in Yogyakarta, during my last visit in August 1997, a priest, architect, social-political activist and writer of numerous novels summarised all this as follows, 'children are no longer the children they used to be, parents are no longer parents as we have known them'.

But the tie to the salvation community, to the native village, remains strong. Those who have moved to the city regularly return to their village. Western music and other forms of relaxation have replaced, for young city people, the traditional stories of the *wayang*. City dwellers are less familiar with the *Mahabharata* and the *Ramayana*. But the old culture still lives in the villages of Java that contain more than half the country's population. The great majority of army officers as well as most soldiers and civil servants are Javanese. Moreover, numerous Javanese farmers have moved to other islands. Not only are an increasing number of Javanese words being adopted in to the official language of the country, but bahasa Indonesia is also being shaped by Javanese attitudes.

All the chaos that the economy has brought into the lives of so many has led to an urge for renewed spiritual contact with the original culture. During my last visit I was repeatedly assured that the *wayang* stories are more popular now than they have been for the last twenty years. It is not essential to attend one of the shadow plays: the *Mahabharata* and the *Ramayana* can also be heard from morning to evening on the countless transistor radios. Over the last few years the *Ramayana* has been the more popular.

One characteristic of the old adat is that young people may not criticise their elders in public. But in the *wayang* serious philosophical discussions alternate with humorous passages. These contain criticism of current events.

Capitalism is the product of a culture grafted onto Calvinist roots (Max Weber). When this economy is imposed on another culture that has not undergone the same developments as Western countries, disruptions can occur. It may seem for a time that cooperation between Western capitalism and a small feudal elite ('crony-capitalism') is successful. But it is now apparent that the first crisis that comes along is enough to put millions of people out of work for a long period. The economy must fit in with the culture if a country's apparent prosperity is not to remain vulnerable. Foreign systems inappropriate to the religious and cultural traditions of Asia must be adjusted. As in other cases, so here too, haste makes waste.

Lee Kuan Yew, the long-serving prime minister of Singapore, and Tung Chee Hwa, the leader of Hong Kong after the departure of the British, have repeatedly asserted that 'human rights is not a monopoly of the West'. Eastern countries have their own concept of human rights rooted in their own culture and traditions. It is an infringement of human rights, in particular of cultural rights to make the introduction of Western democracy a condition for granting economic aid.

Unlike Westerners, people in the Hindu culture stress indifference toward this world. An impersonal world-spirit dominates the lives of many hundreds of millions of inhabitants of India. The Indians' fundamental attitudes in soul, heart and life towards material prosperity differ essentially from those of the Westerner. In the 1950s, the Indian share in world trade was 2 percent. The socialism imported from Great Britain, in particular from the London School of Economics, failed. After this an open market economy and globalisation were expected to help the country to progress. The second most populous country in the world now has a world market share of 0.8 percent and a weakened political structure.

Sub-Saharan Africa is completely excluded from the process of globalisation. In 1995, more was invested in China every two months than was invested throughout that year in all of Africa. An indigenous form of socialism, as attempted in Tanzania, ended in failure. Does this mean the Africans should be left to their own devices? Have they no right to both their own culture and prosperity? Neo-liberalism, a free market and deregulation are often associated with freedom for everyone. When a majority of the population of a country is pushed into poverty because this neo-liberal freedom is not appropriate to their culture, it can only be called a false freedom. In Africa countless people suffer from the market system, globalisation, deregulation and privatisation imposed on their countries. Only a small elite enjoys prosperity. As a result, authoritarianism has been raised, in many states, to the level of a national ideology.

Even the religions imposed from outside have not succeeded in removing the African's original spirit, not even after generations of Christianity. This has been adequately demonstrated by the recent history of Rwanda, where hundreds of thousands of Catholics murdered one another. After several generations of Christianity and education, blood ties with the tribe still proved stronger than the water of Baptism. Too little patience and a lost opportunity to forge a link with traditional religions appear to have ousted tribal experiences only temporarily.

In our global village everything is linked. Poverty for the many and riches for the few are often a source of violence against the right to race, religion and equal citizenship. This, in its turn, leads to the impoverishment of hundreds of millions in large third-world cities, to the arms trade that keeps dictators in power in poor countries, to drug trafficking and the enticement of women into prostitution. It makes poor countries hate rich ones. Think here of Shah Reza Pahlavi's imposition of the American economic system in Iran, and the widespread corruption that accompanied it. This explains the great attraction of the Ayatollah Khomeini and the hatred towards the United States. Perhaps it would be a considerable improvement if large international companies hired cultural anthropologists to help plan their global expansion.

Furthermore, it is of the greatest importance for the future of the West to know how we are to interact with Asians and Africans. Nothing less than justice and peace on earth are at risk. The former Prime Minister of South Africa, F.W. de Klerk, is correct when he states that 'the continuing marginalization of Africa is simply not an acceptable option. In a shrinking world, the problems of one region will in-evitably become the problems of other regions, and ultimately of the whole world'. Without seeking to praise every element of the cultural heritage of every people (such as African tribalism) or falling into a romantic, exalted or uncritical view of past Asian and African cultures, it must still be possible to devote more attention to the cultural rights of all peoples. I would like to close with a quotation from the Asian Charter on Human Rights, finalised in Hong Kong in 1997 by non-governmental organisations: 'Human beings have social, cultural and economic needs and aspirations that cannot be fragmented or compartmentalised, but are mutually dependent'.

JUDITH HERZBERG

Welcome in Free World

I'll speak a basic English:
'You cold, warm, hunger have?
You university – oh – yes.
Where? Where is that? No,
sorry, far away, for me.

You can be quiet now.
Your troubles over.
They don't come here
they don't come back
to get you. Here is
safe. No worry.

No, wailing sound
is of a sick car.
Siren of ambulance.
They go to hospital,
normal, in haste,
other cars must make space.

These clothes here
you can keep. They
look so good on you.
You don't believe?
Oh, not your taste.
You have? Sorry -
I thought that over there -
Well. Yes. No, they
are not new.

But for you they are!
New. Yes, and a mattress,
a whole own bed
sheets pillows
towel, soap. No?
Not lie down?
Why not lie down.
You cannot stay
standing. You can't.

You cannot stand
for nights on end just
like that next to bed.
As if waiting for -
someone. No-one
said: dead. Just
we don't know. You
must not worry so.

Yes you can stay.
Stay long? How long?
I cannot say. Stay
means so many
different things anyway.'

*Article 14 of the Universal Declaration of
Human Rights: The Right to Seek Asylum*

Its both fitting and timely, on the occasion of the 50th anniversary of the Universal Declaration of Human Rights, to reflect on the institution of asylum and the international refugee protection regime, which are at the centre of the work of the United Nations High Commissioner for Refugees (UNHCR).

Fitting, because Article 14 of the Universal Declaration states that '[e]veryone has the right to seek and to enjoy in other countries asylum from persecution'. The core of UNHCR's mandate is to provide protection to people who flee their country because of serious human rights violations and to find solutions to their plight. Fitting also because the 1951 Convention relating to the Status of Refugees and its 1967 Protocol are an indispensable part of the global human rights regime.

Timely, because, in my review, the institution of asylum today is under considerable threat. Signs of a diluted refugee protection regime are manifold. Entering a country to seek safety is becoming more and more difficult as states seek to deny access to asylum-seekers, reject them at borders, and erect subtle barriers, such as legislative restrictions and narrow interpretations of the criteria for refugee status. Safety during asylum is also seriously threatened. Forced military recruitment of refugees, abusive detention, deadly attacks on refugee camps, and violence against refugee women and children occur at regular intervals. The images of Rwandan refugees fleeing armed attacks into the tropical forests in Eastern Zaire in 1997 still haunt us today. How many refugees perished due to violence, starvation, sickness or exhaustion will never be known. Moreover, we cannot ignore the fact that the voluntary nature of repatriation is being undermined by an increasing number of forcible returns to situations which are far from safe.

Often, I hear the view expressed that the current refugee protection regime is no longer adequate to meet the new challenges facing states. The changing nature of refugee movements in recent years has contributed to this view that the 1951 Convention is inadequate, but it is a false argument. It undermines not only asylum and the protection of refugees but also weakens the overall human rights regime.

First, the number of refugees has increased significantly. In the second half of the twentieth century the number of refugees grew from 1.5 million in 1951, when UNHCR was established, to 13.2 million in 1997. In addition, UNHCR today is responsible for nearly 10 million returnees, internally displaced persons and other war-affected civilians. Not only these numbers but also the speed and complexity of recent movements, are of concern to states. Rapid mass exoduses in recent years

217

from countries such as Afghanistan, Bosnia, Haiti, Iraq, Liberia and Rwanda have posed complex problems. Asylum states understandably fear the economic, environmental and even security problems caused by such movements. For many receiving states, the degree of international burden sharing is viewed as insufficient and short-lived.

Second, mixed movements of genuine asylum-seekers and of people leaving home for other reasons pose problems for receiving countries. Recent examples include Iraqis, among whom are many Kurds, and Albanians who have sought asylum in Western Europe in recent years. Many of them are fleeing human rights violations while others are escaping economic despair. In some instances, as in the case of the Rwandan refugees in Eastern Zaire, armed elements and people guilty of crimes against humanity are hiding among the civilian refugee population in camps.

Undoubtedly, the increasing complexity of today's forced population movements poses a heavy burden upon states receiving and hosting large numbers of refugees. While appreciating these difficulties, I am convinced that the institution of asylum must be upheld in all circumstances. In the immediate term, it permits people to seek safety from persecution and conflict. In the longer term, asylum provides an essential 'breathing space' to begin the search for solutions to humanitarian crises and to build viable approaches toward reconciling and rehabilitating conflict-torn communities. On many occasions during the last fifty years, the institution of asylum has proven to be an inherently balanced system, capable of adjusting to new needs and circumstances.

Asylum is balanced because it effectively links protection of human rights of refugees to solutions to their problems. The asylum regime, as codified in the 1951 Convention relating to the Status of Refugees, its 1967 Protocol, the 1969 OAU Convention Governing the Specific Aspects of Refugee Problems in Africa, the 1984 Cartagena Declaration on Refugees and other instruments, is undeniably solution-oriented. Usually, asylum is of a temporary nature until a durable solution has been identified: by preparing the ground for voluntary repatriation and consolidating the situation in countries of origin; by supporting lasting refugee integration in the country of asylum; or by facilitating resettlement to third countries.

Another 'balancing' benefit of asylum is that it provides a sound legal basis not only for the recognition of refugees and the protection of their rights, but also for the exclusion of those who do not need or deserve international protection. Refugee instruments make clear that those who have committed abhorrent crimes do not deserve international support and protection. For example, my Office has taken the step, announced late in 1996, of excluding from refugee status Rwandans who have been indicted by the International Criminal Tribunal for Rwanda. UNHCR is also undertaking the screening of Rwandan refugees in several countries of asylum, with the aim of distinguishing those deserving of international protection from those who are not. In my view, this is an aspect of the asylum regime which, while it must be carefully applied, merits greater attention.

Asylum also allows all actors to play a crucial role in the process. The country of asylum has an obligation to provide refugees with international protection. The country of origin has an obligation to welcome back returning refugees and to ensure the protection of their rights, as it must for all its citizens. The international community is required to support these efforts and to share the burden of caring for refugees. Refugees themselves also have an obligation to obey the laws in their country of asylum and to contribute to a solution.

At the same time, asylum adjusts to new needs and circumstances. Over the forty-five years since it came into force, the 1951 Convention has proved to be a flexible instrument that has successfully adapted itself to provide protection in a variety of circumstances. As such, it must remain a 'living' instrument of protection. Even more restrictive interpretations of the Convention in some respects have not prevented it from being applied to new protection needs. For example, gender is not mentioned in the 1951 Convention, yet a number of countries have found innovative, practical and justifiable means to protect women who have fallen victim to gender-related persecution, such as sexual abuse, rape, and female genital mutilation. This development has not, as was feared by some, resulted in a flood of unwarranted claims.

Likewise, in situations of mass population influx not all persons may be considered as refugees under the 1951 Convention but they may, nevertheless, be in need of protection. This was obviously the case with, for example, the vast majority of those who fled the conflict in Bosnia and Herzegovina. When the asylum procedures in the receiving countries were overwhelmed, I appealed to governments to grant protection on a temporary and group basis, until conditions existed in which people could return. Temporary protection was conceived as a practical and flexible tool to respond to large numbers of people in need of protection while the search for solutions was under way. It is one element of a comprehensive humanitarian strategy which in turn is aligned with political conflict resolution. Temporary protection is a means of balancing the protection needs of people with the interests of the states receiving them.

Thus the dynamic nature of asylum allows for pragmatic, creative and realistic approaches in fashioning responses to refugee problems. The challenge lies in finding principled ways to respond to practical concerns; to adjust to the times without giving up the essential meaning and elements of asylum.

Over the past few years, my Office has tried to help create and grasp opportunities for solutions to refugee problems. The international community, through the United Nations and regional organizations, has shown an increased willingness to back humanitarian operations so as to protect and assist a wide range of populations in need, including internally displaced persons. Moreover, attempts to tackle the root causes of refugee flows have directed international attention to preventive measures.

And yet, I believe that much greater recognition must be given to the importance of asylum which bridges the right to remain in one's country as well as to return once the crisis is over. During the conflict in former Yugoslavia I stressed the 'right to remain' or the right not to be displaced as a response to ethnic cleansing. It is by no means a clearly delineated right, but I firmly believe that we must develop the law in this direction to help avert forced displacement.

As to the 'right to return', new ways must be found to ensure full and voluntary implementation in the face of political obstruction which may occur in countries of both asylum and origin. The Dayton Peace Agreement contains many exemplary references to respect for human rights. Unfortunately, many elements relating to freedom of movement and minority returns have not been adequately implemented. For some 1.4 million people, 800,000 of whom are displaced inside Bosnia and Herzegovina, return to their former homes remains an unkept promise. Almost all of those still awaiting return are members of minorities in their original communities. Since the signing of the Dayton Peace Agreement, only some 35,000 people have returned to areas in which they constitute a minority. Political obstruction, insecurity, legal barriers, distrust, house occupation and destruction block their return. UNHCR initiated its 'Open Cities' concept in 1997 to encourage refugee return to minority areas by rewarding those municipalities which welcome minorities. Encouraging minority return is a centrepiece of our strategy for 1998 in Bosnia and Herzegovina, because we recognise that if we make refugee return possible, the institution of asylum itself is strengthened.

The example of Bosnia and Herzegovina also illustrates the undeniably political nature of refugee problems. As such it requires political action to find a solution. But refugee issues are not only or solely political. They have fundamental humanitarian and human rights dimensions, such as establishment of a functioning judiciary, promotion of communal reconciliation, and prosecution of war crimes. Rwanda and Bosnia and Herzegovina are vivid examples of the broader links between human rights, refugee return, and lasting peace.

On the occasion of the 50th anniversary of the Universal Declaration of Human Rights, I wish to make three pleas. First, while managing population movement is a legitimate concern, do not shut out those genuinely fleeing for their lives and freedom. Refugees have no choice but to flee. How can I appeal to countries facing massive refugee inflows which pose a heavy security, economic, social and environmental burden on them, when wealthy industrialised countries close their doors to a relatively small number of asylum-seekers? Second, I urge you to de-dramatise and de-politicise the asylum debate. Do not let racists and xenophobes set the agenda. Asylum issues are manageable, especially in Western countries. The total number of asylum seekers has been falling for the past several years in Europe. It is neither necessary nor helpful to invoke an atmosphere of crisis in setting refugee policy. Third, the international community should look for prevention and solutions to refugee movements, rather than seeking control and adopting deterrent measures.

Asylum is not an end in itself, but a response to protect those in need. It may be implemented differently and flexibly over time, but it still requires a commitment by individual states to uphold respect for the human rights of those forced out of their country. Refugees must be accepted and protected until they can go home or find another durable solution. Over the last fifty years, millions of people have benefited from the practical application of Article 14 of the Universal Declaration of Human Rights. Millions of people, I believe, must be able to rely on it in the future.

Article 21

1. Everyone has the right to take part in the government of his country, directly or through freely chosen representatives.
2. Everyone has the right to equal access to public service in his country.
3. The will of the people shall be the basis of the authority of government; this will shall be expressed in periodic and genuine elections which shall be by universal and equal suffrage and shall be held by secret vote or by equivalent free voting procedures.

MARTEN OOSTING

Universal Government Obligations and the
Protection Afforded by the Ombudsman

HUMAN RIGHTS AS GOVERNMENT OBLIGATIONS

On 10 December 1948 the UN General Assembly made a historic decision. At that time, the formulation of a Universal Declaration of Human Rights was without doubt a pioneering step. Now, fifty years on, the Universal Declaration has become history to such an extent as to have somewhat faded into the background. This is because it has since been elaborated in a number of important human rights conventions that have made its provisions legally binding. The most important of these, in global terms, are the International Covenant on Civil and Political Rights and that on Economic, Social and Cultural Rights, both of which date from 1966. Europe, of course, has its far older European Convention for the Protection of Human Rights and Fundamental Freedoms, dating from 1950. And where the Netherlands is concerned, aside from the self-executing provisions of human rights conventions, the fundamental rights enshrined in Dutch law – primarily in the Constitution – make up an important part of our national legal order. The norms embodied in all these sources of law underscore the significance of the Universal Declaration as a global basis for the safeguarding of – to quote the preamble – 'freedom, justice and peace in the world'.

The Universal Declaration of Human Rights is also – or much of it is – a catalogue of obligations on governments. In the Netherlands, as in many other countries, the government in its capacity of legislator has deemed the Declaration's principles to be so self-evident that it has made them into an essential part of the national legal order through the introduction of a series of legal norms. The related obligations are at the heart of the rule of law.

But legislation is not enough to ensure that human rights are respected everywhere and at all times, as the past fifty years since the proclamation of the Universal Declaration have made only too clear. For government, the Declaration's principles are also directly relevant to the way it carries out its tasks vis-à-vis the general public. After all, the government, in its capacity of executive power, must always ensure that it fulfils – and that its employees fulfil – the obligations imposed on it by the provisions of human rights conventions, and that it promotes the observation of the legal norms concerned.

For many government employees in a country such as the Netherlands, the Universal Declaration itself will be very remote from their everyday working lives. But

223

the preamble contains a fundamental concept that should be a permanent guideline for every executive government agency: that of respect for the human dignity of everyone with whom it comes into contact. The significance of this concept reaches far beyond the thirty articles of the Universal Declaration.

In this respect, one should fully acknowledge the fact that members of the public have many relationships of dependency with the government, which holds monopolies in numerous areas. Therefore, every government employee and agency must realize that the task of government in society in its essence is to serve the people. The implementation of public policy should always be based on an attitude of respect for the human dignity of the person whom it concerns.

It is worth pointing out in this connection that the government's relations with members of the public are not merely relations in law, determined by what is prescribed by law (and in particular by human rights provisions). There is always an element of personal interaction as well. Members of the public must be able to take it for granted that the government will treat them properly. Many complaints about the authorities are based on the individual's sense of not being taken seriously.

The obligations that human rights impose on government set high standards of conduct. The government must create the conditions that will ensure that its organisation and personnel are equal to their task. Only people can ensure that human rights are observed and promoted. This means that the government, in its capacity of executive power, must not only be well-staffed, but that all its employees must be adequately equipped to cope with this aspect of their work; this in turn has implications for their training. The culture within an executive government agency is also of vital importance. The government and its employees must be steeped in an awareness of the significance of heeding human rights provisions. Appropriate internal regulations and procedures, and peer review, can help achieve this.

These measures to be taken within the executive power itself are the prime way of ensuring the government's proper observance of human rights provisions. But past experience has demonstrated the vital importance of complementary external supervision. Thus Articles 8 and 10 of the Universal Declaration articulate the importance of the protection afforded by independent tribunals. In practice, however, this protection is not always sufficient, as cases in the Netherlands and elsewhere have made clear. The Ombudsman has been shown to fulfil an essential role, complementary to that of the courts, in protecting the general public from the government, partly – sometimes primarily – in the realm of human rights. In the rest of my essay I shall deal with the Ombudsman's significance in scrutinising the government's fulfilment of its obligations under human rights provisions, and hence as one of the institutions set up to protect human rights.

THE GOVERNMENT'S OBLIGATIONS AND THE PROTECTION AFFORDED BY THE OMBUDSMAN

The office of the Ombudsman protects individual members of the public from the government. In this capacity it examines cases and decides whether the government has discharged its responsibilities in a proper fashion. Where human rights are concerned, this propriety begins by living up to the provisions on human rights that have been incorporated into the national legal order, including the Universal Declaration. So these provisions are an essential part of the Ombudsman's frame of reference. Most of his investigations are initiated by a complaint made by a member of the public, although he may also be empowered to start investigations on his own initiative. To do his work well, the Ombudsman must have statutory powers of investigation. His independence from the agencies that fall within his area of competence must be assured.

In 1948 there were only two countries with an Ombudsman: Sweden, which had had one since 1809, and Finland, since 1919. In 1955, they were joined by Denmark. Fifteen years on (by around 1970) the number of countries had grown to ten, and after another fifteen (by around 1985) there were about thirty. Now, again almost fifteen years later, there are some eighty countries with an Ombudsman. Besides relatively old democracies they include countries that have shaken off totalitarian rule and face the task of building up new, democratic states that are subject to the rule of law.

In older democratic states which are governed by the rule of law such as the Netherlands, much of the Ombudsman's work relates to a variety of shortcomings on the part of large, bureaucratic government organisations that cannot be directly labelled violations of human rights. The parliamentary ombudsman of the United Kingdom refers to such infringements as 'maladministration, leading to injustice'. Yet even in long-established democracies, it regularly happens that cases must be examined in the light of human rights provisions. At the end of my essay I shall illustrate this in reference to my own experience as the National Ombudsman of the Netherlands. My counterparts in similar countries, like the four Scandinavian countries, have similar experiences.

It is important, when speaking of the Ombudsman's examination of a case in the light of human rights provisions – and of classical human rights in particular – to establish whether his competence includes the police, or if this is the remit of a different independent investigating body. It is also important to know to what extent international human rights conventions have direct application in national legal orders, and to what extent they have been enacted as positive law in domestic legislation, in particular the Constitution. In this respect there is a clear difference between the National Ombudsman in the Netherlands on the one hand, and his counterparts in the United Kingdom and other Commonwealth countries such as Australia, New Zealand and Canada on the other, where the Ombudsman is usually not competent to investigate the police. For this reason alone, the Ombudsman's human rights responsibilities in these countries are bound to be more limited than in countries such as the Netherlands.

The situation in younger democracies will in general be different from that in older democratic constitutional states. In a young democracy, the appointment of an Ombudsman is one of a series of measures taken to create a democratic state subject to the rule of law, in which the protection of human rights occupies a central position. This is often reflected in the name that is given to the institution.

One European example of this is the 1978 Constitution of Spain, the preamble to which expresses a wish to protect the exercise of human rights, and which therefore provides for the institution of a *Defensor del Pueblo*. The main task of the *Defensor del Pueblo* is to protect human rights. A similar development took place a few years earlier in Portugal, where the institution of the *Provedor de Justiça* was established after the collapse of the dictatorship. More recently we have the examples of Central and Eastern European countries, in which a similar development can be traced, especially since the fall of communism. Poland gained an Ombudsman as early as 1988, in the form of a Commissioner for Civil Rights Protection. Slovenia acquired a Human Rights Ombudsman in 1994, and Hungary has had a Parliamentary Commissioner on Human Rights since 1995. As the rule of law evolves further in these new democracies, the observance of human rights provisions can become more firmly entrenched in the implementation of government responsibilities. This means that the Ombudsman's responsibilities in these countries can then extend to cases of improper actions on the government's part – the maladministration already referred to – which cannot be classified as violations of human rights provisions.

Outside Europe too, numerous countries have established the institution of an Ombudsman. Many of them, again, are new democracies, such as a number of Spanish-speaking countries in Latin America that have shaken off military dictatorship and emerged from civil war. These countries have clearly been influenced by the Spanish example. Thus Argentina, Colombia and Peru have each acquired a *Defensor del Pueblo*, and Guatemala and El Salvador a *Procurador de los Derechos Humanos*.

Most of these new democracies with an Ombudsman in Latin America, unlike those I mentioned in Europe, are also developing countries. Furthermore, the police and armed forces still play a prominent role there, added to which the violence that goes along with crime (drug-related crime, for instance) is a serious problem. Corruption in – and the abuse of power by – the government are widespread. On top of this they have serious social problems, such as poverty, illiteracy and other types of disadvantage, often to a particularly marked degree among indigenous peoples. This catalogue of problems is not limited to the younger democracies in Latin America; the same applies, for instance, to Mexico.

In circumstances such as these, the Ombudsman is confronted with serious violations of classical human rights by government officials, and promoting the observance of these rights often means confronting those in power head-on. At the same time, the Ombudsman must work actively to enforce the people's social, economic and cultural rights. In all these areas he also has a definite educational role to play. Unlike his counterparts in older democracies, an Ombudsman working in one of these new democracies has little or no time to deal with complaints about maladministration.

Numerous countries in Africa and Asia also have an Ombudsman. Many are countries that have achieved independence fairly recently, and have followed the example of the former colonial power. This applies both to Commonwealth members – which have the British example of the Parliamentary Commissioner for Administration – and to countries of the *francophonie*, which tend to emulate the French example of the *Médiateur de la République*. But in these regions, in which we are again largely speaking of developing countries, there is less emphasis on the protection of human rights than in Latin America. Thus the Ombudsman's task in the anglophone countries of Africa often focuses on corruption and other forms of maladministration; in some cases, he is not even competent in the area of human rights. A case in point is South Africa, where the new Constitution has generated on the one hand the institution of the Public Protector and on the other hand a National Human Rights Commission, which also has an investigating task. A comparable situation exists in India, which has had a National Human Rights Commission since 1993 that is responsible for the investigative work in this area, while a Bill is before parliament that will institute a National Ombudsman (*Lok Pal*), whose duties will focus on the fight against corruption.

To sum up, in many countries the institution of the Ombudsman has a clear task in relation to human rights. Sometimes this is his main or sole area of responsibility, while in other cases – such as in the Netherlands – monitoring the government's observance of human rights is only one of a more wide-ranging set of respons-ibilities. His primary focus of attention, however, is always on helping to ensure that the government fulfils the obligations imposed on it by human rights, guided by the respect for the dignity and worth of each human being that is the fundamental principle of the Universal Declaration of Human Rights. The rights in this Declaration, as elaborated in international conventions and in national legislation, thus constitute an important part of the frame of reference for many Ombudsmen. I should like to conclude by showing how this applies to the National Ombudsman in the Netherlands.

THE NATIONAL OMBUDSMAN IN THE NETHERLANDS AND HUMAN RIGHTS

The office of the National Ombudsman started work in the Netherlands on 1 January 1982. The Ombudsman investigates the actions of government bodies and their employees in performing government tasks, and then gives its opinion on them. The Ombudsman's protection of members of the public complements the legal protection afforded by the courts.

The National Ombudsman Act contains a single criterion for assessing each case: propriety. Ten years ago, when I first took up the post of National Ombudsman, I elaborated the norm of propriety in a list of requirements, to help explain my decisions. An important underlying principle was that individual members of the public, in their relationship with the government, not only have rights and obligations as dictated by the law, but should also be seen as human beings in other respects, and that their human dignity must be acknowledged. The assessment of whether actions meet the appropriate standards of propriety norm depends on a wide range of factors. It includes an examination of the lawfulness of the actions concerned, the requirement – essential in any state subject to the rule of law – that each and every action on the part of the authorities be in accordance with the law. Thus the checklist of requirements of propriety begins with human rights as enshrined in self-executing international human rights conventions, the Constitution and other legislation. To this extent, the norms laid down by the Universal Declaration are of essential significance to the Ombudsman's findings. I shall illustrate this below on the basis of a few examples.

The norm of respect for human dignity imposes on the government the obligation to take an active approach to persons in relation to whom – or in circumstances in which – there is a special risk of this norm being violated. This duty of care was first enshrined in several of the Universal Declaration's provisions, and later in the above-mentioned human rights conventions and in national legislation.

Thus the government has a special duty of care in relation to persons held in detention – whether in police custody or in prison (see in particular Article 5 of the Universal Declaration) – which applies with added force in the case of sickness or psychological problems. This duty of care includes ensuring that detainees have easy access to medical care where necessary. The National Ombudsman has conducted a variety of investigations in this area, concerning, for example, the care of a seriously ill detainee who died in his cell in distressing circumstances, the supervision of detainees with psychological problems (in relation to the risk of suicide), the decision to call a medical practitioner, and various forms of supervision, including supplying medicine, in relation to persons detained in police custody.

The government's duty of care extends to the living conditions of asylum seekers who are staying in government accommodation pending a decision on their request for asylum. It was also at issue in an investigation that the National Ombudsman conducted into the role of the authorities in health care in the mid-1980s in relation to the risk of the HIV contamination of blood products, in particular of blood-clotting preparations for haemophiliacs. The National Ombudsman also studied, in connection with the government's duty of care, the length of time that detainees subject to a hospital order – who are entitled to expect prompt placement in an institution where they can receive treatment – have to wait before this is effected.

The government has an obligation to pay particular attention to the rights of people in a vulnerable situation and its own corresponding obligations. Besides the example of detention, one must also consider aliens under this heading, especially those who have left their own country because of fear of persecution (see in particular Article 14 of the Universal Declaration). Past investigations in this area by the National Ombudsman have concerned ways of making the right to request asylum at the gate-check at Schiphol airport truly effective, safeguarding the quality of the further interviews of asylum seekers, and respecting the ban on *refoulement*.

When the police and the public prosecution service fall within the competence of the National Ombudsman, as is the case in the Netherlands, the Ombudsman has a special responsibility for ensuring that both police and the judicial authorities fulfil the obligations imposed on them by human rights provisions. Many of the National Ombudsman's investigations have been within this area, and have related to matters including the decision to deprive someone of their liberty and the use of other modes of force and coercion (e.g. handcuffs), and the observance of the right to privacy (see especially Articles 5, 9 and 12 of the Universal Declaration).

As a final example, the fundamental principle of equality and the associated ban on discrimination must not be forgotten (see Articles 1, 2 and 7 of the Universal Declaration). In the National Ombudsman's work this principle has been central to investigations in the area of the supervision of aliens, job placement (re age discrimination) and the implementation of positive discrimination (in relation to women and minorities) in the selection of new government employees.

The above paragraphs concern examples of the government's obligations inasmuch as they can be inferred directly from statutory human rights provisions. But the basic norm of respect for human dignity goes far beyond the various provisions of law relating to human rights. Partly because of this basic norm, a number of requirements relating to due care occupy an important position in the National Ombudsman's assessments. They all share a common characteristic: the government may be expected at all times to do justice to the interests of the individual concerned, and to try to understand these interests. Thus individuals are entitled, in their dealings with the government, to receive an answer to a communication, and to have their case dealt with within a reasonable time. When looked at in this way, the Universal Declaration contains principles – aside from its individual articles – that are a source of inspiration to the Ombudsman in his assessment of the government's fulfilment of its obligations to members of the public.

MORIS FARHI

Armoured Men

born
unborn
stillborn
children

are tossed this way and that

in this dungeon
where
armoured men
defend
country
faith
civilization

OLARA OTUNNU

Protecting the Rights of Children Affected by Armed Conflict

We are on the eve of a new millennium, celebrating the fiftieth anniversary of the Universal Declaration of Human Rights. There will be much to celebrate, because in the modern era our civilization has achieved breath-taking advances in virtually every field of human endeavour. And yet, these quantum leaps in human progress and its potential for good co-exists uneasily with a darker side to our civilization. Witness our capacity to inflict and tolerate grave injustice and our capacity for deep hatred and cruelty towards our fellow human beings. Despite the aspirations of the Universal Declaration of Human Rights, entire communities continue to be destroyed in the quest for power, or in the name of ethnicity, religion, class or race. It would seem the gap between lofty principles and actual reality is wide, and indeed growing.

I believe that a crucial measure of our civilization must be about its human quality, which has to do with how we treat our fellow human beings. Above all, it has to do with how we treat the most innocent and most vulnerable members of our community, those who represent the future of every society – our children. Our record in this respect is mixed. Even though the rights of children are now recognised in an array of human rights and humanitarian instruments, these have not in themselves protected the growing numbers of children who are brutalized and abused in the context of armed conflict.

The international community has failed to apply the most fundamental principles of human rights to the most vulnerable members of society. At this moment in approximately fifty countries around the world, children are suffering from the effects of conflict and its aftermath. Not only are millions of children still the victims of war, far too often they are its principal targets and even its instruments. For all the children deliberately massacred or caught in crossfire or maimed by anti-personnel land mines, many more have been deprived of their physical, mental and emotional needs. Millions have lost their homes and their parents, not to mention years of education and socialization. Some have been permanently traumatized by the events they have witnessed and experienced. In today's armed conflicts, children are specifically targeted in strategies to eliminate the next generation of potential adversaries. To the same end, children, and especially girls, have been made the targets of sexual abuse and gender-based violence on a large scale. Most cynically, children have been compelled to become instruments of war, recruited or kidnapped to become child soldiers, or forced to participate indirectly as cooks,

231

messengers and porters. Children have even be used for mine clearance, spying and suicide bombing. In all, an estimated two million children have been killed in situations of armed conflict since 1987, while three times that number have been seriously injured or permanently disabled. Millions more have been psychologically scarred and socially disabled, and approximately 12 million made homeless. An estimated quarter of a million children under the age of 18 are currently serving as child soldiers in various armed conflicts around the world.

This brutal reality is exacerbated by a qualitative change in the nature and conduct of warfare itself. While in World War I and World War II civilians counted for some 5 and 40 percent of casualties respectively, today up to 90 percent of conflict casualties around the world are civilians, a large and increasing number of them children. The majority of armed conflicts today are internal, being fought by multiple, semi-autonomous armed groups within existing state boundaries. They are characterized by a particular brand of lawlessness, brutality and chaos. In these situations, belligerents routinely ignore the international human rights and humanitarian laws which have traditionally moderated, if not governed, inter-state wars. Many of these conflicts are fought among those who know each other well. In this intimate setting, the village has become the battlefield and civilian populations the primary target. Another feature of these struggles is the 'demonisation' of the enemy community, often defined in religious, ethnic, racial or regional terms, engendering a quality of passion and hate and setting the scene for terrible cruelties and atrocities. The proliferation of light-weight weapons that are easily assembled and borne by children, fuel these conflicts further, causing successive generations of children to be exposed to horrific violence.

While the international community has an obligation to be concerned about the protection of all non-combatants caught in the midst of violent conflicts, there is an urgent need to focus special attention on the plight of children. Children represent the future of human civilization and the future of every society. To allow them to be used as pawns in warfare, whether as targets or perpetrators, is to cast a shadow on the future. From generation to generation, violence begets violence, as the abused grow up to become abusers. Children who are thus violated carry the scars of fear and hatred in their hearts and minds. Forced to learn to kill instead of pursuing education, the children of conflict lack the knowledge and skills needed to build their futures, and the futures of their communities. For society, the lives destroyed and the opportunities lost could have a devastating effect on its long-term stability and development.

The special obligation to protect the rights and welfare of children was recognized in Article 25 of the Universal Declaration itself. This was further elaborated by the adoption of other international human rights and humanitarian instruments such as the Geneva Conventions (1949) and their Additional Protocols, and the Convention on the Rights of the Child. However, the impressive series of instruments that the nations of the world have expended so much effort in developing and ratifying, have neither been respected nor applied. Herein lies the dilemma and the challenge at the heart of this 50th-anniversary year of the Universal Declaration.

I believe a serious and systematic effort by all concerned parties – from governments to the United Nations system to civil society organizations to private citizens – is needed to address the abomination being committed against children in the context of armed conflict. A combination of actions and strategies – normative, political and humanitarian – is required to promote prevention, protection and rehabilitation for the benefit of these children.

First, it is high time to put the old adage that 'an ounce of prevention is worth a pound of cure' into actual practice. Prevention entails strengthening the normative foundation of societies and mobilizing public opinion in order to create a social and political climate that is capable of impeding abuse against children. It is a sad reflection of our times that, in the so-called Information Age, we remain ignorant, or choose to remain ignorant, of the multiple atrocities inflicted against children caught up in conflicts in so many parts of the world. Much greater official and public attention needs to be drawn to those children who have been victimized by the chaos, cruelty and lawlessness that characterize contemporary armed conflicts. Broadening public awareness, engaging public support and directing public outrage against such atrocities, will, I believe, go a long way in exerting pressure on the belligerents who commit them. While the array of international human rights and humanitarian instruments are genuine landmarks and provide a basis for action to protect children victimized by conflict, the gap between these norms and their observance on the ground is unacceptably wide and growing. Governments have the primary responsibility for bridging this gap and for exerting their weight and influence so that these international norms and domestic standards are applied.

Undoubtedly, a greater challenge lies in securing the protection and welfare of children who are actually caught up in the midst of on-going conflicts. When communities are cut off from the outside world and vulnerable to the abuse of belligerents, atrocities are likely to occur and multiply. For this reason, the international community needs to insist on having access to such communities. In addition to their right to life and physical security, children require continued access to relief, health and educational services. Humanitarian relief agencies and human rights organizations must therefore be given access to such populations in distress, to provide them with relief, to bear impartial witness, and to draw attention to rules and norms applicable to the conduct of war. The international community must also insist that facilities normally reserved for children or which have a significant presence of children, such as schools, hospitals and playgrounds, be considered battle-free zones. In one situation of conflict, Sri Lanka, among the main priorities for the protection of children is the continued provision and distribution of humanitarian supplies, the free movement of displaced persons, and firm commitments by the parties to refrain from using children under the age of 18 in combat and from targeting civilian populations and sites.

In those societies emerging from conflict, there is a need to design recovery programmes that heal and reintegrate those whose lives have been shattered by war. Women and children in post-conflict situations have special needs, particularly those who have been extensively exposed to the culture of violence. Only with a systematic programme of healing and reintegration into society will the cycle of violence be broken, and will spiritual, emotional and psychological health be restored. Without healing, the child victims of abuse may grow up to become the abusers of tomorrow and thus transmit hatred and the seeds of conflict from one generation to the next. In this context, the provision of physical, spiritual and emotional care to children whose lives have been damaged by the effects of conflict must constitute an important component of post-conflict recovery programmes, and not merely as an afterthought. Some of the issues that require urgent consideration in post-conflict response programmes are the demobilization of child soldiers and their social reintegration, the return and reintegration of displaced and refugee children, mine-clearance and development of mine awareness programmes, psychological recovery, educational and vocational training, and addressing issues of juvenile justice. In Sierra Leone, for example, demobilization of child combatants, resettlement of internally displaced persons, rehabilitation and support of victims without limbs, and the provision and rehabilitation of health and educational services remain priority concerns for international action.

Even in times of war, in every society fundamental values and rules mattered. Distinctions between acceptable and unacceptable practices were maintained, with taboos and injunctions proscribing indiscriminate targeting of civilian populations, especially women and children. Societies that have experienced prolonged periods of conflict have seen their value systems collapse, with horrendous consequences for the civilian population. These societies must, in the first place, draw from the well-springs of their own traditions and renew their sense of ethical rootedness. In order to nurture this process, it is essential to strengthen the various networks and institutions that traditionally inculcate values and that protect and help to meet the needs of children, such as parents, extended families, elders, teachers, schools and religious institutions. This renewal is an essential process if a society caught in the throes of a deep moral crisis is to regain its moral bearings. This process must then be reinforced by the modern legal regimes that have been developed at the international level.

For example, I grew up in a society where the concept of *lapir* was very strong. Among the Acholi people, *lapir* denotes the cleanliness of one's claim, which then attracts the blessing of the ancestors in recognition and support of that claim. Before declaring war, the elders would carefully examine their *lapir* – to be sure that their community had a deep and well-founded grievance against the other side. If this was established to be the case, war might be declared, but never lightly. But in order to preserve the original *lapir*, strict injunctions would be issued to regulate the actual conduct of the war. One did not attack children, women or the elderly, one did not destroy crops, granary stores or livestock. For to commit such taboos would be to spoil your *lapir*, with consequences that you would forfeit the blessing of the ancestors and thereby risk losing the war itself. Moreover, in declaring war, there was always the presumption of co-existence in the post-conflict period. Therefore in prosecuting a war effort you took great care to avoid committing taboos and acts of humiliation that would destroy forever the basis for future co-existence between erstwhile enemy communities. Tragically today, warfare is unbound from such injunctions. The breakdown of value systems has led instead to a situation of 'total war', in which every person, every structure and every resource is considered fair game in the struggle for power.

Finally, we cannot protect children from the brutality of warfare without addressing the conditions that give rise to conflicts in the first place. Patterns of political exclusion, the existence of gross disparities in the distribution of resources between different regions, sectors and groups in the same country, lie at the heart of violent conflict. We must work to transform these distorted relationships if we are to achieve sustainable solutions to conflicts in which children, women and civilian populations at large are brutalized. This is a long-term project that requires a true partnership to be built between international and national actors, which can result in political, economic and social measures that can generate within communities a sense of hope in place of despair, a sense of inclusion instead of exclusion, a sense of belonging instead of alienation. The celebration of fifty years of the Universal Declaration of Human Rights will ring hollow without tangible commitments to redress the political exclusion and disparities in wealth between and within nations that so often sow the seeds of conflict.

While the understanding that human rights are the foundation of human existence and co-existence, that human rights are universal, indivisible and interdependent, and that human rights lie at the heart of peace and development, is as salient today as it was fifty years ago, the obstacles that prevent their full realization are many and deeply entrenched. In the last fifty years, human rights have been politicized, its universality eroded and its principles selectively applied in the context of national frameworks to serve national imperatives. The absence of tolerance and human rights in our world today is not only a denial of human dignity, it is also the root of the suffering and hatred that breeds political violence and inhibits economic development. For those of us in societies that are blessed with peace, enjoying full democracy and great prosperity, reaping the benefits of an increasingly globalized world, let us begin our efforts by promoting and protecting the rights and welfare of our own children. From this starting point, we can then build a common endeavour to protect and rehabilitate children across the world who have been and continue to be affected by the terrible reality of violent conflict.

Article 22

Everyone, as a member of society, has the right to social security and is entitled to realization, through national effort and international co-operation and in accordance with the organization and resources of each State, of the economic, social and cultural rights indispensable for his dignity and the free development of his personality.

Everyone has a Responsibility

The Universal Declaration of Human Rights reiterated, in the shocked aftermath of the Second World War, what earlier was affirmed in the American Declaration of Independence in 1776, in the Bill of Rights of the United States Constitution, and in the French Constituent Assembly's Declaration, in 1789, of the Rights of Man and of the Citizen. All say that humans possess rights, which civilization must respect.

This argument rests on the notion of 'natural' law, developed in the middle ages, and reaffirmed in the 18th-century Scottish and French Enlightenments. The existence of natural law was held to imply the existence of rights that people possess by virtue of what they are, and because of their natural relationship to one another in society.

A right by definition is something to which one has a just claim. It is 'that which is morally just or due'. This presupposes agreement about what is just and moral. An affirmation of human rights is a statement about the nature of society. In the case of the Universal Declaration, the statement was essentially Western in origin and philosophy.

The Universal Declaration of Human Rights has been criticized as hypocrisy, since many of the governments voting for it in 1948 neither respected, nor intended to respect, any claims by their citizens which limited their power. But even hypocrisy has its uses, and the Universal Declaration has significantly influenced events since 1948 by making the defense of human rights an issue in international relations.

Other criticisms have come from Asia, where it is said that the Western concept of human rights is excessively individualistic and neglects community solidarity. Western commentators have replied by saying that Asian criticisms of these Western ideas are often equally hypocritical, serving simply to defend arbitrary government.

There is nonetheless a legitimate argument which says that the Western emphasis on individual rights can be socially destructive, and neglects the claims of society and community. By affirming an individual 'right', one makes a claim on society which is dissociated from responsibility. We say: You must grant me my pursuit of happiness. However my pursuit of happiness may prove to be at your expense. My freedom of enterprise may ruin you.

The conventional response made in the West is that the rights of one should stop when they infringe the rights of another. But this reflects a Western, adversarial conception of justice. In practice, it usually means that if you infringe my rights I'll sue you, or take your government to an international court.

A group of 24 former chiefs of state or government, including former prime ministers of Thailand, Singapore, Korea, and Japan, and ex-presidents or prime ministers from the United States, Canada, France, Brazil, and other countries, have published a draft Universal Declaration of Human Responsibilities, which they would like to see enacted as a complement to the Universal Declaration of Human Rights.

Their chairman is former German Chancellor Helmut Schmidt. Their document begins by saying that 'the exclusive insistence on rights can result in conflict, division, and endless dispute, and the neglect of human responsibilities can lead to lawlessness and chaos'. It declares that 'the rule of law and the promotion of human rights depend on the readiness of men and women to act justly'.

The fundamental principle the group affirms is that people must be treated humanely. 'What you do not wish to be done to yourself, do not do to others'. Their declaration states that every person 'is infinitely precious and must be protected unconditionally'. It points out that disputes should be resolved without violence and that every person has an obligation to honesty, and to truth in speech and action. The declaration says that people have a responsibility 'to develop their talents through diligent endeavor; they should have equal access to education and meaning-ful work.... All property and wealth must be used responsibly in accordance with justice and for the advancement of the human race. Economic and political power must not be handled as an instrument of domination, but in the service of economic justice and of the social order'.

The most significant aspect of this Declaration of Human Responsibilities, in today's Western intellectual climate, is its unqualified affirmation of the existence of right and wrong. 'No person, no group or organization, no state, no army or police stands above good and evil; all are subject to ethical standards. Everyone has a responsibility to promote good and to avoid evil in all things'.

That takes this declaration out of the realm of platitude. It connects it to the assumption fundamental to the existence of the United Nations itself, as well as to international law and the concept of human rights: that there is indeed a 'natural' law which is connected to the nature of man, and that we owe it respect. That makes it a controversial document, but also makes it a necessary one.

Article 23

1. Everyone has the right to work, to free choice of employment, to just and favourable conditions of work and to protection against unemployment.
2. Everyone, without any discrimination, has the right to equal pay for equal work.
3. Everyone who works has the right to just and favourable remuneration ensuring for himself and his family an existence worthy of human dignity, and supplemented, if necessary, by other means of social protection.
4. Everyone has the right to form and to join trade unions for the protection of his interests.

SONIA PICADO SOTELA

The Involvement of Women in Politics: A Victory in the Gender War and a Human Right

WOMEN'S STRUGGLE AND DEMOCRATIC PROCEDURES

On this fiftieth anniversary of the proclamation of the Universal Declaration of Human Rights, I believe it is important to draw attention to the historic struggle of women to achieve true equality in the exercise and observance of human rights. Article 21 of the Universal Declaration, to which this essay is devoted, is the foundation and inspiration for the basic principles that underlie all true democracies in today's world. Yet these very principles have often served as a basis for negative commitments to freedom in which vast amounts of glib, hollow, calculating rhetoric have been uttered in the name of democracy. There is no historical consciouseess, and this is reflected in the fact that, in the struggle for democracy and human rights, very little account has ever been taken of women.

On this occasion, then, I would like to make a political analysis of Article 21, and in particular paragraph 1, with reference to discrimination on grounds of sex in order to establish a link between these norms related to representation and the unremitting struggle – both passionate and silent – to achieve true political equality. This is a never-ending task which presents familiar and unfamiliar challenges every single day, and I therefore believe it merits special attention – both in tribute to the unflagging efforts of women in the past, and as an encouragement to those who will continue the fight in the future.

It must be remembered that electoral processes, which depend on strict compliance with formal procedures, are merely a starting point on the road to democracy, which is the outcome of an ongoing process that requires the joint, consistent efforts of the whole of society. This aspect of political reality – the evolutionary nature of democracy – is of particular relevance when it comes to the involvement of women in politics. One is struck by the difficulties which society has encountered in giving women full democratic rights. There are still structures which encourage economic, social and political exclusion, particularly of women. We still hear arguments to the effect that women's votes are merely supplementary to men's, and that all that is needed to get women to go to the polls is an effective publicity campaign. When it comes to the election of public officials, there are parties which still put women on their tickets simply because womanhood is associated in the public mind with moral cleanliness – always a good vote-catcher.

For decades women have been involved as grass-roots party workers, performing all kinds of tasks which are essentially an extension of their household duties: sewing flags and party emblems, cooking meals on election day, and house-to-house canvassing. Such work is considered inferior to that of men and is scarcely reflected in terms of appointments to elected posts (for more on this subject, see Line Bareiro, 'Las recién llegadas: mujer y participación política', *Estudios Básicos de Derechos Humanos*, volume IV, IIDH, San José, 1996, p. 221).

Luckily, this picture is now changing. In a long process extending over many years, Latin America has seen major changes in the exercise of political power and its structures, although it must be stressed that much remains to be done. I will now look at developments in a number of these countries, concluding with recent events in my own country, Costa Rica.

The percentage of women members of parliament in thirty-four American countries (not including Cuba) has now risen to 11 percent, a far higher figure than the bare 2 percent recorded some fifteen years ago. Argentina leads the field with 28 percent, thanks to a quota system.

If we accept the basic premise that there is a clear link between women's access to culture – i.e. full education – and their involvement in politics, positive law is the other mechanism which can be used to encourage greater female participation. Constitutional engineering can be used to reverse the process which restricts their involvement, so as to create a situation in which the number of political posts per geographical area is not limited, in which there are no 'closed' lists of candidates for public office, and in which instruments of affirmative action (such as gender quotas) are applied. Here we need to take issue with the usual argument against quotas, which is that they are a form of discrimination against men. It may be discrimination, but it is *positive* discrimination.

THE CHALLENGE IN COSTA RICA

General elections were recently held in Costa Rica, and I would like to draw attention to the most striking feature of the election campaign – namely that the parties with the largest number of votes (the Christian Social Unity and National Liberation) put forward women of high moral and intellectual calibre as candidates for the two Vice-Presidencies which are required to be filled under Article 130 of our Constitution. Since 8 May 1998, historian Astrid Fichel and judge Elizabeth Odio make institutional history by being the first women in Costa Rica to occupy both posts, which have traditionally been held by men (although the country had already had one woman Vice-President in 1986 and another in 1994). It should also be noted that two women representing parties with smaller number of votes were candidates for the Presidency.

My personal experience during these elections was that I was the first woman ever to head the ticket of the National Liberation party for the Costa Rican Congress. The second place on the ticket also went to a woman, the distinguished educationalist Joycelyn Sawyers. She comes from the Atlantic region of the country, whose largely Afro-Costarican population has, for historical and geographic reasons, suffered from discrimination and social exclusion. The two of us occupy our seats since 1 May 1998 and, together with the other twelve women elected (from all parties), will take up the challenge of drawing up a joint agenda to improve the status of women in Costa Rica.

Like most other countries around the world, Costa Rica is currently suffering from a crisis of confidence in political parties and their leaders. There is a kind of ideological breakdown, and the moral integrity of all those who hold public office is constantly being challenged. We need to ask ourselves whether greater involvement of women in election campaigns and political processes is linked to this perception and whether women have been elected to posts traditionally held by men merely in an attempt to increase their parties' legitimacy in the eyes of the electorate, or whether, on the contrary, this is the direct outcome of women's struggle for equality in the field of human rights.

Male politicians are naturally inclined to select people who are like themselves and to focus on the male gender when making appointments to public office. This is the way things are, and the selection of candidates of one's own gender has inevitable implications for appointments to positions of power. As regards the 'open options' policy for which we women are fighting, and which is also being fought for in other parts of America, our recent experience in Costa Rica is surely worth mentioning. I believe that more capable women who had distinguished themselves in the struggle for greater democracy should have stood for the posts I have referred to, including posts in local government. Our encouraging experience needs to be repeated elsewhere, so that public opinion – that double-edged sword of political life – can turn into a compass for democracy and can start to counteract people's increasing loss of confidence and moral sustenance.

COSTA RICA: AN ASSESSMENT

In the light of the challenges facing Costa Rica today, I would like to make an assessment of the situation which has risen since the general elections. There can be no doubt that, despite the apathy I have mentioned, those who ultimately went to the polls showed faith in traditional suffrage which was organised in an impeccable way. In this connection, people constantly told us what a fine example of democratic progress Costa Rica is. Yet merely congratulating ourselves on how smoothly the elections were run will not bring us a step closer to democracy. We need to look at other issues, such as how to get women fully involved in public debate, the exercise of political power, and party structures.

Costa Rica seems more concerned with electoral procedures than with the real business of politics – i.e. changes in power structures or in economic policy. Yet our democracy could be so much more than it is at the moment: a party system in which the fundamental decisions affecting the nation are taken by the two parties with the largest number of votes. What we are challenging are the electoral rules of the party system, not the discussion concerning styles of government or models of development. While I have no doubt that Costa Rica has achieved a great deal, I am equally aware that much remains to be done and discussed – especially now that we are faced with declining turnout at elections, growing apathy and an increasing rejection of traditional politics. If we are to preserve our democracy, there is a great deal we must do to encourage greater involvement, and not only in elections. This is a challenge which affects every aspect of national life, especially when it comes to encouraging a less passive attitude towards this country's real problems.

Beyond Quotas and Procedures:
The Importance of Getting Women Involved in Politics

This is why it is so important to consider what the election of women to certain political posts actually means. Until now the sole aim seems to have been to in-corporate a view of gender which can respond to new challenges and counteract people's loss of confidence in politics and government, so that a particular party can get more votes. The personal dimension of any commitment in this direction needs to be re-examined.

My basic argument therefore goes beyond establishing quotas and more trans-parent procedures for women candidates. The appointment of women to senior positions requires a commitment from society as a whole. Men, hitherto the sole occupants of positions of power, must cease paying lip-service to equality and must specifically commit themselves to a critical process of reflection and investigation concerning gender issues in our society and their close links with true participatory democracy.

In the struggle to redefine politics and power in a democratic society, the full, active involvement of women in their various roles as mothers, wives and constant negotiators in the household and the community may well give a new impetus to the work of government and even bring new light to bear on society's most serious problems, such as corruption, drug trafficking and crime. At the same time, inertia, publicity and patronage encourage political parties to adopt facile confrontational stances during election campaigns. None of this is of any conceivable help when it comes to solving people's real problems. While politicians tend to focus their campaigns on discrediting or disparaging their opponents, what people really want are clear, simple, relevant messages. In response to these shortcomings, women from all the contending parties in Costa Rica are now embarking on a serious campaign to promote the values which are needed in order to tackle the main problems facing our democracy.

DEVELOPMENT VERSUS FORMS OF SOCIAL EXCLUSION WHICH UNDERMINE DEMOCRACY

Clearly, nothing can be achieved as long as women remain excluded from the development process. The overriding importance of this issue has been highlighted by the work of the United Nations, in an effort which began at the Mexico Conference in 1975 and culminated in Beijing in 1995. Specific recommendations have been made regarding political involvement: corrections to electoral systems and measures to help women accede to public office in the same proportion and at the same level as men.

Other forms of exclusion are related to poverty: women continue to be 'the poorest of the poor' and represent approximately 70 percent of the world's rural poor – 1,300 million people in all (Human Development Report 1996, UNDP). In Latin America, the percentage of women in the overall working population rose from 21.9 percent in 1950 to 28.1 percent in 1990. Despite this increase, there is still a huge wage gap, as well as differences in types of work. Most women work in the informal sector, where legal protection is practically non-existent.

In the Vienna Declaration and Programme of Action (1993), governments acknowledged that human rights are women's rights. They promised to guarantee women social and economic rights (their right to peace, development and equality) and to defend their civil and political rights (their right not to be killed, tortured, sexually abused or arbitrarily imprisoned or to 'disappear'). In both cases, however, a gulf has remained between words and action.

WOMEN'S RIGHTS AND HUMAN RIGHTS: THE ACTUAL STATUS OF WOMEN

It has been very difficult to get people to understand and accept that women's rights are human rights – that, when declarations, treaties and conventions speak of 'man', this must specifically include 'woman'. 'Ever since 1789 the Rights of Man have been a symbol of modern democracy and of the emergence of citizenship as a potentially universal quality. However, a century and a half later they were no longer adequate, and they were reformulated as Human Rights by Eleanor Roosevelt. She called them human rights rather than rights of man, in order to emphasise that the previous concept did not only refer to males, and to include women explicitly. The plural, neutral term 'human' embraces both genders, women and men' (Marcela Lagarde, 'Identidad de género y derechos humanos. La construcción de las humanas', *Estudios Básicos de Derechos Humanos,* volume IV, IIDH, San José, 1996, p. 87).

However, it is not enough merely to use different words. When thinking about the involvement of women in political processes, we must remember what their actual status is. Involvement of women in politics means more than just the right to vote and to be elected, the number of parliamentary seats and ministerial portfolios held by women, and the statutes or structures of political parties.

Any genuine commitment to greater involvement of women in politics must mean their actual participation in the drafting and implementation of public policy in such areas as health, education, labour, crime and protection of basic values. It is in these areas that women must play a central, leading role rather than a purely marginal one. And political groups which approach men and women on a more equal basis will attract greater support at the key moment of the electoral process, which is when people are alone with their consciences in the polling booth.

INVOLVEMENT OF WOMEN IN THE EXERCISE OF POWER: THE DEFEAT OF VERTICALISM

Involvement of women now means more than just sitting back and swallowing humdrum rhetoric or – worse – voting en masse, like so many sheep. We must certainly keep on voting, but we women now want more. We must get to the centres of power and give them new impetus; we must show that our input can alter the character of political campaigning, in the direction of truly civic – i.e. civilised – education. We must prove that we can really tackle the problems that people are faced with – people who have had so little experience of expressing their opinions freely (and thus seriously and respectfully) on the matters that concern them. I believe that greater participation by women in politics may ultimately lead to the defeat at the ballot-box of that arrogant verticalism which still forms the basis for party strategy in our democratic society.

We must pursue two goals at once: the broader goal of improving women's actual status, and the more specific goal of incorporating an ever greater number of women into party and government structures and giving them more real power. Men and women must make a joint, conscious effort to attract into politics those apathetic women who, exhausted by the struggle for day-to-day survival, feel alienated and cheated by the global decisions that are being made around them. Women who do not believe in purely electoral triumphs or defeats, and who must become fully involved so that our democracies can be given the boost they so badly need, and so that people's opinions can continue to be freely expressed.

A political culture which is not sustained by the values of tolerance, cooperation, harmonisation and unrestricted involvement is symptomatic of a *flawed* democracy. Electoral democracy must now transcend itself in an effort to achieve greater solidarity and recognise people's real interests.

In her great work *The Second Sex,* Simone de Beauvoir sets out to show that women are not born but made. While there is undeniably a biological difference between men and women, there is also a culture of stereotypes which assigns them to specific roles and prevents them from working together more productively.

Good intentions are not enough. We have an obligation towards future generations to improve living conditions today. Girls and women must no longer be beaten, tortured, abused or mistreated. We must lay the foundations for peaceful, harmonious coexistence based on the enduring democratic values of human dignity and human rights.

Individuals and organisations, women and men must work together as equals to implement these human rights and fulfil these obligations and so improve the overall quality of development in Latin America. These are the goals to which we women aspire, and this is why the exercise of political power by women, and for women, is so essential. Only then will democracy, as enshrined in Article 21, have achieved its goals, and only then will the spirit of the Universal Declaration be fully realised. Understanding, accepting and encouraging the involvement of women in politics is an act of honesty and courage which I believe will restore the health and credibility of our flawed Latin American democracies.

GORAN SIMIC

A Simple Explanation

I am a plum. And you are an apple.
For a long time we've been lying in the same basket
made of dead branches.
And together we smell nicely of a smell
we lend to each other.
Only we can tell which belongs to whom.

I have nightmares that some day I'll wake up
and only your smell will remain,
the one I bear in me.

Therefore,
when I start bothering you, please,
do not persuade the pear to turn its spoilt back on me.
It will force me upward in the basket.
Bear in mind
that the hand that reaches for fruit
sometimes doesn't think of taste.
Wait until I shrivel
because I will shrivel with the smell
that remains after you.

Please.

ELISABETH REHN

My Experiences as Special Rapporteur for the Former Yugoslavia

It was with great pleasure that I accepted the invitation to present my personal comments and reflections on the occasion of the 50th anniversary of the Universal Declaration of Human Rights. In Finland my generation was brought up in the shadow of the tragedy of the Second World War. The dramatic consequences of that war strengthened our belief that a new and more efficient international system for the protection of human rights must be created. The Universal Declaration proclaimed the birth of that system. However, can we say that we have achieved what we were dreaming of?

Looking at the problem of the protection of human rights from my homeland's perspective one can be satisfied. As a former parliamentarian and member of government I can say that human rights, not only those of Finnish nationals, but of all residents of my country, are well protected and safeguarded. At the same time, however, since my appointment as Special Rapporteur to the UN Commission on Human Rights for the former Yugoslavia in September 1995, I have been confronted with the most dramatic violations of human rights in Europe since the Second World War. The thoughts presented below should not be seen as the opinions of the Special Rapporteur (or, moreover, of the Special Representative of the Secretary-General). Following the suggestion of the editors, I am sharing my very personal feelings based on my experiences gathered during the implementation of my human rights mandate. I do not pretend to be systematic or academic in my opinions. With due respect to many outstanding experts in the field of human rights, I believe that sometimes a normal human approach can be more interesting than learned elaborations.

The invitation to become the Special Rapporteur for the former Yugoslavia came as a surprise to me. My decision to accept it was not an easy one. I was aware of at least some of the problems related to the conflicts in the former Yugoslavia. Finnish soldiers took part in peacekeeping missions and in my capacity as Finnish Minister of Defence I visited them occasionally. It was from that perspective that I had been following the situation in the region. On the other hand my appointment came as a result of the resignation of the former Special Rapporteur, Tadeusz Mazowiecki, who resigned in protest after the fall of Srebrenica in August 1995. The fate of that small town in Eastern Bosnia and Herzegovina became a symbol for the most cruel violations of human rights. Thousands of people were killed. The fate of many thousands of others is still unknown. Several thousand lost their homes and were forced to seek refuge. Like so many other people all over the world, I have asked myself – how did such brutal and flagrant violations of the most essential human rights happen right in front of us? Why were we not able to prevent it? Neither the UN, nor any other international organisation – and so many were already present in Bosnia – proved able to protect the life and dignity of thousands of inhabitants of Srebrenica. Does it mean that the most essential human rights set forth in the Universal Declaration are just empty slogans?

With all these unanswered questions and doubts, I decided that it was my duty to work to improve the situation and to offer my contribution. Fortunately, soon after my appointment, the Dayton Peace Agreement (and I was lucky enough to have the opportunity to participate in the negotiations in Dayton) created a new framework which made the work of all of us involved in bringing to an end the conflicts in the former Yugoslavia easier. In that sense my role became a different one compared to that of my predecessor. While still monitoring violations of human rights and intervening in order to stop them, I was far more engaged in the process of helping the victims of those violations. I asked myself what could be done to help those women and children whose loved ones had been killed or were missing. What could be done for victims of rape, torture and post-war trauma? How could we overcome hate, mistrust, and the desire for revenge, so normal in a society torn apart by war?

One of the results of the Dayton Peace Agreement was that the substance of the Universal Declaration as well as of several other international human rights covenants became a part of the internal legal system of Bosnia and Herzegovina. At the same time I had the impression that neither politicians nor ordinary people believed that those standards could be implemented. In fact the very concept of universal human rights was to a large extent alien in a country ruled by the Communist party for decades.

As Special Rapporteur I was confronted immediately with a very complicated problem – how to prioritise my work? Are some human rights more important than others? Neither the Universal Declaration nor either of the International Covenants (one on civil and political rights and one on economic, social and cultural rights) provide answers to this dilemma. Of course it is necessary to protect all rights. However, in the case of a country like Bosnia and Herzegovina one has to prioritise even if such an approach contradicts the principle of equal treatment of all human rights.

In order to explain my doubts let me briefly recall the situation in September 1995. There was still a war going on in Bosnia and Herzegovina. People were being killed by snipers or as a result of other military activity. A large number of people were kept in various detention facilities, some of them in very bad conditions. There was serious discrimination and harassment of people on the basis of their nationality. The media were being used as a propaganda tool for undemocratic and nationalistic ideas. Practically speaking, none of the freedoms and rights declared by the international community as basic human rights were being respected and safeguarded. Let us not forget either that the system of social protection had collapsed and therefore social and economic rights were being seriously violated. In that context the problem of the so-called 'silent emergencies' arose. Elderly people, pensioners, women and children were suffering the most. I asked myself what I could do to change this tragic situation.

My first decision was to try to learn about the human rights situation in the region through direct contact not only with authorities but above all with the local population and in particular with members of vulnerable groups. I wanted to learn what the real situation of those people was, their state of mind, their expectations. Looking back at my mandate I am convinced that this was the correct decision. Thanks to my frequent missions and direct contact with people from all regions and social groups I was able to develop and formulate a proper opinion about the human rights situation.

In all those contacts one aspect struck me – the lack of self-confidence. People had lost the hope that a better future could be achieved through their own activities. They believed that only the 'international community' could bring about improvement. As a result of that attitude the 'international community' was blamed for everything, even for not clearing snow from the roads. While I was very much surprised by that attitude, I soon learned that it was a consequence not only of the tragic experiences of the war, but also the heritage of a Communist system. That system was based on a collective approach. And it is not easy for people shaped by such a system to understand that human rights are individual rights and that an individual is entitled to enjoy those rights.

One additional problem seriously hampered all attempts to improve the situation in Bosnia and Herzegovina, i.e. the mutual mistrust between people belonging to different ethnic or religious groups. During the many meetings I attended, people tended to accuse 'others' of all possible crimes. Always 'they' were responsible for 'our' tragedy. 'We' were always innocent victims. Of course unscrupulous politicians are to blame for that approach. I tried to change it and whenever possible I directed the discussion towards the problems for which my current interlocutors were responsible. But I also learned that mistrust cannot be overcome unless people are fully informed about the facts. Manipulations of the facts is one of the most powerful political weapons. Article 19 of the Universal Declaration is still being blatantly violated. It is difficult to believe, but even today such essential information as the number of victims of the war in Bosnia is unknown. Some people, including – unfortunately – some from the international community, try to cast doubts on the number of massacres in Sarajevo, like the one in Merkele in 1995. It reminds me of the situation in Poland after the Second World War, when those who had the courage to lay the responsibility for killing thousands of Polish Army officers in Katyn on the Soviet Union were heavily punished because according to official propaganda Germans were responsible for that war crime. Only a couple of years ago the Russian authorities admitted the truth. Nothing has been learned from those lessons. In Bosnia and Herzegovina war criminals are still denying their responsibility for killing civilians and are again trying to put the blame on the victims.

Article 3 of the Universal Declaration is one of the most important: 'Everyone has the right to life, liberty and security of person'. In Bosnia and Herzegovina that standard has gained an additional dimension. Under normal circumstances, when we speak about human rights we are referring to the relations between the authorities and citizens. If I am beaten by my fellow citizen I cannot claim that my human rights have been violated, as long as that act of violence is prohibited by law and law enforcement institutions are ready to offer me protection and remedy. In Bosnia, however, a great number of acts of violence, committed by so-called 'unknown perpetrators', have not only been left unpunished by the authorities, but one was actually under the impression that the authorities encouraged such acts. I asked myself so many times why people were attacking those who tried to return. Why were they throwing stones at their vehicles, why were they burning their rebuilt homes etc? Quite often the people who commit such acts have themselves been victims of similar crimes. According to official propaganda these are the 'spontaneous' reactions of people who do not want to live alongside members of other ethnic groups. However, in reality those people are being used to pursue a policy of ethnic division which suits the interest of some politicians.

During my frequent trips, in particular to the United States, I was very often asked by journalists, politicians and ordinary people why we as foreigners had to be involved in that conflict. National governments should be responsible for the protection of the human rights of their citizens. Why outsiders? Let us be frank: who among those of us working in Bosnia and Herzegovina, have not asked ourselves these questions? Such doubts are particularly strong when we are confronted with politicians who block all efforts to build a civil and peaceful society in Bosnia. But when I met with women and children expelled from Srebrenica, the families of missing persons, people displaced from their homes, I lost all my doubts. It is our duty to help them. I cannot peacefully enjoy my human rights in Finland while the rights of the people of Srebrenica are being brutally violated. Never before had the first sentence of Article 1 of the Universal Declaration – 'All human being are born free and equal in dignity and rights' – meant more to me.

Article 24

Everyone has the right to rest and leisure, including reasonable limitation of working hours and periodic holidays with pay.

The Universal Declaration of Human Rights: The International Keystone of Human Dignity

In the fifty years since its adoption the Universal Declaration of Human Rights has become the keystone of the international community's commitment to a truly human quality of life for all people.

The Universal Declaration, adopted on 10 December 1948 in Paris, distinguished itself from other great 'constitutional' documents - such as the Code of Hammurabi, the Magna Carta, the French Declaration of the Rights of Man and of the Citizen or the American Declaration of Independence - in two fundamental respects. It was the first international articulation of the rights and freedoms of all members of the human family. For the first time in the history of humankind nations had come together to agree on the substance of the rights of all human beings. They did so in the aftermath of the barbarities of the Second World War, out of respect for the dignity of each human being and because they perceived the close connection between violation of human rights and national and international peace. The emphasis throughout the Universal Declaration was on rights and freedoms applicable to every person everywhere.

Secondly, the Universal Declaration - the 'common standard of achievement for all peoples and all nations' - treated human rights not only as universal but also as indivisible. In other words, it regarded both civil and political rights, on the one hand, and social, economic and cultural rights, on the other, as demanding the same level of protection and as interdependent and interrelated. In doing so, it laid the essential conceptual foundations of the international law of human rights, set the human rights agenda of the United Nations for this century and beyond and awakened the great forces in civil society to the cause of human rights.

Thus the Universal Declaration proclaims in its preamble that 'recognition of the inherent dignity and of the equal and inalienable rights of all members of the human family is the foundation of freedom, justice and peace in the world'. Economic, social and cultural rights are set out with the same degree of affirmation and conviction as civil and political rights. Freedom of speech and belief are enshrined in the Universal Declaration, but so are freedom from fear and want. Fair trial and the right of participatory and representative government sit shoulder to shoulder with the right to work, to equal pay for equal work, and the right to education. Both sets of rights are proclaimed as 'the highest aspiration of the common people'. All the people.

Today the Universal Declaration of Human Rights stands as a monument to the convictions and determination of its framers who were leaders in their time. It is one of the great documents in world history. The *travaux préparatoires* are there to remind us that the authors sought to reflect in their work the differing cultural traditions in the world. The result is a distillation of many of the values inherent in the world's major legal systems, philosophical traditions and religious beliefs including the Buddhist, Christian, Hindu, Islamic and Jewish traditions.

The Universal Declaration has exerted a moral, political and legal influence throughout the world, far beyond the aspirations of its drafters. It has been the primary source of inspiration for post-war international legislation in the field of human rights. All of the United Nations human rights treaties as well as the regional human rights conventions - the European and American conventions and the African Charter on Human and Peoples' Rights - have been directly inspired by the Universal Declaration. Virtually every international instrument concerning human rights contains at least one preambular reference to the Universal Declaration, as do many subsequent declarations adopted by the General Assembly of the United Nations.

Its detailed provisions have served as a model for many domestic constitutions and laws, regulations and policies that protect human rights. National courts throughout the world have had recourse to the provisions of the Universal Declaration in the interpretation of provisions of national law or directly applicable international law. Parliaments, governments, lawyers and non-governmental organizations through-out the world invoke the Declaration when human rights are discussed.

Many of the provisions of the Universal Declaration have become part of customary international law, which is binding on all states whether or not they are signatories to multilateral conventions concerning human rights. Thus what started its existence as a solemn but non-binding proclamation of rights and freedoms has, at least in some respects, if not all, acquired through state practice the status of universal law.

Twenty years after its adoption, its tenets were authoritatively endorsed by the 1968 Proclamation of Teheran as constituting 'an obligation for the members of the international community' and became part of international law with the entry into force in 1976 of the International Covenant on Economic, Social and Cultural Rights and the International Covenant on Civil and Political Rights. Most recently 171 countries participating in the 1993 UN World Conference on Human Rights reaffirmed their commitment to the Universal Declaration in the Vienna Declaration and Programme of Action, emphasising and endorsing its inspirational role as the basis for United Nations standard-setting. It also inspired other world conferences, including the World Conference on Women, which re-emphasised in its final document that women's rights are human rights. Indeed one of the functions of the office of the High Commissioner for Human Rights established by the General Assembly in 1993 is to promote and protect the rights and freedoms contained, *inter alia,* in the Universal Declaration of Human Rights.

In short, the Universal Declaration has, since its adoption, assumed the mantle of a constitutional instrument, giving specificity to the concept of human rights in the United Nations Charter and radiating its benign influence throughout the planet.

However, we must be honest and recognize that there has been an imbalance in the promotion at the international level of economic, social and cultural rights and the right to development on the one hand, and of civil and political rights on the other. Extreme poverty, illiteracy, homelessness and the vulnerability of children to exploitation through trafficking and prostitution are telling indictments of leadership in our world as we end this millennium. I have committed myself as High Commissioner for Human Rights to work together, I hope, with a global alliance for human rights to redress that imbalance. 1998 is a good year to begin to forge this alliance.

One needs to look no further than the preamble of the Universal Declaration to realize that, while the world around us is evolving at a pace more rapid than at any other time in human history, the premises on which the Declaration is founded will remain valid and immutable forever. Test their relevance against the bitter realities of today's world events. The preamble continues to articulate our response. It speaks of 'barbarous acts which have outraged the conscience of mankind'. It points out that 'it is essential, if man is not to be compelled to have recourse, as a last resort, to rebellion against tyranny and oppression, that human rights should be protected by the rule of law'. It reminds us of the connection between human rights observance and 'friendly relations between nations'. It ends with a phrase that goes to the heart of the commemoration of the 50th anniversary: that 'a common understanding of the rights and freedoms is of the greatest importance for the full realization of this pledge'.

No one reading these phrases today can fail to be struck by their insight into the connection between denial of human rights and peace - domestic and international - and their enduring actuality.

But today's world is more complex than it was fifty years ago. There are now many more participating states than there were in 1948 and more strident and concerned voices from civil society. The agenda set by the Universal Declaration is surprisingly apt for these new complexities - whether they are linked to the rights of indigenous peoples or the right to development or discrimination on grounds of gender or on the basis of sexual orientation - but who could have imagined in 1948 that we would use the 50th anniversary of the Universal Declaration as an opportunity to reposition these fresh concerns and others in our order of priorities?

In December 1997, on a trip to Cambodia, I visited the Tuol Sleng Museum in Phnom Penh. It had been a school, but became a place of torture and inevitable death for over 16,000 people during the Khmer Rouge period from 1975-1979. As I looked at the iron beds with torture implements, saw the graphic photographs of how they had been used, and walked past row upon row of photographs of young girls and boys, of old people, of people from every walk of life – civil servants, peasants, intellectuals, soldiers, students – as I saw the piled up clothes and shoes it brought back so vividly my visit to Auschwitz, my visit to Hiroshima in 1995, and the terrible aftermath of the genocidal killing in Rwanda which I saw on my first visit there in 1994. How often have we said 'never again'? This, surely, is the strongest argument for the universality and indivisibility of human rights. It also reminds us of the need for eternal vigilance in safeguarding those rights.

My vision of the Universal Declaration, however, strays beyond its legal and political influence. Nelson Mandela recently reminded us that the Universal Declaration was adopted only a few months after the formation of the first apartheid government. He said – and I quote:

> For all the opponents of this pernicious system, the simple and noble words of the Universal Declaration were a sudden ray of hope at one of our darkest moments. During the many years that followed, this document ... served as a shining beacon and an inspiration to many millions of South Africans. It was proof that they were not alone, but rather part of a global movement against racism and colonialism, for human rights, peace and justice.

It is often said that rights which exist on paper are of no value. But paper, vision, commitment and action are the powerful tools of peace. The pages of the Universal Declaration, as Nelson Mandela observed, have been a source of courage to the downtrodden by showing them that they are not alone! They also interrogate our sense of solidarity. Notwithstanding the cruel fact of the persistence of human rights violations throughout the world, this document has served and will continue to serve as a reminder that the world community cannot turn a blind eye to the suffering of the oppressed and the destitute and that it has a mandate to concern itself and, where possible, offer succour – beyond all frontiers.

It is in this context that the search for global ethical standards and human responsibilities brings fresh insights into the interpretation of the preamble and articles of the Universal Declaration of Human Rights as a living document. It is right that we should focus more on duties and obligations, but I do not believe it is necessary to seek a new declaration. Instead we need to recognize and recommit ourselves, to the extent to which these values are implied, to creating through the Universal Declaration of Human Rights 'a common standard of achievement for all people and all nations' which can be reinforced by greater emphasis on these values as applying to individuals and communities in all our civil societies. This anniversary year is a most appropriate time to receive commentaries on the Universal Declaration from the different religious, philosophical and cultural traditions.

It is thanks to the Universal Declaration that human rights have established themselves everywhere as a legitimate political and moral concern, that the world community has pledged itself to promote and protect human rights, that the ordinary citizen has been given a vocabulary of complaint and inspiration, and that a corpus of enforceable human rights law is developing in different regions of the world through effective regional mechanisms.

I would venture to suggest that it has become an elevating force on the events of our world because it can be seen to embody the legal, moral and philosophical beliefs held true by all peoples and because it applies to all. It is precisely this notion of 'universality' – in the widest sense – that gives it its force. Its universal vocation to protect the dignity of every human being has captured the imagination of humanity. It is this vision which explains the enduring mission of the Universal Declaration and its unsurpassable dominance as a statement of legal principles. We tamper with it at our peril.

I am aware of the gap in perceptions over just what we mean by 'human rights', especially when the term focuses specifically on civil and political rights or, at the other end of the spectrum, emphasizes the importance of the right to development.

The right to development should guide us in a holistic approach to human rights. Realizing this right is essential if we intend to protect people against alienation in economic, social and political life. Although from country to country the needs in terms of human rights can vary greatly, the international community should make it a priority to further conceptualize and implement economic, social and cultural rights.

We must learn that human rights, in their essence, are empowering. By protecting human rights, we can create an environment for living in which each individual is able to develop his or her own gifts to the fullest extent. Providing this assurance of protection, in turn, will contribute to preventing so many of the conflicts based on poverty, discrimination and political oppression which continue to plague humanity. The vicious cycle: violations of human rights – conflicts – which in turn lead to more violations – must be broken. I believe we can break it only by ensuring respect for all human rights. The reaction to conflict always comes too late from the perspective of those whose rights have been violated. Now is the time for us to assume collective responsibility and develop the institutions and processes to anticipate, deter and prevent gross human rights violations.

As we commemorate the 50th anniversary of the Universal Declaration of Human Rights we must keep firmly in mind that human rights are women's rights too and the United Nations must be the uncompromising guardian of women's human rights.

The words of the Declaration coupled with those of the 1993 Vienna Declaration and Programme of Action and that of the 1995 Beijing Platform for Action stand in sharp contrast to the daily reality of life for so many. Women throughout the world have experienced the fact that declarations and conventions are not enough to guarantee their human rights. It is past time to move from fine words to firm action by international organizations, national and local governments and civil society to ensure that the rights of women everywhere are fully honoured.

The best hope for realising the human rights of women lies in the efforts of

257

women themselves. In recent visits to Uganda, Rwanda, South Africa, Cambodia, Japan and Iran I have met women committed to demonstrating that human rights principles belong to all and are compatible with diverse cultures and traditions. The solidarity women have for their sisters in other countries is a powerful force and this year I would particularly call for a focus on the women in Afghanistan.

Of the 1.3 billion people living in poverty 70 percent are women; the majority of the world's refugees are women; female illiteracy is invariably higher than male illiteracy; women and girl children are becoming commodities in cross-border prostitution rackets and the pornography industry. Millions of girls are still subject to genital mutilation, women in every country are regular victims of domestic violence and every day women are targeted in armed conflicts.

While addressing these realities we must avoid viewing women merely as victims of violations and conflict. Women are also the true peacemakers and peacebuilders – at the negotiating table and in war-torn communities everywhere.

Fighting for women's human rights is a positive struggle which recognizes the quality of a woman's contribution in every aspect of the community: in politics, industry, commerce, education, academe, agriculture and the home.

The United Nations' role as the guardian of women's rights must go beyond rhetorical support. Practical and creative measures to realize the human rights of women – civil and political rights, economic, social and cultural rights and the right to development – are a priority for my Office and must be for every part of the United Nations.

We are all the custodians of human rights. Their protection cannot remain the sole responsibility of governments or the United Nations. We must all find our own way to do what is required. We need a global alliance for human rights - a partnership linking governments, civil society, and international organizations. Working together, assisting and drawing lessons from each other, helping people to realize their rights - that's what the Universal Declaration teaches us; that is what it challenges us to do.

SEAMUS HEANEY

From the Republic of Conscience

I

When I landed in the republic of conscience
it was so noiseless when the engines stopped
I could hear a curlew high above the runway.

At immigration, the clerk was an old man
who produced a wallet from his homespun coat
and showed me a photograph of my grandfather.

The woman in customs asked me to declare
the words of our traditional cures and charms
to heal dumbness and avert the evil eye.

No porters. No interpreter. No taxi.
You carried your own burden and very soon
your symptoms of creeping privilege disappeared.

II

Fog is a dreaded omen there but lightning
spells universal good and parents hang
swaddled infants in trees during thunderstorms.

Salt is their precious mineral. And seashells
are held to the ear during births and funerals.
The base of all inks and pigments is seawater.

Their sacred symbol is a stylized boat.
The sail is an ear, the mast a sloping pen,
The hull a mouth-shape, the keel an open eye.

At their inauguration, public leaders
must swear to uphold unwritten law and weep
to atone for their presumption to hold office -

and to affirm their faith that all life sprang
from salt in tears which the sky-god wept
after he dreamt his solitude was endless.

III

I came back from that frugal republic
with my two arms the one length, the customs woman
having insisted my allowance was myself.

The old man rose and gazed into my face
and said that was official recognition
that I was now a dual citizen.

He therefore desired me when I got home
to consider myself a representative
and to speak on their behalf in my own tongue.

Their embassies, he said, were everywhere
but operated independently
and no ambassador would ever be relieved.

NIGEL RODLEY

The Universal Declaration of Human Rights: Learning from Experience

For an international lawyer, the significance of the Universal Declaration of Human Rights lies in its belated completion of an underlying value system that had been kept fractured for some two hundred years. After a period in which its first modern articulators, notably, the great Dutchman, Hugo de Groot (Grotius), looked partly to a natural law based on human dignity for a framework of principles in which to set down the rules binding nations, the behaviour of governments or sovereigns forced scholars and practitioners to accept that international law was no more than the rules by which the governments agreed to conduct their relations. There was nothing in this system that prevented governments waging war on each other or from treating their citizenry as arbitrarily or brutally as they chose.

Yet international law was still seen as embodying humane values. To the extent that it could and did establish rules to cover problems that arose in interstate relations, it was providing for the peaceful adjustment of disputes, a decidedly better solution than armed conflict.

The Kellogg-Briand Pact (Pact of Paris, 1928) closed a major gap in the edifice by outlawing recourse to war as a legitimate tool of statecraft. Eleven years later the Second World War broke out. The Charter of the United Nations which followed it strengthened the prohibition of resort to armed force to settle disputes and introduced into the field of general international law the obligation to promote respect for and observance of human rights and fundamental freedoms. Here was a recognition of a lesson from the war, that governments that were allowed to treat their own citizens as things beyond international concern could end up also treating other states and their populations with similar disregard. The Universal Declaration of Human Rights was the document that ensured that the Charter's human rights clauses did not remain a dead letter.

The Declaration itself contained elements that reflected the experience of the Second World War, while building on the historic models of the French *Déclaration des Droits de l'Homme et du Citoyen* and the American Bill of Rights. For example, in Europe under Nazi German control the phenomenon of torture, long thought abolished, resurfaced as a tool of government. Article 5 of the Universal Declaration responded: 'No one shall be subjected to torture or to cruel, inhuman or degrading treatment or punishment'.

The next step in our learning process was the realization that, just as the promotion of respect for human rights could be seen as a safeguard against war, human

261

rights too needed safeguards. Again, taking the prohibition of torture as an example, we soon learnt that as long as people who are arrested or detained remain at the unsupervised mercy of their captors and interrogators, they are at great risk of being tortured. So one protracted exercise in standard-setting, launched in 1975 and completed in 1988, was the establishment of a Body of Principles for the Protection of All Persons under Any Form of Detention or Imprisonment. The Principles are an integral part of the United Nations General Assembly's work to prevent torture.

Despite these advances, the dead hand of tradition for at least two decades prevented the United Nations from moving beyond the standard-setting phase to one of implementation, a term used to connote monitoring and holding to account. Many governments felt, as a few still do, that it was improper intervention in their internal affairs for the international organization to examine their human rights performance, unless this was agreed to under a treaty to which the government concerned was a party. At the universal level, the key general treaties, the International Covenants on Economic, Social and Cultural Rights and on Civil and Political Rights were only adopted in 1966 and took ten years to secure the 35 ratifications or accessions that brought them into force. As far as the former was concerned the only monitoring mechanism was by scrutiny of states' periodic reports. The latter used the same technique, but also permitted states to accept on an optional basis interstate and individual complaints. Even now, only 93 of the 140 states parties have accepted the right of individual petition under the (first) Optional Protocol to the Civil and Political Covenant. The interstate complaint procedure has yet to be used.

So for much of the UN's life it was left to non-governmental organisations (NGOs) like Amnesty International to try to hold governments accountable for their violations of the norms contained in the Universal Declaration of Human Rights. The NGOs themselves were not satisfied with UN inertia in the face of its members' flouting those norms. They kept calling for action and questioning the legitimacy of the UN's practice of turning 'a blind eye' to the violations. By the late 1960s certain relatively friendless countries' human rights records were starting to be subjected to scrutiny by the UN, notably, its Commission on Human Rights. But, then as now, some countries were immune from scrutiny because of voting patterns in this Commission.

This in turn led to the establishment in the 1980s and 1990s of 'thematic machinery' which would look at types of violation on a country-by-country basis. The first of these was the Working Group on Enforced or Involuntary Disappearances (1980), followed by the Special Rapporteur on summary, arbitrary and extrajudicial executions (1982) and the Special Rapporteur on torture (1985). Several others have been created since, but the first three have developed the range of practices that are followed in greater or lesser degree by the others: making urgent appeals to governments, transmitting substantiated cases to governments for their comments, reporting annually to the Commission on Human Rights with their country-specific observations, and undertaking and reporting on missions to countries that agree to invite them. One mechanism, the Working Group on Arbitrary Detention (1991), draws conclusions on individual cases.

Despite the existence of these mechanisms, the first three dealing with what might be called criminal violations of human rights, the practices continue. This has led to calls for action to put an end to impunity for the perpetrators.

The Vienna Declaration and Programme of Action adopted by the 1993 World Conference on Human Rights acknowledged as an issue of major importance the question of impunity for violations of human rights. It 'view[ed] with concern the issue of impunity of perpetrators of human rights violations' and affirmed that states 'should abrogate legislation leading to impunity for those responsible for grave violations of human rights such as torture and prosecute such violations, thereby providing a firm basis for the rule of law'.

But does it not seem strange that the question of punishment should have entered so positively the vocabulary of human rights discourse? After all, among the most potent symbols in human rights demonology have been 'cruel and unusual punishments' often handed down after unfair trials for sedition by 'Star Chambers', in other words, the arbitrary and oppressive action of an overweaning state that could not tolerate individual freedom of speech, conscience, association and assembly. The human rights project, in short, has been suffused with an ethos that sought to inhibit state power, especially its powers of compulsion enforced through the criminal law. Indeed, a definition of human rights that arguably best encapsulates the concept of human rights is that they consist in precisely those rights that insulate the individual from state power or, at any rate, mediate the power of the state in its relation with the individual. So why should the proponents of more effective protection of human rights be looking to national and international criminal tribunals to assist their cause?

No simple answer suggests itself, but a number of elements that could contribute to the formulation of an answer might be posited. First of all, there has been a general revulsion at the spectacle of murderers, torturers and kidnappers ensconced in presidential palaces purporting to absolve themselves of the crimes they knew they were committing by means of amnesties or similar techniques of avoidance of criminal responsibility which they grant themselves or procure for themselves from civilian authorities anxious to replace them at the helm of government or fearful of their being replaced by the forces responsible for the crimes. I recall my own con-frontation with this revulsion during a mission for Amnesty International to Chile in the mid-1980s, when I met numerous torture victims, witnessed their physical and other scars and confronted the cynical reality that the only constitutional route to a return of civilian, popularly chosen government was by accepting a constitution that effectively guaranteed the persistence of the amnesty granted in 1978 by the military junta to itself and its forces. At the time, Amnesty International had not taken a position on such amnesties and I myself had favoured a neutral position for the organisation. After the Chile experience I came off the fence and I note with satisfaction that Amnesty International subsequently came out against pre-trial amnesties for human rights crimes within its mandate.

Yet the problem of impunity was not new to me. On the contrary, the existence of *de facto* impunity was the evident pre-condition for the crimes in question to take place, as they did (and still do) in all too many countries. Indeed, as I have already noted, much human rights activity in this area is aimed at erecting safeguards against extreme violations, such as the UN Body of Principles for the Protection of All Persons under Any Form of Detention or Imprisonment. What was especially offensive about the formal amnesty was the project of giving legal form to the impunity. For those who hold law as expressing some form of moral consistency, legitimacy, here was a poisoning of its well-springs, a perversion of its purpose. Just as the world reacted with greater intensity to apartheid, institutionalised racial discrimination, than it did to everyday racism, reprehensible through this be, so it rejects *de jure* impunity with more vehemence than it does the *de facto* version.

It was perhaps a similar sense of disgust that led to the joint intervention by the Special Rapporteurs on torture, on summary, arbitrary and extrajudicial executions and on the independence of judges and lawyers, as well as the Chairman of the Working Group on Enforced or Involuntary Disappearances, in respect of two Peruvian laws of 1955. These granted amnesty to official personnel for crimes committed in the 'struggle against terrorism', and excluded judicial review of the application of the amnesty. Joint interventions by mechanisms established by the Commission on Human Rights were at that time rare, especially ones involving so many of them. So was the use of the urgent appeal mechanism in respect, not of an incident involving an actual violation within their mandate, but of a law that had yet to be acted upon. The widespread use of torture, murder and enforced disappearance committed by the Peruvian security forces had been on a scale that could not implausibly have allowed them to be characterised as crimes against humanity; and the government in whose name they had been committed was absolving its agents and officials from responsibility for them.

A further element, especially for international lawyers, is the existence of the beacon of Nuremberg. There, for the first time international justice was brought to bear on those acting in the name of the state who were responsible for atrocities that shocked the conscience of mankind. The corporate veil of the state was pierced and behind the abstract entity were revealed the individuals who dreamt up and executed acts that were too awful to have been considered for legislative enactment. The principles of Nuremberg were not only the victory of justice over the intolerable fiction of the unassailable state, as well as an affirmation of the supremacy of a higher positive law, they were also the base upon which a positive international law of human rights could be built, namely, the identification of duties of those sharing in the exercise of power to respect, at least to a minimal extent, the dignity of those subject to that power.

Another relevant element has been the growing realisation that the 'cycle of impunity' can be the breeding ground for cycles of atrocity. Indeed, I first heard the term used by the United Nations Secretary-General's Special Representative in Burundi at the time, Ahmedou Ould-Abdallah, at the height of the genocide in Rwanda. Here was a UN peacemaker, the sort of diplomat who might normally be expected to be seeking to cobble together some arrangement reflecting a balance of hostile forces, appearing to lament the absence of something far more radical, a calling to account of the leadership and others within those forces responsible for the atrocities. This was a few days before the Security Council was to create a commission of inquiry that, on the model of how the international criminal tribunal for the former Yugoslavia was set up, was to lead to the establishment of the tribunal for Rwanda.

It may be that the constitution of both tribunals were initiatives designed to give the appearance of action, while avoiding the necessary (military) action that could have ended the carnage, but it was also a recognition of the need to address the cycle of impunity. And while there was something distasteful about creating *ad hoc* bodies, the basis was being laid – partly as a result of the distaste – for the establishment of a permanent international criminal tribunal.

It may not be overoptimistic to expect the adoption in 1998 of a Statute of an international criminal court, a fitting commemoration of the 50th anniversary of the Universal Declaration. It is likely to include war crimes and crimes against humanity within the court's jurisdiction. War crimes certainly include human rights crimes committed in international armed conflict and probably also in non-international or civil armed conflict. Crimes against humanity cover the same crimes, when committed as part of a systematic practice, even in the absence of armed conflict. As far as states parties to the eventual statute are concerned, its very existence would prevent national amnesties immunizing perpetrators from international jurisdiction.

By so doing, it would also remove from politicians and diplomats the temptation to trade impunity for (a usually spurious) peace. This is one carrot that must be taken off the menu of peacemakers' inducements. This goal could, of course, be undermined if serious currency were given to informal suggestions that national amnesties be considered a bar to the court's jurisdiction. Such an initiative would legitimise the Faustian fact that the amnesties typically represent ('we shall return sovereignty to the people and go back to our barracks – until we decide to come out again'). Moreover, its juridical effect would be to turn fundamental doctrine on its head: international law and legal norms would be trumped by national law. In other words, there would be no international law on crimes that shock the conscience of mankind applicable to countries that legislate to that effect. This preposterous notion should be rejected.

It should be remembered that even a permanent international penal jurisdiction will be able to try only a fraction of the criminals. National jurisdictions will remain of key importance. And, since it will rarely be the territorial state that initiates the proceedings, a burden falls on other states availing themselves of universal jurisdiction. Unfortunately, many, if not most, states do not have the legislation that would permit their courts to exercise such jurisdiction.

A task for human rights activists and lawyers in the next century will be to encourage states to adhere to the statute of the court and to enact the legislation needed to ensure the availability of universal jurisdiction over human rights crimes. This will show that we are still learning.

1. Everyone has the right to a standard of living adequate for the health and well-being of himself and of his family, including food, clothing, housing and medical care and necessary social services, and the right to security in the event of unemployment, sickness, disability, widowhood, old age or other lack of livelihood in circumstances beyond his control.
2. Motherhood and childhood are entitled to special care and assistance. All children, whether born in or out of wedlock, shall enjoy the same social protection.

NAWAL EL SAADAWI

The Right to Life

I was a pupil at secondary school when the Universal Declaration of Human Rights was adopted in Paris on 10 December 1948. I did not hear anything about it at my school. None of the teachers mentioned it. Maybe the newspapers that appeared in Cairo discussed it, but we did not read the newspapers at our school, a boarding school for girls in Helwan, a small town south of Cairo. From the window of the dormitory I used to look out over the desert and the sand hills. On the other side were the British military barracks. At night they appeared like black, blurred shadows from which beams of lights searched the heavens and the earth, catching the faces of the girls who stood at the window like prisoners behind bars. We used to hide from the searchlights behind the shutters but they still got through the cracks and openings. Even if we hid under the beds we could not escape the beams, or the loud voices of the British soldiers, their mocking laughter, and their flirtatious words in English which we did not understand, although from the way they pronounced them we somehow sensed that these words were distasteful and mean. Their loud bursts of laughter were crude and coarse, and disturbed the tranquillity of the night in the small town of Helwan, as it slept quietly in the arms of the desert, which extended like an ocean of sand to the Nile.

Nobody in the school talked to us about the rights of human beings – be they man or woman, young person or child, or pupil. When we had to line up in the morning before entering our classrooms, the headmistress marched past us with an angry face, looking grim. Behind her the deputy headmistresses or the superintendents of the boarding house, like the British soldiers, followed on iron heels, on the face of each of them a rigid smile, a smile which was bigger than the one on the face of the headmistress, and in the hands of each of them you could see a long ruler, as sharp as a sword, which might suddenly descend on our fingers while we were standing in the queue for the morning call, trembling with fear.

When I was a child I did not know that I was a 'human being' or that I had 'rights' which I might possibly assert. In school, when we stood in the morning queue, we used to sing every day about 'God – the King – the Fatherland'. In the classroom we heard from all our teachers that obedience was a duty to God, to the King and to the Fatherland, and that death in the service of God, the King and the Fatherland was not death but meant great glory and the admission to eternal paradise in the heavens high above. We naturally believed everything we heard in school, especially what we heard from the directress or the headmistress whose stern face made her appear like the directly authorized representative of God, the King and the Fatherland. Disobeying her orders meant disobeying the orders of God, the King and the Fatherland. We could not see these three, because the word 'God' was just a word we heard or read, and the word 'Fatherland' was also just a word, and the King we could only see on photographs printed in the papers. The headmistress, however, was, to us, the incarnation of the three of them, in the shape of a woman with bulging eyes behind the lenses of her spectacles, and thick hands with strong fingers which held a long stick in the shape of a ruler.

My friends and I loved to walk and to play in the school's courtyard, like all children of that age. We also used to love singing and dancing, and playing the lute, the piano, the *tabla* drum, the tambourine, the violin or any other modern or traditional musical instrument. We could only pursue these hobbies during the holidays or in the free hours after our studies. Nevertheless, the instructions of the headmistress were harsh: she forbade all these hobbies, saying that they corrupted a girl's morals.

The long summer holidays I spent in my family's home in a small town called Menouf that looked like a village, in the middle of the Egyptian Delta. Adolescent girls in Menouf were not allowed to go out into the street or the fields to play, or to ride a bicycle, as the boys did. My brother Tal'at, who was just one year older than I, played outside the whole summer long, and he had the right to go out into the street and the fields. He rode his bicycle, and stayed out late with his friends at the cinema and the theatre. I asked my mother why my brother enjoyed these rights although he had failed his examinations in school, whereas I was denied them, having to spend the holidays in the kitchen even though I had excelled at school. The only answer my mother gave was 'because he is a boy and you are a girl'. I asked my father the same question. His answer was similar to my mother's, but he added: 'This is a divine command which you have to obey without discussion'. However, my mind could not be content with blind obedience, especially since the command was not fair. How could it be fair that I had to do my best in school for a whole session, and then have to work in the kitchen and clean the house during the holidays, whereas my brother had only played at school, and then could spend his holidays playing as well, without having to work in the house like me, without even having to make his bed or clean his room or wash the plate from which he had eaten? Did I really have to do all these things in his place? Was it possible that God had ordered such an injustice?

I asked God this question in my dreams and in my prayers to him, but God did not answer me. My father said that God did not have a tongue, or ears, or a body. I asked my father: 'By whose tongue then does God speak so that man may hear Him?' My father said: 'God speaks through the tongue of the Prophets and the Apostles and those who have the right to command'.

At school I learned that 'those who have the right to command' are our fathers. They held parental authority over the affairs of the school girls. I knew of the relationship between God and my father, because my father was the one through whose tongue God spoke at home. Similarly, at school it was the headmistress who spoke in his name. Disobeying my father meant disobeying God, and it meant disobeying the headmistress, and all this meant disobeying the King and the Fatherland as well.

After I came of age, having graduated from secondary school and become a medical student, I began to understand the historical connection between the forces in heaven and on earth, in school, the home and the Fatherland.

Since my father was a Muslim who believed in the three books of God (the Qur'an, the Gospels and the Torah) I inherited his faith from him, and I read all three books. I was astonished by the great similarities between them, especially where the rights of women and men were concerned. I discovered that in all three religions women enjoy fewer rights than men. However, the Torah is even more unfair to women than the Gospels and the Qur'an. For instance, there is a verse in the Torah which says that the impurity of the 'blood of the mother' who has given birth to a daughter continues for 64 days, which is twice the period of impurity of the 'blood of the mother' who has given birth to a son, which lasts only 32 days. Equally, the verses of the Torah emphasize that our Mother Eve was the first person who committed the great sin and ate from the tree of knowledge which God had forbidden her.

However, in his third book, the Qur'an, God does not treat Eve so unfairly. The text of the Qur'an says that the Devil, Satan, 'caused Adam and Eve to slip', both of them, and so they both ate from the tree. In the Qur'an, the tree has no name, and we do not know whether it was the tree of knowledge or another tree. In addition, in the Qur'an God did not consider Eve alone guilty of sin and included Adam in his condemnation. Also the verse of forgiveness says: 'God accepted from Adam words, and He relented towards him'. The words 'towards him' in the Qur'an are in the male singular, not the plural as in the preceding verse which dealt with their disobedience. Thus we understand that Adam alone was allowed to repent and seek atonement. Eve, however, was excluded from God's forgiveness.

Why did God forgive Adam, and not Eve, in spite of the fact that they had committed their sin together? Do women not have human rights like men? Or are we to understand that men are human beings, and women are not?

It was in 1956 that I read the Universal Declaration of Human Rights for the first time. It gave me a shock, similar to the shock I felt when, as a child, I first read God's three books. In December 1956 I was a young doctor in a health unit in the village of Tahla, in the Egyptian Delta. I had been trained, in the village military camp, to handle weapons, so that I could volunteer in the war, in defence of the Fatherland, which to us meant the town of Port Said that had been hit by British, French and Israeli bombs. It was our patriotic duty to bring this threefold aggression to a standstill. Later it proved to have been a fourfold aggression (in which the United States of America had participated indirectly and secretly). At that age, I was in my first youth, I imagined that the first article of the Universal Declaration of Human Rights should have forbidden a large state to attack a small state with bombs, or that it should have forbidden a group of large states to attack a small state in Africa – a small state without an army equipped with modern weapons. I would have imagined that the second article would have forbidden economic imperialism just as military occupation of any country in the world is forbidden. Since my childhood I had known that Great Britain had sent troops to occupy Egypt in 1882, and that Great Britain had transformed Egypt into a cotton farm, to serve its interests, against the interests of the Egyptian people, especially the poor *fellahin* (peasants). Since my childhood I had heard my grandmother, herself a poor peasant woman, sing with the women of the village: 'Precious one, precious one, may a great disaster befall the British'. I imagined that the third article of the Universal Declaration of Human Rights would have outlawed the double standards that apply in the world between different states, locally within one state, and even apply within the family.

In the preamble to the Universal Declaration of Human Rights I read general phrases about the equality between people, regardless of colour, race, nationality, sex or religion ... and so forth.

These general phrases, however, were not translated into clear, well-defined articles and rights. They are all just generalities in prose, like verses from the religious books, or articles in state constitutions.

The language of the Universal Declaration is male, even though its text proclaims men and women to be equal. The word 'human' is used in its male form, as if only men are human. Moreover, in the Universal Declaration there is an article which clearly proclaims that the family is the basic unit on which society is built and must be protected by the state and society. But the word 'family' refers to the patriarchal family, which is dominant thoughout the world, where men control women. Women are deprived of their basic human rights, the first of which is to be considered human like men, and to have the same rights within the family.

I found nothing in the Universal Declaration of Human Rights that gave me back the human rights that were taken away from me when I became a wife and a mother. At the end of 1956 I had my first experience of marriage and motherhood. I found out that a mother is deprived of many rights which the father enjoys simply because he is male. It is not just that children are named after their father only, and do not have the right to hold their mother's nationality. The husband has the absolute right to repudiate his wife, and the right to marry more than one woman. In the event of divorce he has the right to the care of his children after they reach a certain age, and he has the right to parental authority over them after he has repudiated their mother. The mother does not have the right to parental authority over her own children, not even if their father dies, because she is not male, and parental authority can only be entrusted to males.

I suffered from this law in Egypt after my first husband repudiated me. I had the right to look after my daughter, and the right to care for her until she had reached the age at which the right of care had to be transferred to her father. In 1971 my daughter was fifteen, attending secondary school, and was selected for the school tennis team that was to travel to Algeria for a girls' tennis tournament. But my daughter could not go. Her father was her legal guardian, and he was the only person with legal authority over her. He had to approve her travelling outside Egypt. My daughter had not lived with her father since the divorce, she had lived with me, and for some years we had not even known her father's address. I, her mother, was not entitled to give her permission to travel because I am a woman and so could not be her legal guardian.

After the death of my father, in 1959, I received the right to look after my sisters who were under age. But I could not be their legal guardian. I had to look for a man, any man, in my family to be their guardian, even though he did not live with them, even though I lived with them and had taken upon myself the responsibility of supporting them financially and protecting them from trouble.

The laws on the family in Egypt (and in many other countries) deprive a wife and mother of some of her basic human rights, such as the right to travel in freedom. Even today Egyptian law still denies women this important human right. For instance, I cannot renew my passport without the approval of my husband, but my husband can renew his passport without my approval. In Egypt, this is called 'the Law of Restraint', which means that a husband has the right to 'restrain' his wife.

Until recently women in Europe and America did not enjoy human rights within the institution of the family, or within marriage. The Universal Declaration of Human Rights confers no rights on women in their public and private lives.

I have reread the Universal Declaration of Human Rights at different stages of my life up to the moment when I wrote these lines in December 1997. The Declaration is now half a century old. I believe that it needs to be developed, in keeping with the movements to liberate peoples and women, and I believe that new articles should be added, to reflect the rights of peoples in confrontation with governments and states and the rights of children and women within families so that they can move towards greater justice and greater happiness.

The Universal Declaration should contain a basic article outlawing double standards between states and individuals. 'Rights' should be fundamental in the world, not 'force'. Every state should be obliged to execute a programme of nuclear and chemical disarmament, and to forego the use of all weapons of mass destruction, not excluding the weapon of economic blockade, or the economic sanctions imposed by large states upon smaller states, which only claim victims among children, women and the poor, not among the powerful in the state or in the government. For instance, why does the United States of America force nuclear disarmament upon Egypt and a number of other Arab and African states, and compel them to sign special agreements to that effect, while, at the same time, it does not require nuclear disarmament of Israel, and does not require it to sign the same agreement? Why does the United States of America not give up its own nuclear arsenal, in order to be an example to others?

Why has an economic blockade been imposed upon the State of Iraq to punish it for failing to implement UN resolutions and why does the State of Israel go completely unpunished, although it does not execute any of the United Nations resolutions? It is common knowledge that in Iraq today 500 children die every day as a result of the economic blockade. Nevertheless the world is celebrating the promulgation of the Universal Declaration of Human Rights half a century ago. Does 'human' refer, in the eyes of the world, solely to white men in the Northern hemisphere? Do the children and women in the Southern hemisphere have no human rights?! Do they not have the right to life, the right not to die?

AFSHIN ELLIAN

The Autumn Melodies

fear creeps into the words
through the river bed into the bedding
the bed of a vision
over there in the woods
in the bundling of people and plants
there in the woods
in the river valley
of lost hopes and dreams
there in the woods
lie horizontally the green plants
the tangled stories
there in the woods
is
a grave of mass
a mass of grave
      things are unsettled again
        today over this mass grave

the dogs do not bark
the eagles do not fly
the last leaves do not fall
      things are unsettled again
        today over this mass grave

now it is autumn
do you remember, the autumn
the death and the falling, the autumn
      things are unsettled again
        today over this mass grave

the forester saws and saws
the wood in the house
the wood in the ashes
      things are unsettled again
        today over this mass grave

the smoke bit into
the eyes of a cloud
a young cloud
      things are unsettled again
         today over this mass grave

the forester's wife hangs
flesh in the smoke
little cloud little cloud
rub rub out your eyes
      things are unsettled again
         today over this mass grave

the shepherd prays
in a silk garment
on a forehead of an autumn
      things are unsettled again
         today over this mass grave

the crystal silence
breaks through a grey
dark light
every autumn sways round the crystals
the shatters of the light

Ah me, every man is a wish
Oh, how tiny is man
Oh, how fragile is the wish
Oh, how tragic is Promethea
      things are unsettled again
         today over this mass grave

falling, a rain
a droplet of tear
yellow and yellow
on the head of
the crystal autumn
on the head of a tree
      things are unsettled again
         today over this mass grave

***

a leap
to lap
all leaps:

on the square
   of yesterday Louis the Fifteenth
the square
   of the red morn of the Revolution
the square
   of the morrow noon of Concorde
on the square flies
for the last time
flies
with wings of hair
flies
the head of Marie Antoinette
   the eyes her eyes your eyes
     cry a snowy tear

      ***

you, beloved
   my rose
     has too once flown
       on a grey square

      ***

what did the flying head say?
asked a woodcutter from the bazaar
she calls on the God
that she does not believe
called a priest from the bazaar
no my dear customer
called a merchant from the bazaar
she calls on the concealed elements
in the palace of the money
no my comrade
called a revolutionary from the bazaar
from his fine throat

she calls on the followers to battle
no my brother
called an imam from the bazaar
from his beard
she calls on the largest devil
she calls on the largest dove
for the flight
no my fellow citizens
called a lawyer from the void
she calls
and she called on the magic word
droits de l'homme
she called and called and called
– you, all, do know -
the light the enlightenment
but lit by
the red light of the knife
of Guillotine lightning
      the afternoon
            and deluminates the morning
                that light she called
                    the delumination falls
                        the delumination rises

the eyes of Marie Antoinette
moved for the last turn
towards the light which lightens
the eyelids turned
      in the heel of the light

Oh, my God, the desolation
de l'homme l'homme homme
the 'home home home'
I want to go to the rosehouse
Oh, my God, the Desolation
      things are unsettled again
            over the human landscape

a leap
to the woods:

the forester breaks a branch
a female dear
leapt onto a branch
a thunder resonates
in the light
an echo lightens:
'I am tired of being a man'.*

*This line is taken from a poem by Pablo Neruda.

PIERRE SANÉ

An Unfinished Revolution

THE WORK OF AMNESTY INTERNATIONAL

Wei Jingsheng, a prisoner of conscience in China, was unexpectedly released from prison in November 1997. It was the latest chapter in one of Amnesty International's oldest campaigns for an individual. At the time Wei was 47 years old and had spent more than half his adult life behind bars. Amnesty International groups worldwide had been working for his release since 1979, when he was sentenced to 14 years imprisonment for 'counter-revolutionary' crimes. Wei Jingsheng was released on parole in 1993 after serving his first sentence, but was arrested once again in April 1994 and held for nearly 20 months without charge. In December 1995 he was sentenced to a further 14 years imprisonment for 'engaging in activities in an attempt to overthrow the government'. He has never used or advocated violence. His release, almost exactly 12 years before it was due, was the best possible reward for all the work done on his behalf by Amnesty International members and others. Soon after he was freed he explained to Amnesty International how he had learned about the support he was receiving and the effect it had:

> A guard who never usually spoke to me struck up a conversation. We chatted casually for a bit and then I asked him very nonchalantly, 'I guess fewer letters have been coming for me lately, right?' The guard then looked at me and exclaimed incredulously, 'Fewer? Old Wei, you get *so* many letters!' When he finished saying this he realized what he had told me and suddenly stopped speaking and hurried out of the room.... The mental inspiration this gave me greatly surpassed any small improvement in my living conditions.

Such successful campaigns do not imply that Amnesty International is always the subject of praise. Amnesty International is guilty of 'sloganeering, slanging off at people, abusing them', proclaimed the Australian Minister of Foreign Affairs, Alexander Downer. 'It might make you feel good, but it doesn't achieve anything.' What sparked these remarks was Amnesty International's energetic campaigning in Australia as part of its work on the human rights of refugees worldwide, one of the organization's major campaigns of 1997. The Minister was particularly incensed at a report which exposed Australia's unfair treatment of asylum-seekers.

The Minister was wrong, however, to believe that such campaigns achieve nothing. Even in his own country, his comments provoked the Senate to pass a resolution calling on him to 'direct his energies to more vigorously tackle the human rights abuses in East Timor ... and to review Australia's stance on East Timorese asylum-seekers'. In October 1997 the Senate passed another motion noting Amnesty International's main recommendations on how Australia should improve its procedures for asylum-seekers.

The 1997 campaign for refugees' rights highlighted the strength, diversity and imagination of the Amnesty International movement. The million-strong force of Amnesty International members and supporters is now active in 176 countries and territories of the world. In 105 of these countries and territories, they are organized in more than 4,300 local Amnesty International groups, over 3,400 youth and student groups, and several hundred professional and other groups. In 55 countries and territories the groups are coordinated by sections.

These activists mobilize their communities, put pressure on governments, support victims and their families, lobby for legal reform, and raise public awareness through the media and human rights education work. Alongside traditional campaigning methods such as letter-writing, each group looks for new and more effective ways of making their distinct contribution to promoting and protecting human rights. A group in a small village may focus on solidarity work with victims of torture in a faraway country. Children can give immense joy to prisoners and their families by sending drawings and cards. A group in a large town may organize joint initiatives with other non-governmental organizations (NGOs) to campaign on a particular human rights issue, or stage a concert to raise funds and promote awareness of human rights. Some members concentrate on public education, others work with sympathetic members of parliament to introduce laws to protect human rights. All these activities, as well as the policies and overall strategies of the movement as a whole, are decided by Amnesty International members themselves through internal democratic structures.

THE SIGNIFICANCE OF THE UNIVERSAL DECLARATION

It is 50 years since the Universal Declaration of Human Rights was proclaimed by the General Assembly of the United Nations. Developed in response to the atrocities of the Second World War, the Universal Declaration represented a collective determination never to return to those dark days. It was an important milestone in a discourse that stretches back through thousands of years of human history: what are the qualities that make us human and what rights, obligations and responsibilities do these create in our relationships with each other? The Universal Declaration sets out the human rights which are fundamental to the dignity and development of every human being. These range from economic rights, such as the right to work and to an adequate standard of living, to political rights, such as freedom of opinion, expression and association. They include civil rights, such as equality before the law, and social or cultural rights, such as the right to education and to participate in the cultural life of the community. The Universal Declaration proclaims that all these rights belong to all people.

Much has been achieved in the last half century. Struggles against colonialism and apartheid have changed the map of the world. Mass movements against race and gender discrimination have transformed societies. The rights enshrined in the Universal Declaration have become a rallying cry for human rights defenders and ordinary people throughout the world. They have been elaborated upon and codified in international human rights treaties and declarations, as well as many national constitutions and laws. They have provided a foundation for UN and regional initiatives to secure peace and to reduce poverty, combat illiteracy and safeguard health.

In 1993, at the UN World Conference on Human Rights in Vienna, 171 governments adopted by consensus a declaration stating:

> All human rights are universal, indivisible and interdependent and inter-related.... While the significance of national and regional particularities and various historical, cultural and religious backgrounds must be borne in mind, it is the duty of states, regardless of their political, economic and cultural systems, to promote and protect human rights and fundamental freedoms.

It is true that the codification of the international human rights discourse has been stimulated by political and philosophical developments in the West over the past few centuries. It does not follow, however, that the underlying tenets are of restricted relevance. The terminology may be culturally specific, but not the principles themselves. As Burmese opposition leader Daw Aung San Suu Kyi wrote in her book *Freedom from Fear*:

> It is difficult for the Burmese people to understand how any of the rights contained in the 30 articles of the UDHR can be seen as anything but wholesome and good. That the Declaration was not drawn up in Burma by the Burmese people seems an inadequate reason, to say the least, for rejecting it. If ideas and beliefs are to be denied validity outside the geographical and cultural bounds of their origin, Buddhism would be confined to North India, Christianity to a narrow tract in the Middle East and Islam to Arabia.

But for most people the rights in the Universal Declaration still are little more than a paper promise. A promise that has not been fulfilled for the 1.3 billion people who struggle to survive on less than one US dollar a day; for the 35,000 children who die of malnutrition and preventable diseases every day; for the billion adults, most of them women, who cannot read or write; for the prisoners of conscience languishing in jails in every region of the world; or for the victims of torture in a third of the world's countries.

Many governments in the developing world insist on the primacy of economic growth which, they say, necessitates strong government and the subjugation of the individual's interests to those of the community. They argue that only when a country has attained a certain level of economic development can it afford the luxury of civil and political freedoms.

But economic growth is no guarantee of economic or social rights. Many governments in the developed world have dismantled elements of their welfare provision, justifying their actions on grounds of economic competitiveness. They have greatly reduced access to free education, health care and social security, leaving many homeless and hungry, even within the wealthiest nations. Article 7 of the Universal Declaration guarantees that '[a]ll are equal before the law and are entitled without any discrimination to equal protection of the law', a principle enshrined in constitutions and legal systems the world over. But this basic civil and political right is compromised when economic and social rights are denied, skewing the legal system against the poor and socially marginalized groups.

On 10 December 1997 Amnesty International launched a year-long campaign to raise awareness of and mobilize support for the rights enshrined in the Universal Declaration. As part of this campaign, which coincides with the 50th anniversary of the Universal Declaration, the movement began collecting signatures from people all over the world pledging that they will do everything in their power to ensure that the rights enshrined in the Universal Declaration are realized. Millions of people are expected to sign what will become the world's largest book of signatures. It will be presented to the UN as an expression of the commitment of people from all cultures to the promotion and protection of fundamental human rights.

ECONOMIC RELATIONS AND ARMS SALES

The assumption has been that civil and political rights could be defined by law and enforced in courts, since it is argued that they largely require the state to refrain from doing certain things to its citizens. By contrast, economic, social and cultural rights, it is argued, impose positive obligations on states which are not so susceptible to determination by the courts. They are more in the nature of calls on states to achieve certain goals, the argument runs, and the degree of the state's efforts to do so can neither be measured easily nor separated from the exigencies of circumstance.

This argument is based on two misconceptions. First, it is wrong to argue that civil and political rights do not place positive obligations on states to take action. States have a duty not only to protect human rights, but also to promote them actively. For example, the prohibition on torture requires at the very least training of law enforcement officers and inspection of detention centres. Second, it is clear that many economic, social and cultural rights do have elements which can already, in the law and practices of some states, be invoked in court. It is striking how little effort has been made to provide meaningful administrative or judicial remedies to those whose economic or social rights have been violated. Even those governments which say they give economic rights priority over civil and political rights have failed to support the development of standards or mechanisms which would enhance their population's enjoyment of these rights.

Amnesty International continues to develop its campaigning work to persuade governments and companies to use their influence on the authorities of countries with which they have economic relations to promote and protect human rights. Although Amnesty International takes no general position on sanctions or boycotts, the organization has opposed in specific instances the transfer of military and security equipment and of training and personnel that could reasonably be assumed to contribute to human rights abuses.

In a speech to the UN Security Council, I stressed the problem of human rights abuses being fuelled by arms, security equipment and mercenary inflows. I pointed out that analyzing arms flows to areas of armed conflict can help determine responsibility for human rights violations and, if action is taken, abuses can be prevented. I recommended continued monitoring of transfers, particularly of light weapons, to the whole of Central Africa in order to encourage observance of international human rights standards and humanitarian law. Similar efforts could be made in relation to Afghanistan and other areas where armed conflict has fuelled human rights crises.

In May 1997 Amnesty International and other Nobel Peace Prize laureates launched an International Code of Conduct on Arms Transfers, which set out human rights and other international principles for the control of international arms transfers. By late 1997 over 600 NGOs had endorsed a European Union (EU) version of the Code. Several EU governments and many members of the European Parliament expressed support for establishing harmonized arms control mechanisms based on criteria governing arms exports agreed by the Council of Ministers between 1991 and 1992.

In addition, businesses have a responsibility to use their influence to try to stop violations of human rights by governments or armed political groups in the countries in which they operate. Amnesty International has drawn up a checklist of human rights principles for companies, based on international law, for inclusion in company codes of conduct. International financial and economic institutions such as the International Monetary Fund (IMF), the World Bank and the World Trade Organization (WTO) should also ensure that human rights are taken into account in the development of their policies and projects.

REFORM AT THE UNITED NATIONS

Human rights work in the conference rooms and corridors of the UN in Geneva is gradually being complemented by a human rights program of action in the field, at the UN headquarters in New York and in political and economic debates around the world. The UN human rights program now has more staff working in the field than in its offices in New York and Geneva.

In July 1997 the UN Secretary-General, Kofi Annan, launched a package of UN reforms. Despite some voices of dissent to the integration of human rights into all the activities of the UN, the reform package was endorsed by the UN General Assembly in December. The UN reforms, the appointment of a new UN High Commissioner for Human Rights, a UN Secretary-General who has strongly articulated the moral and human rights foundations of the UN's mission, the 50th anniversary of the Universal Declaration of Human Rights, and the 1998 review of implementation of the Vienna Declaration and Programme of Action have combined to provide unique opportunities for human rights activists.

If however the rhetoric of integration is to be translated into a reality, all UN departments, funds and programs need to look at how their own work could enhance human rights promotion and protection. Responsibility for this cannot be left entirely to the UN High Commissioner for Human Rights. The High Commissioner's resources are stretched too thinly to address properly the human rights needs of post-conflict countries or development work. The UN Secretary-General will need to monitor progress closely to ensure that the culture of isolation is broken down and that human rights are taken into account in all areas of work.

As to the role of human rights in peace-building and security, I had the opportunity to address members of the UN Security Council in September 1997 on human rights in armed conflict. It was the first time that a human rights organization addressed members of the UN Security Council and it is hoped that this breakthrough will lead to presentations by other relevant organizations. I stated that there is a tendency to see human rights work as somehow an obstacle to political progress in peace-making and peace-keeping. But in fact human rights work can be part of the tool box needed to tackle emerging conflict and help the Security Council know what action might be taken to avert conflict. If the Security Council wants to grasp the causes of and solutions to armed conflict it should continue to pay greater attention to the human rights violations which lead to armed conflict, which fuel armed conflict, which can be a weapon of war within armed conflict, and which, if not addressed, will lead to further conflict and further threats to international peace and security. Examination of human rights reports should be part of the process of preventive action and diplomacy. During an armed conflict, accurate and timely human rights investigations can dispel propaganda and rumours which only fan the flames of conflict.

TOWARDS AN INTERNATIONAL CRIMINAL COURT

The worldwide effort to establish a permanent international criminal court – the missing link in the interlocking chain of international justice in peace and war – has moved into a new phase since December 1996, when the UN General Assembly decided to convene a diplomatic conference in Rome in June 1998 to adopt a statute for such a court. Amnesty International, together with more than 300 other members of the NGO Coalition for an International Criminal Court, urged governments to strengthen the draft statute for the court.

Much progress has been made in reducing more than 300 pages of proposals to a manageable consolidated text for discussion at the diplomatic conference. In addition, there is an emerging consensus that the court will have jurisdiction over the 'core crimes' of genocide, other crimes against humanity and serious violations of humanitarian law in both international and internal armed conflict; and possibly aggression.

Nevertheless, many other issues are still fiercely contested. How they are resolved will determine whether the court is an independent, fair and effective institution or, on the contrary, a set-back for international justice. For example, the Permanent Members of the UN Security Council argue that they should each have a veto over any prosecution in a country that the UN Security Council is considering under Chapter VII of the UN Charter (threats to or breaches of international peace and security). Many other countries now agree with Amnesty International that, although the UN Security Council should have the power to refer a situation to the international criminal court for investigation, as this avoids further *ad hoc* courts and ensures that court orders can be enforced in any state, it should not have any power to prevent a prosecution.

Amnesty International has also argued that the prosecutor should be able to initiate an investigation based on information from any source, including victims and their families. Many countries now agree with that position.

A FUTURE OF ACCOUNTABILITY

There is little point in integrating human rights into the activities of other parts of the UN if those UN political bodies which already have a mandate to deal with human rights do not discharge their basic duty to hold their peers accountable to international standards. The UN's record so far has been very mixed. Trade considerations and the political pressures of regional solidarity meant that most states avoided direct confrontation at the Commission. Dialogue and quiet diplomacy dominated, but all too often turned into silent diplomacy.

At the launch of Amnesty International's report on Algeria in November 1997, I told UN diplomats in New York that there is no other country where the violations are so extreme where there has been no international scrutiny let alone action – no visits by experts, no monitors, not even a resolution passed. Such indifference in the face of the daily slaughter becomes increasingly untenable, for it is an indifference that has contributed to a worsening of the situation by allowing impunity to prevail. In the absence of any concrete action, the condemnation of the violence and the expressions of regret for the loss of lives are sounding more and more like hollow rhetoric.

To promote the Universal Declaration and defend the principles of universality and indivisibility in the next century, Amnesty International and the broader human rights movement of which it is part, will need to rise to the challenges presented by a fast-changing world environment. Article 28 of the Universal Declaration states: 'Everyone is entitled to a social and international order in which the rights and freedoms set forth in this Declaration can be fully realized'. Achieving such a world is the task before us.

One of the indications that there may be a more hopeful future for human rights was the adoption in April 1998 of a UN declaration on human rights defenders. After many years of preparation and debate, the international community finally recognized that people – those whom we often call activists, dissidents, or just human rights reporters – have a right not only actively to defend the human rights embodied in international and national law, but more importantly the right to be protected against persecution for promoting and reporting on those rights. Such promotion and reporting is at the heart of Amnesty International's work. We are an organization which is greatly dependent on what people on the spot can tell us, and often through us tell the world. It is this international community of human rights defenders, a community which in principle includes all of us, which will provide the key to the observance of the Universal Declaration of Human Rights from its fiftieth year onwards.

1. Everyone has the right to education. Education shall be free, at least in the elementary and fundamental stages. Elementary education shall be compulsory. Technical and professional education shall be made generally available and higher education shall be equally accessible to all on the basis of merit.
2. Education shall be directed to the full development of the human personality and to the strengthening of respect for human rights and fundamental freedoms. It shall promote understanding, tolerance and friendship among all nations, racial or religious groups, and shall further the activities of the United Nations for the maintenance of peace.
3. Parents have a prior right to choose the kind of education that shall be given to their children.

HELMUT SCHMIDT

*The Interdependence
of Freedom and Responsibility*

The Universal Declaration of Human Rights started out as a declaration of moral principles, meeting a worldwide need after the defeat of the dictatorial imperialism of both Hitler and Japanese military. Soon after the decision by the United Nations in 1948 the Universal Declaration was gradually transformed into international law. It has thus provided solid and reliable foundations for legal claims to basic human rights for countless millions of individuals. This is an enormous achievement. It deserves praise for all who have contributed to this success.

At the same time we must not forget that billions of individuals still do not enjoy basic rights. There are several reasons for this deplorable situation. One lies in the fact that the concept of basic rights for each and every individual stems from European sources, from the era of enlightenment in particular, and from the American revolution. Like the concepts of the separation of powers within a state, of the 'contrat social', of democracy and of the 'open society', the concept of human rights has its historical origins in the West.

Although most of us Westerners believe human rights to be universal by nature or by God's law, irrespective of a person's creed or colour, it is obvious that many people on other continents have different opinions or maintain a sceptical distance vis-à-vis the concept. Some religious, spiritual and political leaders in Asia and Africa misinterpret the institutionalisation of human rights as just another instrument for the attempted prolongation of Western dominance over former colonies. Some religious and spiritual leaders misinterpret the idea of human rights as infringing their religious beliefs or their ethical traditions. Some political leaders misinterpret the idea as being intended to undermine the fabric of their societies and in particular their structure of political governance.

All in all, these criticisms often appear unjust and unfounded in Western eyes. But this does not change the facts. It remains a fact that many societies have traditionally perceived human relations in terms of obligations rather than rights. This is true, in general terms, for much of Eastern thought. While traditionally in the West the concepts of freedom and individuality have been emphasized, in the East the notions of responsibility and community have prevailed. The fact that a Universal Declaration of Human Rights was drafted, but no Universal Declaration of Human Responsibilities, undoubtedly reflects the philosophical and cultural background of the document's drafters, who represented the Western powers emerging victorious from the Second World War.

While rights relate more to freedom, obligations are associated with responsibility. Despite this distinction, freedom and responsibility are interdependent. Responsibility, as a moral quality, serves as a natural, voluntary check on one's freedom. In any society, freedom can never be exercised without limits. The more freedom we enjoy, the greater the responsibility we bear, toward others as well as ourselves.

Sadly, this relationship between freedom and responsibility has not always been clearly understood. Some ideologies have placed greater importance on the concept of individual freedom, while others have set great store by unquestioning commitment to the social group. Without a proper balance, unrestricted freedom is as dangerous as imposed unrestricted social or political duties. Great social injustices have resulted from extreme economic freedom and capitalist greed, while at the same time cruel oppression of people's basic liberties has been justified in the name of political ideals and society's interests.

Both extremes are undesirable. At present, with the disappearance of the East-West conflict and the end of the Cold War, with the failure of the Soviet experiment and the hope for the gradual humanization of capitalism, humanity has a chance to come closer to a balance between freedom and responsibility. We have struggled for freedom and rights. It is now time to foster both responsibility and human obligation.

The InterAction Council, a truly international group of former heads of state and government from all five continents, believes that the globalization of the world economy is being accompanied by the globalization of problems. The Council abhors the notion of the inevitability of a future 'clash of civilisations'. Instead, global interdependence demands that we must live with each other in peace. Human beings need rules and constraints. And only a common minimal code of ethics can make collective peace possible. Without ethics and self-restraint humankind would revert to the jungle. The world is in need of an ethical base on which to stand.

The world faiths have much in common. On the basis of these commonalities the InterAction Council endorsed the recommendation that in 1998, on the 50th anniversary of the Universal Declaration of Human Rights, the United Nations should consider a Declaration of Human Responsibilities to complement its earlier crucial work on rights.

The initiative to draft a Universal Declaration of Human Responsibilities is not only a way of balancing freedom with responsibility, but also a means of reconciling ideologies and political views that are deemed antagonistic by many both in Asia and in the West. The basic premise, then, should be that humans deserve the greatest possible freedom, but they should also develop their sense of responsibility to its fullest in order to correctly administer their freedom.

Globalization has given new urgency to ethical teaching, because violence on our television screens is now transmitted by satellite across the planet. Because speculation in distant financial markets can devastate communities and economies.

And because the influence of private tycoons now transcends the power of governments. Unlike elected politicians, there is no accountability for such private power except these economically powerful individuals' personal sense of responsibility. Never has the world needed a declaration of human responsibilities more than today. Rights and duties are inextricably linked. Regardless of a particular society's values, human relations are universally based on the existence of both rights and duties.

Article 27

1. Everyone has the right freely to participate in the cultural life of the community, to enjoy the arts and to share in scientific advancement and its benefits.
2. Everyone has the right to the protection of the moral and material interests resulting from any scientific, literary or artistic production of which he is the author.

MAX VAN DER STOEL

Some Remarks on Human Rights
at the Dawn of the New Millennium

As the Charter of the United Nations has often been referred to as a sort of 'Constitution' for the world, so the Universal Declaration of Human Rights should be viewed as a sort of revolutionary document proclaiming the limits of authority of state over the personality of each and every human being throughout the world. Indeed, in combination with the UN Charter, the Universal Declaration of Human Rights established a new world order based not only upon the reaffirmation of the Westphalian idea of sovereign equality combined with the twentieth-century foreswearing of the aggressive use of force among states, but perhaps first and foremost on the moral determination that 'recognition of the inherent dignity and of the equal and inalienable rights of all members of the human family is the foundation of freedom, justice and peace in the world'. From this last assertion flows in teleological fashion the whole compendium of the contemporary international law of human rights both at the universal and at the regional levels.

The Universal Declaration was a long time in coming and, for those who suffered and died during the Second World War, it came too late. It is perhaps a sad truth of human development that progress is far too often the child of terrible events. At least by 1945, the world had witnessed enough of such events to come to the common position that arbitrary distinctions and arbitrary rule would have to be checked by the fundamental requirements of humanity as constituted in the dignity of every human being. The world knew all too well what had gone wrong and what values ultimately need protecting. Notwithstanding some ideological distinctions which hampered the subsequent elaboration of binding human rights treaties, the Universal Declaration captured the essence and breadth of public concerns in articulating 'a common standard of achievement for all peoples and all nations'. It became, as such, the benchmark against which to judge the progress of all civilized societies.

Not surprisingly, the declaratory nature of the Univeral Declaration gave rise after 1948 to an extended period of standard-setting as the norms proclaimed in the Universal Declaration were more precisely detailed in a host of related declarations and a handful of treaties ranging from the 1951 Convention relating to the Status of Refugees (which assured safety for those fleeing persecution) to the 1989 Convention on the Rights of the Child. Of course, the principal conventional articulation of the norms of the Universal Declaration are to be found in the two Covenants of 1966. The well-known story of the division of the subject matter of the Universal Declaration into two separate treaties reflecting roughly the so-called first and second 'generations' of human rights (i.e. civil and political in the former case and economic, social and cultural in the latter case) managed to stall progress at the global level for several years. Nonetheless, the Universal Declaration was successively appearing as a fundamental reference in an ever-growing number of national constitutions. In so doing, the Universal Declaration found expression in applicable domestic law either directly or indirectly through related constitutional provisions and through specific laws.

With the catalogue of international human rights standards now quite thick and detailed, the pre-occupation of the community of human rights advocates has rightly focused increasingly on implementation. At the universal level, a half-dozen expert committees established by human rights treaties monitor the compliance by states parties with their obligations, mainly by means of scrutiny of state reports submitted on a periodic basis. More has been achieved at the regional levels of Europe and the Americas where courts have been established to judge individual and inter-state complaints. Although the oldest of these, i.e. the European Court of Human Rights, has been functioning for several decades, it is only now in the process of becoming a full-time and fully professional court. Still, while the UN treaty bodies remain very much part-time and poorly supported, they have contributed important decisions and an invaluable quasi-jurisprudence which has been noted by governments and national judicial bodies far and wide.

Perhaps the inspiration and application of the Universal Declaration is even more apparent in the many non-treaty-based mechanisms. The UN technique of appointing independent experts as 'special rapporteurs' and members of 'working groups' concerning various themes and geographical situations of human rights allows for the direct evaluation of state practices relating to the respect of human rights. While the system of special procedures which has since evolved remains still tentative and fragile, it has undeniably achieved a great deal – especially in terms of the application of the Universal Declaration. One particularly good example of this is the case of the appointment in 1992 of a UN Special Rapporteur on the situation of human rights in Myanmar (Burma); at that time, Myanmar was party to almost no human rights treaty and so the Special Rapporteur assessed the situation in the country against, *inter alia*, the Universal Declaration which he rightly characterized as giving fuller expression to the human rights obligations arising from the UN Charter. The so-called 'country mechanisms' are also capable of assessing respect of those rights articulated in the Universal Declaration which are not, or not adequately, re-articulated in human rights treaties, e.g. the right to a nationality (Article 15 of the Universal Declaration) and the right to own property (Article 17 of the Universal Declaration). From this perspective, the Universal Declaration re-mains not only the inspiration to other instruments and techniques of im-plementation, but it is also directly applied.

One of the more recent and rapidly increasing uses of the Universal Declaration is its utility as the reference point for the 'standard of achievement' relating to democracy. Specifically, the third paragraph of Article 21 of the Universal Declaration famously proclaims that 'The will of the people shall be the basis of the authority of government'. In an increasingly interdependent world, this provision is gaining importance as the arbitrariness of government in one state gives rise to resistance, instability and ultimately spill-overs affecting neighbouring states and the international community as a whole. As we witness these events within and between states, we constantly observe reaffirmed the validity of the first preambular paragraph of the Universal Declaration as quoted above, i.e. that respect for human rights 'is the foundation of freedom, justice and peace in the world'. This is not just so in relation to the critical questions of peace and justice – although it is evidently so for these questions (see my essay 'Peace and Justice, Power and Principle: From Nuremberg to The Hague', *The Finnish Yearbook of International Law*, volume VII, 1996, pp. 334-340). Recent events in the world have also demonstrated that arbitrariness and non-accountable governance is at the root of major economic crises which strike hard at the welfare of huge numbers of persons. It is interesting to note, for example, that leading politicians from some East Asian states currently in economic turmoil have attributed a main cause of their problems to the lack of 'legitimate' or 'good governance'.

In the absence of a specific 'right to democracy', Article 21 of the Universal Declaration remains the essential reference point at the global level. Certainly, the practical determination of 'legitimate' authority and 'good' governance relies to a large extent on the level of respect of a host of other human rights including especially the freedoms of thought, expression, association and assembly. It is also clear that legitimate authority is not merely that endorsed by periodic elections since these can be, have been and still are stage-managed in many states. The fundamental point (and, indeed, the controlling norm) remains that for authority to be wielded with legitimacy it must accord with, or at least be granted on the basis of, the *genuine* will of the people. This is only discernable in the context of the general respect of human rights where free-thinking and secure adults may know, consider and act upon matters of public interest. It is also *in general* a matter of human rights because it is inextricably linked to the notion that the dignity of the human being should not be subjected to the arbitrariness of power; the authority of government is exactly the manifestation of political power affecting almost all aspects of life including life itself and, as such, the individual must at least indirectly consent to such authority over his or her own life. This is a matter of consistency, the logic of which proceeds directly from the Universal Declaration.

Of course, until the end of the Cold War, it was hardly possible to bridge the ideological divide between the two main interpretations of 'legitimacy', 'democracy' and even the hierarchy and relative importance of human rights. The Cold War also prevented progress in relation to some of the more difficult subjects such as the protection of minorities. In one sense, the revolutionary nature of the

Universal Declaration was partly to be found in its insistence on the inherent dignity of *everyone* irrespective of race, colour, sex, language, religion, political or other opinion, national or social origin, property, birth or other status. It has been convincingly argued by academics that the principle of non-discrimination goes a very long way in responding to the most serious concerns of persons belonging to minorities. Indeed, the whole human rights approach as adopted by the United Nations after the Second World War arises from the extreme nationalism and racism which resulted in the oppression of minorities throughout the world and was the motivation behind the holocausts suffered by certain of them. It was the intention of the drafters of the Universal Declaration to do away with ugly and threatening distinctions which had nothing to do with the universal essence of the human experience. Not surprisingly, therefore, the Universal Declaration does not mention minorities.

Nonetheless, it was almost immediately recognized that problems involving minorities persisted. On the one hand, these problems could not be simply wished away through the language of individualism: the human being is also essentially a social being who is, in fact, dependent upon communities. But, on the other hand, it was not clear how this social dimension of the individual conceived in groups could be reconciled with the recent terrible experience or how one could avoid placing the individual beneath the oppressive yoke of the socialist collective. As a result, the UN member states charged a group of independent experts to study the matter in the UN Sub-Commission on the Prevention of Discrimination and the Protection of Minorities.

While the Sub-Commission started its work in the early days of the UN, and while numerous valuable studies have been prepared by its members, it was not until the end of the Cold War that the UN managed to develop some positive content of minority rights in the form of the 1992 UN Declaration on the Rights of Persons Belonging to National or Ethnic, Religious and Linguistic Minorities. Until then, the UN had produced (in addition to the principle of non-discrimination) essentially only one relevant provision of one treaty, i.e. Article 27 of the International Covenant on Civil and Political Rights which is formulated in a negative construction obligating states parties not to deny certain stipulated freedoms. The UN is still struggling to give additional meaningful content to those limited minority rights which have been recognized and to establish adequate supervisory mechanisms.

Within Europe, much more progress in the area of minority rights has been possible since the end of the Cold War. This is no doubt because the participating states of the Helsinki process have committed themselves since 1990 not only to respect for human rights, but moreover to democratic governance and the rule of law. On this basis, the participating states were able to elaborate an impressive positive content of minority rights in the Copenhagen Document of the Conference on the Human Dimension. These political commitments were subsequently transposed into binding obligations of international law in the form of the Framework Convention on the Protection of National Minorities as elaborated by the Council of Europe. The Universal Declaration is the ultimate inspiration for both instruments. As our understanding of the democratic process and the full extent of human needs and life in dignity becomes better developed, so we will be able to further refine the relevant standards of behaviour. In my work as High Commissioner on National Minorities of the Organization for Security and Cooperation in Europe, I have been witness to the need for such refinement. The complex problems which are often at the root of conflicts and social antagonisms causing instability within and between states can be addressed only with the assistance of a more precise understanding of international standards. The application of existing norms and standards can yield through reasoned and consistent interpretation practical solutions to many problems. This can be achieved through judicial decisions within states and through opinions provided by competent international bodies. However, policy-making can be guided in advance by a more informed understanding of the policy implications of existing norms and standards. It is in this connection that I have encouraged internationally recognized independent experts to draw up recommendations regarding the rights of national minorities in the spheres of education and the use of language. The resultant recommendations – called, respectively, The Hague Recommendations Regarding the Education Rights of National Minorities and the Oslo Recommendations Regarding the Linguistic Rights of National Minorities – proceed from and are consistent with the inspiring provisions of the Universal Declaration.

The full and progressive realization of the rights included in the Universal Declaration is, unfortunately, not a matter of certainty. There are constant challenges both to the substance and to the implementation of the Universal Declaration. Recently, the entire notion of universality has been questioned by the governmental representatives of certain states, particularly Malaysia. Aside from old arguments that the Universal Declaration and other human rights instruments were elaborated and adopted by former colonial states without the participation or acceptance of the very many states which gained independence in the last forty years, the fundamental argument is that existing human rights instruments reflect 'Western values' and, as such, fail to take account of 'Eastern' or 'Southern values' including especially collective (and even state) rights. They also propose that emphasis should be placed on second and third generation rights rather than civil and political rights. These arguments have been countered even by human rights advocates from the East and South who affirm that the values of the Universal Declaration remain those of fundamental interest to persons throughout the world (see the speech by Dato' Param Cumaraswamy, 'The Universal Declaration of Human Rights: Is It Universal?', published in the *Human Rights Law Journal*, volume 18, 1997, no. 5-8). It may also be observed that no state has dissociated itself from the Universal Declaration while an increasing number have ratified the various treaties; e.g., over 190 states are now party to the Convention on the Rights of the Child. This would seem to indicate that, as a matter of positive international law, the norms and standards of the Universal Declaration as further articulated in specific treaties are increasingly (rather than decreasingly) *universal*. This is to say nothing of the Vienna Declaration and Programme of Action of June 1993 by which some 170 UN member states participating in the World Conference on Human Rights expressly reaffirmed the universality of all human rights and emphasized 'that the Universal Declaration of Human Rights, which constitutes a common standard of achievement for all peoples and nations, is the source of inspiration and has been the basis for the United Nations in making advances in standard setting as contained in the existing international human rights instruments'.

Another recent challenge to the Universal Declaration comes in the form of a new discussion about the responsibilities of individuals. These so-called 'human responsibilities' (as opposed to 'human rights') are no doubt inspired by the current concern especially in the Western world about the dissolution of 'community values' and the atomization of society. While there is much to be considered in these concerns, one is wary of solutions which impose duties on individuals vis-à-vis the state, their families, their neighbours, and even themselves. How are these to be implemented? And how is one to be protected against abuse by relevant authorities? Certainly, everyone is obliged to respect the rule of law. But the Universal Declaration and all of human rights have been developed to limit the extent to which the overwhelming and often anonymous power of the state may weigh upon the individual to the detriment of his or her dignity. It does not follow from existing social problems that the state needs to be protected through imposition of further duties on individuals or, in other terms, the reduction of individual liberties and rights.

The Universal Declaration and all that it has inspired aims to ensure a minimum respect for the dignity of everyone. It foresees and implies a certain socio-political order which is open and relatively free. It does require the rule of law. But human beings may choose within that freedom to develop their talents and organise their lives in community with others; the Universal Declaration stands as a bulwark against the abuse of authority by the state. It also points the way to the fuller development of society in justice and in peace, and so it merits reading and reading again. The full content of such an order respectful of all human rights is open-ended. Its full realization may well depend upon some enlightened political leadership, but, ultimately, it depends upon the vigilance of each of us. In this sense, the Universal Declaration remains as current, as strong and as fragile as it did when it was proclaimed fifty years ago.

Article 28

Everyone is entitled to a social and international order in which the rights and freedoms set forth in this Declaration can be fully realized.

The Universal Declaration and the Media

Eleanor Roosevelt said it best: 'Promoting respect for human rights is a fulfilling – but never fulfilled – obligation'. And today, as we celebrate the 50th anniversary of the Universal Declaration of Human Rights, we should reflect on how much this exalted doctrine has changed the principles by which we are judged. No clearer statement of man's visceral yearning of freedom has ever been penned.

In 1948, nations came together to establish a series of provisos which would define the basic standards of protection for human rights, dignity and freedom. Fifty years later, through a series of trials and tribulations, wars and conflicts, détentes and reconciliations, we, citizens of the world, have come to crystallize the truth and depth of the Universal Declaration. Most notably, we have witnessed the remarkable end of the Cold War and the emergence of new nations which are grappling to define constitutional rights and freedoms. Inevitably, they will look to the Universal Declaration to map out their intriguing futures.

At a time in history when the world is rapidly being transformed into a global village, it is important to particularly note Article 19 of the Universal Declaration which states that all people should be free to '... receive and impart information and ideas through any media and regardless of frontiers'. In the coming millennium, we should be cognizant of the reality that free flow of information will be the catalyst to change for the few vestiges of authoritarianism. It is a freedom which should be cherished and protected with earnest and unwavering certitude.

We have come far. But by no means are we finished. On this historic anniversary, let us acknowledge the profundity of our achievements while we aim for no less than absolute freedom and dignity for human kind. After all, when even a few of us remain in chains, who alone can say he is truly free?

LECH WAŁĘSA

Faith, Hope and Charity

This year it is fifty years since the adoption of the Universal Declaration of Human Rights. The golden jubilee – a fine anniversary, and an occasion not only for celebration, but also for reflection. I would like to share some of my reflections with you.

As we know, a human being is entitled to human rights merely by virtue of the fact that he or she is a human being, not because these rights have been conferred by the power of law. Human rights are universal and inalienable. Hence they have a history that goes back long before 1948 – a history that reaches back to the beginnings of the human race.

What exactly are we celebrating this year? We are observing the anniversary of an international agreement that tells us we must recognise the universality of human rights. Have we been successful in this? Unfortunately not. Whole tracts of the globe do not observe these rights.

Let us look at part of the preamble:

> Whereas recognition of the inherent dignity and of the equal and inalienable rights of all members of the human family is the foundation of freedom, justice and peace in the world,

> Whereas disregard and contempt for human rights have resulted in barbarous acts which have outraged the conscience of mankind, and the advent of a world in which human beings shall enjoy freedom of speech and belief and freedom from fear and want has been proclaimed as the highest aspiration of the common people,

> Whereas it is essential, if man is not to be compelled to have recourse, as a last resort, to rebellion against tyranny and oppression, that human rights should be protected by the rule of law.

For the whole of my adult life I have campaigned for human rights. And I have noticed a strange phenomenon. Since human rights are universal, they do not bear the mark of politics. However, there are human rights campaigners who are politically committed. I have noticed that the main source of pressure to observe human rights is moving from the Left to the Right. There was a time when the struggle for these rights was founded on the ideology of the Left, but now it has shifted to the Right. The Communists' attitude to human rights is not insignificant in this regard. Seven Communist states (including Poland) abstained from voting on the Universal Declaration. More than a hundred million people paid with their lives for that earthly embodiment of the left-wing utopia – more than were consumed by two World Wars.

But it is also difficult to overestimate the importance of the fact that the faithful have changed their attitude to human rights. If you are convinced that man was formed in the image and likeness of God, then it is easy to accept that by virtue merely of existing you are entitled to a right to life, liberty and security (Article 3). It is somehow automatically understood that human beings are born free and equal in dignity and rights (Article 1). I am thoroughly convinced that the Universal Declaration of Human Rights is in harmony with and underpinned by natural law.

It is precisely this shift in the political complexion of social sensibility which seems to me most characteristic of the last half century – the half century of the Universal Declaration of Human Rights. It shows that politics is not (and cannot be) judged only according to expediency. No politician has the freedom to ignore expediency, but politics is above all the realisation of values. I have fought for this view of politics all my life and that is why I have fought for human rights, guided all along by the three theological virtues: faith, hope and charity.

NEVZAT ÇELIK

Sleep and Torture

put your hand on my forehead when I sleep
wet your hand in cool water put on my forehead
protect me from the horror of my dreams
I say I would rather die in a carnation's delicateness
I say I would rather walk shaping my shadow
I keep being a dry tree all day long
probably I would fight against the thief who sneaks into my house
do protect me against the government that would come to protect me
with all your health with all your beauty
just think of you sleeping by me
just think of me sleeping by you
they are taking me away from your scent from your skin
just think they are shooting me every night

wet your hand in cool water put on my forehead
they are shooting breaking throwing me
a flower a bird walked to the painting
a banana a vase a broken watermelon
my body they killed
not as clear as a color contrast
my face is covered with a newspaper page
they are holding my arm and dragging me
I hear a rustling but my flesh doesn't hurt
I say this is the end finally the end
whenever I say this is the end
a pair of wings under my arms
I am turning back to my being silent all day

wet your hand in cool water put on my forehead
please understand my being silent all day
my being longtime silent the hoarseness of my voice
the sentence gets dirty when you spell it out yet
I am turning back to my being silent all day
call me my darling I like the way you call me my darling

look at me as a mother would
take good care of me with the fear of loosing
take back the carnation you had put into water back in the evening time
get among my screams hold me
tell me it will pass tell me it will end tell me it will be
console me as you'd console a child growing up
in mountain villages with the hope of a bicycle

JAAP WALKATE

Torture: Zero Tolerance!

> *No one shall be subjected to torture or to cruel, inhuman or degrading treatment or punishment.*
>
> Universal Declaration of Human Rights, Article 5

THE PROHIBITION OF TORTURE: PART OF INTERNATIONAL LAW

In the hierarchy of the Universal Declaration of Human Rights – if any such hierarchy exists – the right not to be subjected to torture or cruel, inhuman or degrading treatment or punishment is the third most important right, directly following the right to life, liberty and security of person and the right not to be held in slavery or servitude. It is, of course, closely related to these rights.

The Universal Declaration places a strong *moral obligation* on all member states of the United Nations – including those not present when the Declaration was adopted in 1948 – to follow up and implement the rights contained therein. The word 'moral' was used by the drafters themselves.

However, in the UN context a moral obligation also becomes a *political obligation*, both for member states individually and for the UN as an international organization. The Universal Declaration has been carefully elaborated in two treaties (covenants) which confer a *legal obligation* on those member states that ratify them to incorporate the treaties into their domestic legislation. The prohibition of torture enshrined in Article 5 of the Universal Declaration has been incorporated into Article 7 of the International Covenant on Civil and Political Rights (1966), a formal treaty which has been ratified by 140 states parties.

Moreover, Article 5 – like many articles of the Universal Declaration – has become the subject of a specific declaration and a specific convention and has been elaborated or cited in other declarations, codes and resolutions of the UN. As such, the prohibition of torture and other cruel, inhuman or degrading punishment or treatment has become very much part of (binding) international law. The most important instruments in this context are: the UN Declaration on the Protection of All Persons from Being Subjected to Torture and Other Cruel, Inhuman or Degrading Treatment or Punishment (1975), the UN Principles of Medical Ethics relevant to the Role of Health Personnel, particularly Physicians, in the Protection of Prisoners and Detainees against Torture and Other Cruel, Inhuman or Degrading Treatment or Punishment (1982), and the UN Convention against Torture and Other Cruel, Inhuman or Degrading Treatment or Punishment (1984) which entered into force on 26 June 1987 and has been ratified by 105 states. On 12 December 1997, the UN General Assembly proclaimed 26 June as annual UN International Day in Support of Victims of Torture.

The UN has done everything in its power to act firmly against torture and maltreatment, and to create conditions for their total eradication. The Convention against Torture, for example, has labelled torture a form of international crime that can be prosecuted by any state party in whose territory the perpetrator is found (Article 7).

TORTURE IS WIDELY PRACTISED

While the prohibition and unlawfulness of torture and maltreatment are fully guaranteed by solemn international declarations and treaties, the reality in many countries is still a far cry from this. Reports on the occurrence of torture and maltreatment in detention centers are numerous and appalling. Newspaper articles, reports by non-governmental organizations, such as Amnesty International, reports by the Special Rapporteur on Torture and other Special Rapporteurs – and piles of them exist – all indicate that torture and maltreatment are widely practised in the majority of UN member states.

The reports I receive – as a member of the Board of Trustees of the UN Fund for Victims of Torture – from the various treatment centers for torture victims around the world keep me in touch with reality. In some countries, torture is actually institutionalized, with training centers for torturers and specially designed torture technology, sometimes developed in highly industrialized countries. It would be inappropriate to discuss torture methods here, because they are the products of utterly sick and depraved minds. And every year I am shocked to read about new techniques that have been 'scientifically' developed with the purpose of doing more damage to the individual concerned and of making rehabilitation more difficult.

In this context it should be pointed out that existing cultural patterns accepting the use of force, violence, brutality or even bestiality have an enormous and direct influence on police practices and lax government policies. Violence breeds violence. The enforcement of international law under such domestic circumstances may be difficult and require more than the enactment of national legislation; an active hands-on policy to discourage the use of force may be needed. But governments often use the cultural context – including religious aspects – as a pretext for non-compliance with their international obligations. Such pretexts are simply unacceptable.

Ignorance about the rights of detainees fosters acceptance of violations of these rights; where there is ignorance, there will be no protests about abuses. Tolerance of police brutality leads to more of the same, especially when the police are less interested in finding the truth than in arresting someone, preferably someone who confesses to the crime, guilty or not.

THE PRECEDENCE OF INTERNATIONAL LAW

What can we do to improve protection?

First and foremost, we must continue to emphasize the precedence of international law over domestic law. The interpretation and implementation of international law along the lines of domestic law or religious convictions is not acceptable and goes against the grain of the very international order which brought forth the Universal Declaration. It would have each of us march to the beat of a different drummer.

Let us also uphold the Universal Declaration as the pillar of a just international order as envisaged by the Charter of the United Nations. Chapter IX (Article 55) of the UN Charter clearly relates the universal respect for, and observance of, human rights to higher standards of living, full employment and conditions of economic and social progress and development. Should not every individual, regardless of place of birth and class, race, nationality, political opinion, religion and sex, enjoy the rights and fundamental freedoms of the Universal Declaration? Why should we treat the enjoyment of such rights as a privilege of the happy few while the Universal Declaration speaks of 'everyone'? This is not only unjust, because it violates the notion that all men are created equal, but it is also unwise, because it keeps people from developing their talents and, therefore, their country. People in shackles are a millstone around their government's neck and an obstacle to progress. Indeed, countries that have endeavored to live up to the norms and principles of the Universal Declaration and to strictly enforce human rights and fundamental freedoms have done well in terms of social and economic development.

TORTURE POLICIES MUST BE DENOUNCED

Governments that deny their people adequate protection from the abuse of power should not be allowed to continue doing so with impunity. Non-compliance with international human rights norms and rules must be denounced.

The mobilization of public shame is still a viable instrument to maintain international law and to shock the accused government, as it were, into compliance. It has its effects. Nobody likes to be exposed publicly, governments being no exception. UN resolutions on human rights violations are detested by the governments concerned. When accused of misconduct, most governments protest their innocence. At best they show embarrassment and promise to do better. In such cases Article 5 of the Universal Declaration is recognized as the prevailing norm. This in itself is encouraging because it means that these governments implicitly accept the underlying norms and rules. Were they to turn their backs and shrug off the rebuke, they would place themselves outside the normative system.

The European Union (EU) too feels very strongly about human rights, and generally includes the topic in the agendas of consultations with third countries, citing the various declarations the EU member states have adopted on human rights. No country with a poor human rights record will escape close scrutiny of its performance in its dealings with the EU. In such dialogues, domestic problems are sometimes raised that may hinder full implementation. What is most important is that the subject is actually discussed. If the government concerned shows the political will to improve its record, then many possibilies open up, including suggesting ways of improvement.

First, governments engaged in an active policy to eradicate the practice of torture should make sure that this policy is widely known. It should be publicized in all police stations, detention centers and, where applicable, military barracks, and it should be enforced by all commissioned officers and officials. No one should be left in any doubt that perpetrators will be brought to justice. The message to the public must be clear: torture is not an instrument of policy of the government and shall not be tolerated under any circumstances. No excuses accepted, no exceptions made, no impunity granted. In short: *zero tolerance!*

Everyone must be held responsible for his or her own deeds – as laid down in the Convention against Torture. There are *no excuses*: an order from a superior officer or a public authority may not be invoked as a justification of torture (Article 2). *No exceptions* will be made because under international law, as expressed in the International Covenant on Civil and Political Rights (Article 4) and the Convention against Torture (Article 2), no derogation from the no-torture rule is allowed, not even in the case of a public emergency that threatens the life of the nation, such as war, civil strife or terrorism. Furthermore, *no impunity* should be granted to the perpetrators of torture. They should have no hope of escaping justice, and suffering of torture victims should not be prolonged by the knowledge that their torturers are still at large, or soon will be.

Second, an intensive campaign should be launched at all levels in the hierarchy of the military forces and police organizations to educate and train their members in the correct treatment of detained people. The distribution of texts is important, but training in how to read and to apply them is more important still. Ignorance may not be used as a pretext for non-compliance by law enforcement officials.

Third, of equal importance is the need to educate the general public so that people understand the rights they possess and are able to claim them. This is the most difficult undertaking, especially in countries with low literacy levels: to adopt a different mentality and to learn new ideas and concepts is often quite the opposite of what people are used to. In accepting a degree of brutality in police operations (arrest and detention) the victims of such brutality are, cynical as it may sound, 'part of the problem', in that they do not object to the violation of their integrity by law enforcement officials. In order to be able to protest about such actions they have to know their rights.

In this respect I fervently hope that the declaration the UN is currently drafting on human rights defenders will be adopted by the General Assembly on the occasion of the 50th anniversary of the Universal Declaration. This would also be a boost for the Declaration itself!

OPTIONAL PROTOCOL ON THE ABOLITION OF CORPORAL PUNISHMENT

There is another subject which merits attention in this context: corporal punishment. The Universal Declaration does not mention corporal punishment or the death penalty. Both are in my opinion aggravated forms of torture or of cruel, inhuman and degrading punishment. The International Covenant on Civil and Political Rights mentions the death penalty as a lawful sanction if certain conditions are fulfilled, but there is no reference to corporal punishment. In the meantime, however, an Optional Protocol on the abolition of the death penalty has been added to the Covenant. It would make sense for a similar addition to the Convention on Torture: an Optional Protocol on the abolition of corporal punishment.

There are many references to the unlawfulness of corporal punishment in international documents, such as: the Geneva Conventions (1949) and the Protocols Additional thereto (1977), the Standard Minimum Rules for the Treatment of Prisoners (1957/1977), the Principles of Medical Ethics relevant to the Role of Health Personnel, particularly Physicians, in the Protection of Prisoners and Detainees against Torture and Other Cruel, Inhuman or Degrading Treatment or Punishment (1982), the general comment of the Human Rights Committee on Article 7 of the International Covenant on Civil and Political Rights, and case law of the organs of the European Convention on Human Rights (1950) that could be used to formulate a new protocol. Such a protocol would give lawyers, judges, prison governors and others a good idea of the cases in which corporal punishment – such as lashes with a whip, rod or cane, the amputation of limbs, blinding or stoning, and the use of chains and fetters – is considered unlawful punishment. It may be clear from this that I do not consider the forms of corporal punishment mentioned above to be 'lawful sanctions' under domestic law, as referred to by way of exception in the last sentence of Article 1 of the Convention against Torture.

However, I fully realize how difficult such an undertaking will be, given the opposition it will encounter from countries that practise corporal punishment as a sanction under national and/or religious law. It will be as difficult as the drafting and adoption of the Second Optional Protocol to the Covenant on Civil and Political Rights, aimed at the abolition of the death penalty. The latter Optional Protocol, adopted by the UN General Assembly in 1989 and ratified by more than 30 states parties, clearly sets an international norm with regard to the protection of human dignity and integrity. An optional protocol on the abolition of corporal punishment would do the same and would be a welcome additional instrument to promote the full implementation of Article 5 of the Universal Declaration.

THE REHABILITATION OF TORTURE VICTIMS

The systematic use of maltreatment all over the world produces a large number of victims who have been seriously traumatized and are in urgent need of psychological, medical and other assistance in order to overcome the effects of torture. We do not know the exact number of victims, but there must be hundreds of thousands; we do not know the exact cost of the necessary treatment and assistance, but it runs into tens of millions of dollars. Fortunately, there are small and medium-sized centers for the treatment of torture victims in many different countries, staffed by physicians, psychologists, lawyers and social workers, often on a voluntary basis. What is needed is money to assist the survivors of torture and their families.

The UN General Assembly assumed a form of collective responsibility for the rehabilitation of torture victims by establishing a Fund in 1981 to receive contributions for the distribution, through established channels of assistance, of humanitarian, legal and financial aid. This Fund depends entirely on voluntary contributions from governments, private organizations, institutions and individuals. It does not receive any financial support from the regular UN budget. Over the past 16 years a group of donor states have contributed to the Fund annually. This has enabled the Fund to establish a system for the equitable distribution of the funds to a great number of treatment centers in a variety of countries. Many centers are located in countries where victims have sought refuge (which accounts for the number of centers in Western countries), but at the same time many centers have been set up in countries where torture is practised. This may pose specific problems. In one country, for instance, medical doctors treating torture victims face arrest by government agents and are often forced to reveal their patients' names to the authorities so that they can take action against these victims and their families.

The staff of treatment centers often find it hard to cope with the mind-boggling stories of their patients. Having to do so puts them under a constant strain. It is not uncommon for both staff member and victim to break down during treatment, when the victim's emotions are relived. The staff work under horrendous pressure, with too many clients, little money, and too little time. The accommodation at these centers – I speak from personal experience – is generally very modest. Sometimes the staff members themselves have been torture victims, which gives them a special drive and – more importantly – special expertise. This is not work that can be done by any medical doctor or psychologist. It takes special training to make the right diagnosis. Often highly refined methods of torture have been applied, which leave no physical scars. However, the deeper the wounds of mind and soul, the more difficult it is to assess the patient's statements. Moreover, victims do not always admit to having been tortured, often being ashamed of what has occurred (in the case of sexual torture, for instance) or of the fact that they succumbed and 'confessed'. This is why training seminars and conferences are organized by professional associations or well-established centers, such as the Rehabilitation Center for

Torture Victims in Copenhagen, Denmark, to disseminate knowledge on special methods for effective treatment.

UN FUND WELCOMES DONATIONS

As Chairman of the Board of Trustees of the Fund, I am most grateful for the initiative taken by the former Minister for Foreign Affairs of the Netherlands, Mr Hans van Mierlo, to publish this commemorative book, part of the revenue from which will flow into the Fund. Financial contributions (whatever the amount) are most welcome, and anyone – not only governments – can make a donation. The Fund is in constant need of money. So far it has been unable to honor more than 50 percent of the requests received from treatment centers. Associations, charitable institutions, churches, schools, all of them may help by organizing activities to raise money for the UN Fund or to sponsor one or more centers and hence give more direct financial support. The UN International Day in Support of Victims of Torture to be held annually on 26 June provides an appropriate occasion for fundraising activities.

As long as torture persists – and long thereafter – professional help will be badly needed because the effects, as we now know, take a long time to heal, sometimes even more than an entire generation. The Fund will need our support for a very long time to come!

1. Everyone has duties to the community in which alone the free and full development of his personality is possible.
2. In the exercise of his rights and freedoms, everyone shall be subject only to such limitations as are determined by law solely for the purpose of securing due recognition and respect for the rights and freedoms of others and of meeting the just requirements of morality, public order and the general welfare in a democratic society.
3. These rights and freedoms may in no case be exercised contrary to the purposes and principles of the United Nations.

HALIMA WARZAZI

'Impossible n'est pas marocain'

When I left Cairo University in 1957, my degree in my hand, I had not yet heard of the Universal Declaration of Human Rights. Having done almost all my studying in French, the only declaration I knew anything about was the French Declaration of the Rights of Man and of the Citizen of 1789 while, from childhood, the Islamic faith had taught me to observe the limits that allow the members of the society in which I grew up to live in peace and harmony with each other. I had also learnt that for a Muslim, life is the most precious possession we have and that the protection of life and the well-being and peace of mind of the individual are all-important. The boundaries of good and evil are clearcut, and each of us has a duty to show respect for others in our daily lives and the right to expect the same from them.

Today we call it human rights, but for me, at that time, these were maxims that I had had instilled in me from the cradle. What is more, they were laws that must not be broken. That was all I knew about rights, be they women's rights, children's rights, the rights of the elderly, the poor or people in general.

It was when I arrived at the United Nations in 1959 that I first heard of the Universal Declaration of Human Rights and embarked on a long career in the field of human rights. In the circumstances, it could scarcely have turned out otherwise. Following the paternalist logic of governments determined to demonstrate their progressive views by appointing women delegates, mine had, quite naturally, appointed me to the Third Committee of the General Assembly, the 'Women's Committee' as it was then mockingly called. And yet, speaking of women, the overwhelming majority of delegates were men. For almost three months, these men studied social, cultural and humanitarian issues which had nothing to do with ribbons and lace.

I was struck even then, in 1959, by the fact that while these issues may seem anodyne, each delegate saw them in the light of his or her own civilisation, culture, faith and, especially, ideological affinities. Accordingly, these were highly politicised questions which gave rise to endless controversy and discussion, notably on matters relating to human rights.

During these ideological battles, the Universal Declaration served as a frame of reference when it was necessary to find common ground or justify a conflicting opinion. The fact that it had been adopted so enthusiastically by the member states in 1948, with only eight unfortunate abstentions, and had acquired ever more declarations of support over the years was ample justification for our use of it in this way.

As country after country declared independence they made it their duty to acknowledge the Universal Declaration in their constitutions. Moreover, from 1960 onwards, with more and more African and Asian delegates arriving at the United Nations, it was pressed into the service of the new member states which were keen to participate in the management of world affairs but had decided first to persuade the Organisation to address all the problems affecting them, which had been virtually ignored or overlooked since 1948.

Racial discrimination and apartheid in particular (which became official policy in 1948) were anathema to the countries described collectively at the time as the Third World. They took as their starting point Article 2 of the Universal Declaration which proclaims that everyone is entitled to all the rights and freedoms set out therein without distinction of any kind, such as race, colour or national origin.

The International Convention on the Elimination of All Forms of Racial Discrimination and the International Convention on the Suppression and Punishment of the Crime of Apartheid refer, incidentally, to Articles 1 and 2 of the Declaration in the second paragraph of their preambles. The fight against apartheid came to an end just recently. Regrettably, the fight against racism and its new forms must continue. Hence the decision of the General Assembly at its 52nd session (1997) to convene a World Conference which between now and 2001 will address these intractable problems. Part of the Conference's mandate is to chart the progress made in the fight against racism, racial discrimination, xenophobia and racial intolerance, particularly since the adoption of the Universal Declaration.

The Universal Declaration of Human Rights played an unprecedented role in the formulation of the international human rights covenants. It was the torch that lit up the long road, strewn with traps and obstacles, which the international community had decided to take in order to achieve the goals it had set itself in the wake of the Declaration's adoption.

In 1966 when I was elected chair of the Third Committee at the 21st session of the UN General Assembly, the draft covenants which had started life in May–June 1949 in the Commission on Human Rights had in the course of those seventeen years been passed to and fro countless times between the Commission on Human Rights, the Economic and Social Council (ECOSOC) and the General Assembly. At the time I did not realise that in my new capacity I would be contributing to the start of a new era, both in the field of human rights and with regard to the deeply rooted traditions of the United Nations.

I thus became the first female chair of the Third Committee from a Third World country. I was also the youngest and most junior person ever to hold the post, being at the time a mere counsellor and a long way down the ladder from the post of ambassador. Despite being a woman and despite my youth, I knew what I wanted and lacked neither the will nor the strength of character to get it. Those who thought they detected an air of vulnerability in my smile and my traditional women's clothing soon changed their minds, beginning with the secretary of the Committee and Mr Schreiber, the director of human rights, who were supposed to assist and advise me during the entire session.

I remember shortly after assuming the chair of the Third Committee asking Mr Schreiber, who turned out to be a very pleasant person, what the most important point on our agenda was. '*Point 62 on the draft international human rights covenants or, to be more precise, the articles concerning the implementation of each of the two covenants and the final clauses*', he replied, '*but it's an extremely difficult matter and will need a lot more time*'. '*A lot more time*', I said. '*Okay, we'll have them ready by the end of this session.*' I realise, looking back, that I had absolutely no idea of the magnitude of the task awaiting me. Mr Schreiber was dumbstruck for a moment, then said: '*But that's impossible!*'. Still unsuspecting, I silenced him by echoing Napoleon's famous words: '*Impossible n'est pas marocain*'.

And that is how, one fine morning, I came to submit point 62 on our agenda to the Third Committee, while emphasising the importance of the draft covenants which translated the principles of the Universal Declaration of Human Rights into formal legal obligations and appropriate means of international implementation. The negotiations took two months. Armed with the Universal Declaration and the precious rules of procedure, I chaired one stormy debate after another, made all the more difficult by countless noisy points of order.

I often wondered, when things got difficult, what on earth I was doing there. I made the Committee meet two or even three times a day. From the beginning, the members of the drafting group would meet on Saturdays and Sundays. I would go and sit in a corner with a book while they talked for hours on end. I wanted to give them my moral support as they worked through the weekend. The days passed and progress was slow, but I refused to give in to the feelings of exhaustion, confusion, weariness, impatience and doubt.

We had to finish off these drafts once and for all, and produce the covenants that would address the weighty concerns of the ordinary person, now that the great of the world had enshrined their priorities in the Universal Declaration of Human Rights. I was determined above all to achieve this goal by playing all the trumps I had to the greatest effect in the service of this cause. I did indeed enjoy the support and solidarity of the delegates from the Third World countries, since I was one of them. Even so, the majority of them had always been very susceptible to the pressures and arguments put forward by the socialist delegates who, we should not forget, had little sympathy for the draft covenant on civil and political rights.

In addition, ever since my arrival at the UN, I had cultivated solid friendships with both the European delegations and the representatives of certain socialist countries. These friendships proved to be of inestimable value during the two months of negotiations, enabling me to follow step by step everything that was being discussed and decided among the Europeans and the socialists. Forewarned, I could thus counter every delaying tactic and every manoeuvre or motion that would have jeopardised the completion of the draft covenants.

Both covenants were adopted unanimously on 16 December 1966, embodying the principles set out in the Universal Declaration and, by codifying them, ensuring that they would be universally implemented. It should be said, nonetheless, that the Universal Declaration of Human Rights is unique among its kind. It has been the source of inspiration for all the human rights standards that have enriched international law since 1948. The fight against oppression, domination, exploitation, racism, sexism, torture, intolerance – religious or otherwise – slavery in all its forms, old and new, and extreme poverty has drawn strength from it, a fight that has been waged in the name of hundreds of millions of human beings, and especially the most vulnerable groups in society, and is still continuing today.

Today, the Universal Declaration of Human Rights is an international code of conduct, reflected in numerous constitutions and in legislation. It is the mainstay of those who thirst for justice and are fighting for human rights. Its fiftieth anniversary will be celebrated all over the world. But this old lady still has a difficult task on her hands: to guide fresh generations towards a more peaceful, tolerant, just and generous – in a word, a more human – world.

Article 30

Nothing in this Declaration may be interpreted as implying for any State, group or person any right to engage in any activity or to perform any act aimed at the destruction of any of the rights and freedoms set forth herein.

DAVID WEISSBRODT

Reminiscences on
the Universal Declaration of Human Rights

I recall my first acquaintance with the Universal Declaration of Human Rights in 1960. I was in the tenth grade at a school in Stockbridge, Massachusetts, which had an inscription over the portals of the front door: 'All human beings are born free and equal in dignity and rights. Universal Declaration of Human Rights, Article 1'. That lesson was reinforced by my school chores. Every morning I awoke early to raise the United States and the United Nations flags in front of the school. But my school classes never mentioned the Universal Declaration and I was unaware of the remainder of its content.

My education on the Universal Declaration of Human Rights continued in 1968 when I participated in the first human rights course at the University of California at Berkeley under the leadership of Professor Frank Newman and with the partici- pation of Professors Thomas Buergenthal, Egon Schwelb, and Karel Vasak. Among the students in that class were Dinah Shelton who now teaches human rights at Notre Dame University and Jon van Dyke who teaches international law, including human rights, at Hawaii University. That course taught me about the Declaration's provenance, content, context, and its overall impact. For example, I learned that the primary human rights document is not the Universal Declaration of 1948, but the United Nations Charter of 1945.

It seemed that the Universal Declaration had entered the pantheon of core inspirational utterances of humankind, along with the Ten Commandments, the Sermon on the Mount, the Magna Charta, the US Declaration of Independence, and the French Declaration of the Rights of Man and of the Citizen. During the era of the late 1960s, US citizens were questioning the wisdom of their government's actions, particularly in South East Asia, but also at home. The Universal Declaration and its progeny represented an alternative source of law, inspiration, and action. During the student turmoil of Berkeley in 1968, the Universal Declaration seemed particularly prescient in providing that 'it is essential, if man is not to be compelled to have recourse, as a last resort, to rebellion against tyranny and oppression, that human rights should be protected by the rule of law ....' In my first enthusiastic response to the full text of the Universal Declaration, however, I ignored its occasionally sexist language and its very broad exclusions in Articles 29 and 30.

I was aware that the Declaration omitted monitoring and enforcement pro- visions. Following adoption of the Universal Declaration, the UN Commission on Human Rights drafted the Covenant on Economic, Social and Cultural Rights, the

Covenant on Civil and Political Rights, and an Optional Protocol to the latter Covenant. These three treaties were adopted by the General Assembly in 1966 and entered into force in 1976. The International Bill of Human Rights, which includes the Universal Declaration and the three treaties, comprises the most authoritative, comprehensive, and nearly contemporaneous interpretation of the human rights obligations that governments undertake in joining the UN. It also contains provisions which have been recognized as reflective of customary international law.

After graduating from law school, I had several opportunities to apply aspects of the Universal Declaration in my work. While clerking for the Supreme Court of California, I encouraged the court to use the Universal Declaration, for example, in interpreting the concept of vested rights under California law. While there have been some additional efforts to use the Universal Declaration and other international human rights law in US courts over the past 30 years, there still has been no really successful use of international human rights law to protect the rights of people in the United States.

My spouse and I were privileged to work for a year with Niall MacDermot at the International Commission of Jurists in Geneva where we cited the Universal Declaration in appeals to governments which had violated human rights and which had not yet ratified relevant human rights treaties. For example, we cited the Universal Declaration in dealing with the events in East Pakistan during 1971-72 which ultimately created Bangladesh.

Upon returning to the USA, I became active in Amnesty International, which in those days used the Universal Declaration of Human Rights almost exclusively as its basis for appeals on behalf of prisoners of conscience and to end torture. As a volunteer lawyer and then a professor I had a chance to use the Declaration in representing people fleeing from repression in such countries as South Africa and Chile.

Moreover, I had the opportunity to testify in Congress in favor of US ratification of the two Covenants which arose from the Universal Declaration. I explained to the Senate Foreign Relations Committee that the two Covenants distinguish between implementation of civil and political rights, on the one hand, and economic, social, and cultural rights, on the other. Unlike the latter rights, the former are immediately enforceable. For instance, governments that ratify the Covenants must immediately cease torturing the residents of their countries, but they are not immediately required to feed, clothe, and house them. These latter obligations are generally to be accomplished only progressively as resources permit. However, certain provisions of the Covenant on Economic, Social and Cultural Rights require immediate implementation, for example, the prohibition of discrimination and the freedom of scientific research and creative activity under Article 15(3).

Furthermore, I explained to the Senate that after completing the International Bill of Human Rights, the United Nations has drafted, promulgated, and now helps to implement more than 80 human rights treaties, declarations, and other instruments which provide greater specificity to the Universal Declaration. They extend to subjects such as genocide, racial discrimination, discrimination against women, religious intolerance, the rights of disabled persons, the right to development, and the rights of the child. Human rights law has thus become the most codified domain of international law.

As a human rights advocate and teacher, I have been able to use the Universal Declaration both directly and indirectly. On a number of occasions I have served as an international trial observer and human rights factfinder in such countries as Canada, Congo, Guinea, Guyana, Hong Kong, Kenya, Malaysia, the Philippines, and the USA. Several of these trials failed to comply with the essential guarantee in Article 11 of the Declaration which provides: 'Everyone charged with a penal offence has the right to be presumed innocent until proved guilty according to law in a public trial at which he has had all the guarantees necessary for his defence'.

On the 40th anniversary of the Universal Declaration in 1988, the University of Minnesota Human Rights Center was inaugurated. Two of its principal activities have been particularly related to education about the Universal Declaration: the Partners in Human Rights Education Program and the University of Minnesota Human Rights Library on the World Wide Web.

The Partners Program, a joint initiative of the Human Rights Center and Minnesota Advocates for Human Rights, was established in 1992. It has provided human rights training to school teachers, lawyers, and community members including law students, who have taught human rights and responsibilities to children in Minnesota, the Dakotas, and Wisconsin through hands-on Community Action Projects. The Center, through Human Rights USA, is now trying to bring its human rights education model to a larger number of communities to achieve a new level of awareness about the relevance and meaning of human rights in the United States, and to foster citizen action to guarantee these rights, particularly during the 50th anniversary of the Universal Declaration. The Partners Program is beginning to provide the human rights education for students which I found lacking in my own education years ago.

The University of Minnesota Human Rights Library on the World Wide Web (http://www.umn.edu/humanrts) was established in 1995 in response to the growing availability of Internet throughout the world, particularly in universities and nongovernmental human rights organizations. Indeed, electronic mail has become an indispensable tool for sharing information and for initiating extremely quick responses to human rights crises. While scholars and advocates in the developing world have trouble in acquiring expensive books, they are getting computers which are already necessary in their work. The Human Rights Library contains the Universal Declaration of Human Rights in several languages as well as a core collection of many human rights treaties, jurisprudence, and other materials from the United Nations, the Inter-American Commission on Human Rights, the Inter-American Court of Human Rights, the Organization for Security and Cooperation in Europe, the African Commission on Human and Peoples' Rights, and other sources. In addition, the site provides links to a wide range of inter-governmental and nongovernmental organizations dedicated to international human rights. The Human Rights Library has made this collection available 24-hours per day, seven days per week, without charge on the Internet through the World Wide Web. Thousands of people each week from over 100 nations read, download, and print these documents at the push of a button.

My latest opportunity to apply the Universal Declaration has occurred in connection with my service, since 1995, as a member of the UN Sub-Commission on Prevention of Discrimination and Protection of Minorities. In its earliest years the Sub-Commission assisted in drafting the International Bill of Human Rights and other human rights instruments inspired by the Universal Declaration. In more recent years it has contributed to the implementation of human rights by monitoring indigenous rights through its Working Group on Indigenous Populations, by developing a more profound understanding of minority rights through its Working Group on Minorities, and by identifying governments which have engaged in gross violations of human rights.

The Sub-Commission is only one of many human rights procedures and bodies established under the authority of the United Nations Charter for monitoring the implementation of the Universal Declaration and other human rights law. Moreover, six treaty bodies have been established which professionally and painstakingly monitor the implementation of human rights. These treaty bodies regularly review reports by states parties as to their compliance with the respective treaties. Most of them issue general comments and recommendations that reflect their experience in reviewing the states reports and thus provide authoritative interpretations of the treaty provisions. The treaty bodies also issue conclusions as to each state report that provide useful interpretive indications. Further, three treaty bodies may receive communications complaining about violations of those treaties and thus issue adjudicative decisions interpreting and applying treaty provisions to individuals.

To the jaundiced eye of the person in the street, however, these international implementation techniques may seem pretty weak and perhaps too respectful of government prerogatives. But in a domain where governments ultimately decide what restrictions on their own activities they will respect, it is truly remarkable that those governments have been willing to construct procedures limiting their own capacities to function and have given individuals so many rights.

From the perspective of impact on the individual, the most important means of implementing international human rights law is through national legislation, courts, and administrative agencies. In this context, we have quite a long way to go to bring the Universal Declaration and its progeny into the daily functioning of legal systems and practices. The Universal Declaration's European descendant, the European Convention on Human Rights, has gone furthest in becoming part of the general legal culture of the nations of Europe.

In conclusion, the Universal Declaration has become part of a worldwide culture of human rights which is more pervasive than any religion, political philosophy, or even economic system. We have, however, quite a long way to go in bringing reality to the rights which are set forth in the Universal Declaration. Indeed, the Malaysian Prime Minister and a few others have even proposed amendments to dilute the Declaration. While the Declaration represents the drafting of only the 51 governments which were members of the United Nations in 1948, the human rights treaties which were inspired by the Declaration have achieved extraordinarily broad ratification and thus demonstrate the universality of the declaration and culture of rights which it heralded. The world should resoundingly reject efforts to undermine the Universal Declaration and should, instead, continue to build upon the foundation which the Universal Declaration of Human Rights established.

JACK MAPANJE

Seasons Greetings for Celia (BC)

They say when God closes one door
He opens a window to let in the sun

Celia, your seasons greetings arrived
In time of despair, after I had signed

My life out by signing the Detention
Order insisted upon by Life-President

Who wishes us to rot, rot, rot forever
In this prison but your white and red

Roses invoke that War of the Roses I
Battled to comprehend to achieve my

A-levels, the green English landscape
Summons the Romantics I explored

Under the billowing smoke of paraffin
Tin-can lamps once upon the tough terrain

I thought I had left behind and how did
You hope to be remembered when you

Mark your name merely as Celia (BC)?
If the parentheticals are the British Council,

10 Spring Gardens, London, I recall no-one
By that name there, my British Council

Programme organiser with whom I shared
My London Magazine poems was called

Sheila, I think, and why, why of all those
Bags and bags of protest mail which harass

The Post Office Sorting Centre everyday
As oblique couriers convey, why did only

Your postcard from London and another
From The Hague, choose to slip past our

Strict mail sorters at this crucial moment,
What bribe did you offer the Officer-in-

Charge of prison for him to chance me to
His office to peruse your mail from over-

seas, defying the edict from the life-despot
And risking his life and mine? No matter

Your seasons greetings Celia have thawed
Our anguish furnishing these rancid prison

Walls with much sought after night jasmine
Now the cliché glowers: somewhere some-

one we do not know cares – and that dear
Celia is all the prisoner needs to know!

HARRY WU

China's Gulag – The Laogai

Deng's Communism – Extending a Legacy of Oppression

The Universal Declaration of Human Rights was adopted in 1948. In 1949, Mao's Communist Party took control of China. Measured by the standards of the Universal Declaration, it is clear that the Chinese Communist Party has never treated the people it controls as well as it should. There are those who would argue that the human rights situation in China has improved as the nation has opened its doors to foreign investment and some people there have even become rich. These same people, I fear, either have not read the Universal Declaration of Human Rights or have chosen to ignore it. In any case, a close look at recent Chinese history shows how far that nation is from observing the Universal Declaration.

Deng Xiaoping has passed away, but his style of market-oriented Chinese communism continues to thrive. Since the establishment of the People's Republic of China in 1949, the country has known only one other form of government: Mao's comparatively orthodox communism, with its emphasis on isolation and 'class struggle'. Much has been made of the differences between Mao's and Deng's systems. The truth is that they are fundamentally the same. Both methods rely on the politics of totalitarian despotism and the economics of public ownership, in which the state controls resources and major means of production. Mao and Deng only differed in their modes and methods of ruling. The biggest of these differences stemmed from Mao's refusal to implement the type of capitalism that Deng permitted in his later years.

With its roots in Mao's leadership, today's Chinese communist system is characterized by a massive totalitarian bureaucracy which oversees the public ownership of the means of production. Modern China remains under the firm control of the Chinese Communist Party – even with the continuation of Deng's economic reforms – which denies the average Chinese person the right to free speech.

The Chinese government's violation of Article 5 of the Universal Declaration of Human Rights is particularly flagrant. It states that 'No one shall be subjected to torture or to cruel, inhuman or degrading treatment or punishment.' In my 19 years in China's system of forced labor camps – the 'Laogai', as it is known to the Chinese people – I personally endured beatings, torture and near-starvation. I knew other prisoners who found suicide preferable to continued existence in the camps. In the years since, I have carefully studied the Laogai and have found no reason to believe that the Chinese government has developed any respect for Article 5 as it has expanded China's economy. The Chinese Communist Party has also demonstrated little or no tolerance for dissent.

Consider the cases of a group that I will call the 'three W's'. I am the first 'W'. In 1957, while attending university in Beijing, I spoke against the Soviet Union's invasion of Hungary. For this I was labeled a 'counterrevolutionary', was sent to the Laogai in 1960, and spent 19 years there.

In 1979, the year I emerged from the Laogai, the second 'W', Wei Jingsheng, was sentenced to 15 years for publicly suggesting that China needed democracy. In 1989 I was in the USA and Wei was in the tenth year of his sentence, when the third 'W', Wang Dan, received his first 4-year sentence for being a student leader of the 1989 Tiananmen Square protest.

Interestingly enough, the Chinese government imprisoned each of us in three different decades for peacefully expressing our opinions, but we all received our second sentences in the 1990s. After releasing Wei in 1993, the Chinese authorities arrested him again in 1994 and sentenced him to 14 more years in prison. Wang, upon his release, hoped to enroll at the University of California at Berkeley in the USA, but he was forced to return to prison instead; a Chinese court found him guilty of 'subverting the government' by writing an article critical of the regime. He was sentenced to 11 years of imprisonment.

Of the 'three W's', I am the only one who was fortunate enough to be an American citizen at the time of my second arrest. It was this status that ultimately drove the despots in Beijing to expel me from China rather than force me to serve the 15-year sentence I received in August 1995 for 'stealing state secrets'. Wei and Wang were exiled to the USA in November 1997 and in April 1998 respectively. The stories of the 'three W's' show that despite the economic developments taking place in China, the totalitarian communist system Mao installed has not changed.

THE LAOGAI

China's leaders have a deep-seated fear of real democracy and human rights. It is common knowledge that tyrannical systems need a method of suppression to maintain power. Since the dawn of the People's Republic, Chinese authorities have never hesitated to use the Laogai in their efforts to maintain domestic political control. Literally, the word means 'reform through labor', but it has come to stand for the Beijing regime's vast system of politically imposed slavery. Today, the fundamental policy of the Laogai bureaucracy is 'forced labor is the means, while thought reform is the goal'. The main task of the camps continues to be punishment and reformation of criminals in a manner useful to the state. More specifically, the Chinese Communist Party's economic theory postulates that human beings remain the most instrumental productive force. Except for those who must be exterminated physically out of political considerations, human beings must serve as submissive 'productive forces'. Violence can force submission, but psychological and spiritual acquiescence is best. In effect, the Laogai is not simply a prison system. It is a political tool for maintaining the Communist Party's totalitarian rule. As the Chinese Ministry of Justice's 1988 Criminal Reform Handbook states: 'The nature of the prison as a tool of the dictatorship of classes is determined by the nature of state power'.

Mao Zedong stated that 'Marxism holds that the state is a machine of violence for one class to rule another. Laogai facilities are one of the violent components of the state machine. They are tools representing the interests of the proletariat and the people's masses and exercising dictatorship over a minority of hostile elements originating from the exploiter classes'. By the same token, Communist Party documents support forced labor in the Laogai with the aim of reforming prisoners into 'new socialist people'. This evidence shows that the brutal and oppressive system of the Laogai stems from a radical communist ideology markedly different from Western reformatory ideas.

How has Chinese history reached this sad point? It is not by simple virtue of the fact that it is under the control of a communist party. In theory, the communist system proposes to 'help' people by 'reforming' them. By demanding a monopoly on political power, China's communist leaders made the implementation of their system a crime.

Driven by ideology, party directives, and the whims of dictators, the Chinese Communist Party has designed and maintained a repressive machine meant to control and eliminate dissenters. Religious believers, and those with contrary political views or a different concept of society, have suffered and continue to suffer. Since the creation of the Laogai in 1949, I estimate that approximately 50 million Chinese have been its victims. Today, there are approximately 6 million people in the Laogai and more than 1,000 Laogai camps have been identified.

In China the world's most extensive system of forced labor camps persists today in the form of the Laogai. We cannot ignore the continuing brutality of the Laogai. If we truly want to see an end to the totalitarian despots in China, we must first address and eliminate their main instruments of repression.

Statement on the royalties of the book

Countless violations of human rights take place every day in all parts of the world. As a contribution to the international struggle to end these violations, the royalties of this book will be donated to:

⋆ the UN Voluntary Fund for Victims of Torture
   and
⋆ the UNFPA Trust Fund for the Elimination of Female Genital Mutilation.

The UN Voluntary Fund for Victims of Torture

The United Nations General Assembly established the Voluntary Fund for Victims of Torture in December 1981. The Fund supports thousands of torture survivors and their families through professional centres that provide medical, psychological, social, economic and legal assistance. Voluntary contributions from governments, non-governmental organizations and individuals are not enough and victim assistance programmes have sometimes had to be interrupted.

For further information on torture, victims of torture and the activities of the Fund, see the essay entitled: Torture: Zero Tolerance! *by Jaap Walkate, Chairman of the Fund's Board of Trustees*, pp. 304–310.

The UNFPA Trust Fund for the Elimination of Female Genital Mutilation

In September 1997, the United Nations Population Fund (UNFPA) appointed Waris Dirie, supermodel and a victim of female circumcision, as its Special Ambassador for the Elimination of Female Genital Mutilation (FGM). In almost all countries where FGM is practised, UNFPA runs programmes and initiatives in cooperation with governments to abolish this harmful practice. To support the work of its Special Ambassador, UNFPA established a Trust Fund for the Elimination of FGM in March 1998.

For Dirie's personal account, see her essay entitled: My Story, pp. 117–119.

Ali Alatas, Indonesia

Minister for Foreign Affairs of the Republic of Indonesia. Indonesia's Ambassador and Permanent Representative to the United Nations in New York (1982–1988) and in Geneva (1976–1978). Graduate of the University of Indonesia, Law Faculty, and the Foreign Service Academy, Jakarta, Indonesia.

Philip Alston, Australia

Professor of International Law, Head of the Law Department at the European University Institute in Florence, and Global Law Professor at New York University. Chairperson of the UN Committee on Economic, Social and Cultural Rights. Has taught at several universities, including the Fletcher School of Law and Diplomacy and Harvard Law School. Has degrees in law and in economics from the University of Melbourne and a doctorate from the University of California, Berkeley.

Christiane Amanpour, United Kingdom

Chief International Correspondent for CNN. Contributing Correspondent for 'CBS 60 minutes'. Recent assignments have sent her to Iran, Sarajevo, Haiti, Algeria and Rwanda. Received wide acclaim for her extensive reports on the former Yugoslavia. Awarded a number of prizes. Recently named a Fellow of the Society of Professional Journalists. Holds a BA in journalism, University of Rhode Island, USA.
(© 1994 CNN, Inc. All Rights Reserved. Photo: Andrew Eccles)

Abdullahi An-Na'im, Sudan

Professor of Law at the Emory University Law School, Atlanta, Georgia, USA. Internationally recognized scholar of Islamic law and human rights. Fellow of the Law and Religion Program at Emory. Former Executive Director of Human Rights Watch Africa. Author of various books and articles. Studied in Khartoum, Sudan, and in Cambridge, England. Gained a PhD in law from the University of Edinburgh, Scotland. Has lived in exile since 1989.

Kofi Annan, Ghana

UN Secretary-General since 1 January 1997. Previously Under-Secretary-General for Peace-Keeping Operations. Carried out various sensitive diplomatic assignments. Strong commitment to economic development and social justice. Studied in Kumasi (Ghana), Geneva (Switzerland), Minnesota and Massachusetts (USA).
(© UN/DPI. Photo: Milton Grant)

Aung San Suu Kyi, Burma

Human rights activist and leader of the National League for Democracy. Symbol of the struggle for democracy and freedom in Burma. Won the Nobel Peace Prize in 1991. Placed under house arrest by the ruling military junta for leading a pro-democracy uprising (1989-1995). Awarded various prizes and awards and several honorary doctorates. Studied politics at Delhi University, India, and philosophy, politics and economics at Oxford University, UK.
(Photo: ABC Press/Camera Press)

Bishop Carlos Filipe Ximenes Belo, East Timor

Won the Nobel Peace Prize 1996 together with José Ramos Horta for their work towards a just and peaceful solution to the conflict in East Timor. Titular Bishop of Lorium and Apostolic Administrator of Dili, East Timor. Author of various books. Received several awards and honorary doctorates from various universities. Studied philosophy and theology in Lisbon, Portugal and Rome, Italy.

Tony Blair, United Kingdom

Prime Minister of the United Kingdom. Elected Leader of the Labour Party in July 1994. Entered Parliament in June 1983 at the age of 30. Studied law at Oxford. Practiced as a barrister until 1983, specializing in employment and industrial law. Joined Labour Party in 1975.

Emma Bonino, Italy

Member of the Commission of the European Union responsible for Fisheries, Consumer Policy and Humanitarian Affairs. Chair of the transnational Radical Party (1991-1993) and secretary of the party (1993-1994). Former member of the Italian Parliament and of the European Parliament. Holds a degree in foreign languages and literature from the Bocconi University of Milan, Italy.

Theo van Boven, the Netherlands
Professor of Law at Maastricht University, the Netherlands. Member of the UN Committee on the Elimination of All Forms of Racial Discrimination. Held numerous positions in international organizations. Author of various publications on human rights issues. Holds a PhD in law from the University of Leiden, the Netherlands, as well as several honorary doctorates from other universities.

Ina Brouwer, the Netherlands
Director Coordination Equal Opportunity Policy of the Netherlands Ministry of Social Affairs. Previously member of the Lower House (1981-1986, 1989-1994). Worked as a lawyer specializing in social security, labor law and women's rights. Taught economics and social studies at secondary school level. Author of various articles and a book. Studied law at Groningen University, the Netherlands.
(© Fotopersbureau Hendriksen/Valk, The Hague, The Netherlands)

Thomas Buergenthal, United States of America
Professor of International Law at The George Washington University Law School, Washington D.C. Member of the UN Human Rights Committee. Former Judge and President of the Inter-American Court of Human Rights (1979-1991). Member of the UN Truth Commission for El Salvador (1992-1993). Author of many books and numerous articles on human rights and international law.

Jimmy Carter, United States of America
President of the United States (1977-1981). Founder of the Atlanta-based Carter Center, a nonprofit organization that brings people and resources together to promote peace and human rights, resolve conflict, foster democracy and development, and fight poverty, hunger and disease throughout the world. The Carter Center's accomplishments include support for strengthening the UN human rights system, advocacy on behalf of victims of human rights violations and monitoring of democratic elections.
(Photo: Charles Plant)

Nevzat Çelik, Turkey

Poet. Spent eight years under arrest for alleged membership of a left-wing group. Member of Turkish Trade Union of Writers. Became a honorary member of American Pen Center Club in 1987. His books of poems include The Dawn Song, Song of Life Sentence, Wish the Rain did not Fall, and Life that Hops on the Water. Has received several awards and prizes for his work.

His Holiness the Dalai Lama, Tibet

Tenzin Gyatso, spiritual and temporal leader of the Tibetan people, and 14th Dalai Lama. Resides in exile in Dharamsala, India. Received the Nobel Peace Prize in 1989 for his struggle for the liberation of Tibet and for his commitment to furthering the causes of non-violence and human rights. Has written two autobiographies, including Freedom in Exile, and authored several books on Buddhism, philosophy, human nature and universal responsibility. Doctor of Buddhist Philosophy.

Pieter van Dijk, the Netherlands

Member of the Netherlands Council of State and judge of the European Court of Human Rights. Previously Professor of the Law of International Organizations at Utrecht University. Founder of the Netherlands Institute of Human Rights. Author of numerous books, articles and publications in the field of international law and human rights. Holds a PhD in law from the University of Leiden, the Netherlands.

Sharon Dijksma, the Netherlands

Member of the Dutch Lower House for the Labour Party. Youngest member of Parliament in Dutch history. Member of the Board of BNN (broadcasting organization for young people) and Vice-President of Socialist International Women. Former youth representative of the Netherlands delegation to the UN General Assembly. Studied law at the University of Groningen, the Netherlands.

Waris Dirie, Somalia

Fashion supermodel and social activist. Appointed Special Ambassador for the Elimination of Female Genital Mutilation for the United Nations Population Fund (UNFPA). Fled Somalia at the age of 14. As Special Ambassador Waris Dirie participates in a UN-led campaign ('Face to Face') designed to publicize the plight of millions of women denied basic human rights.
(© Photo Simon Rowe, Forest Hill, Delaware, USA)

Asbjørn Eide, Norway

Member of the UN Sub-Commission on Prevention of Discrimination and Protection of Minorities. Founder and former Director of the Norwegian Institute of Human Rights, Oslo. Author of several studies for the UN Sub-Commission on Prevention of Discrimination and Protection of Minorities. Author and editor of several books on human rights and on conflict and peace research. Doctor juris h.c., Lund University, Sweden. Holder of an LLM from the University of Oslo, Norway.

Afshin Ellian, Iran

Writer of poetry and scientific articles. Forced to leave Iran in 1983. Has lived in the Netherlands since 1989 and became a Dutch national in 1995. Graduated in 1996 from the University of Brabant, Tilburg, the Netherlands, in criminal law, international law and philosophy. Currently works at the Law Faculty of the University of Brabant.

Anna Enquist, the Netherlands

Writer and psychoanalyst. Her poetry volumes include Soldiers' Songs, Hunting Scenes and A New Farewell. She has also written two novels, The Masterpiece (1994) and The Secret (1997). Enquist has received a number of prizes and awards for her poetry and novels.
(© Photo Bert Nienhuis, Amsterdam, The Netherlands)

Moris Farhi, Turkey

Writer. His works include television scripts, poems, novels, a film, and a play. Became a member of English Pen in mid-70s. Chair of International Pen's Writers in Prison Committee. Obtained a BA from the Istanbul American College and a diploma from the Royal Academy of Dramatic Art in London.

Basil Fernando, Sri Lanka
Writer. Executive Director of the Asian Human Rights Commission and the Asian Legal Resource Centre based in Hong Kong. Worked with a UNHCR sponsored project in Hong Kong and for the office of the UN Centre for Human Rights in Cambodia. Has written several books and articles on political and human rights issues as well as poems and short stories. Graduate of the Law Faculty of the University of Ceylon, Colombo, Sri Lanka.

Agnes Gergely, Hungary
Writer. Lectured on the translation of poetry at Budapest University of Liberal Arts, Hungary. Author of poetry, novels and non-fiction. Obtained an MA and a PhD in literature from Budapest University of Liberal Arts. Awarded several prizes for her work.
(© Photo Nora Fabian, Foto Pont Portré Stúdió, Budapest, Hungary)

Mikhail Gorbachev, Russian Federation
President of the International Foundation of Socio-Economic and Political Studies and President of Green Cross International, an environmental organization. Former President of the Soviet Union (1990-1991). Awarded the Nobel Peace Prize in 1990 for improving East-West relations. Author of various publications. Holds a law degree from Moscow State University.

Iain Guest, United Kingdom
International consultant. Has worked for the UN as spokesman and consultant, in Cambodia, Haiti, Bosnia and Rwanda. Specialist in peace-building. Has written widely for newspapers and magazines, and is a regular commentator on National Public Radio. Author of several BBC television documentaries. Studied at Oxford University, United Kingdom.

Václav Havel, Czech Republic
First President of the Czech Republic. Previously President of Czechoslovakia. One of the leaders of the Civic Forum opposition movement. Co-founder and one of the spokesmen of the Charter 77 human rights initiative. Incarcerated several times for his beliefs. Author of various books and plays.
(Photo: Jírí Jírú)

Seamus Heaney, Northern Ireland

Writer. Awarded the Nobel Prize for Literature 1995. Born Co. Derry, Northern Ireland. First book, Death of a Naturalist, 1966. Since then has published many volumes of poetry, also criticism and translations. Former Professor of Poetry at Oxford University. He is the Ralph Waldo Emerson Poet-in-Residence at Harvard University.
(© Photo: Caroline Forbes)

Cor Herkströter, the Netherlands

Former Chairman of the Committee of Managing Directors of the Royal Dutch/Shell Group and former President of the Royal Dutch Petroleum Company. Special interests have been the USA, Human Resources and Organization, Legal, Planning, Environment and External Affairs. Initiated in the company a discussion about its compliance with human rights. Studied at the Netherlands School of Economics.

Judith Herzberg, the Netherlands

Writer. First book of poetry published in 1963, many more followed. Also writes plays and film scripts. Taught scriptwriting in Amsterdam and Jerusalem. Her work was translated into English, French, German and Turkish. Most recent play: De Nietsfabriek (The Nothing-Factory). Awarded many prizes.
(© Photo: Bettina Keller, Berlin, Germany)

Rosalyn Higgins, United Kingdom

First female judge of the International Court of Justice. Former Professor of International Law, University of London and former member of the UN Human Rights Committee. Awarded various honorary doctorates and received many prizes and awards for her work. Author of numerous publications on international law. Holds a JSD from Yale University, USA.
(© D Vorm, Leidschendam, The Netherlands)

Hans Küng, Switzerland

Professor Emeritus at Tübingen University and President of the Foundation Global Ethic, Tübingen-Zürich. Challenged the conservatism of the Vatican regarding subjects such as papal infallibility and birth control. Former Professor of Ecumenical Theology at Tübingen University (1960-1996). Visiting lecturer in many parts of the world. Holds honorary doctorates from several universities. Author of various works.

Catharine MacKinnon, United States of America
Lawyer, teacher, writer, activist, and expert on sex equality. Professor at the University of Michigan Law School and Visiting Professor at the University of Chicago Law School. Her scholarship has been foundational in creating women's law as a field. Pioneered sexual harassment as a legal claim. Currently represents Bosnian Muslim and Croatian women seeking international justice. Has a BA from Smith College and a JD (law) and a PhD (political science) from Yale.
(Photo: Miguel Fairbanks)

Jonathan Mann, United States of America †
Dean of the School of Public Health, Allegheny University of the Health Sciences in Philadelphia. Founding Director of the François-Xavier Bagnoud Center for Health and Human Rights and Professor of Epidemiology and International Health, Harvard School of Public Health. Founding Director, Global Program on Aids, WHO. Received his MD from Washington University, St. Louis, and his MPH from Harvard School of Public Health, USA.

Jack Mapanje, Malawi
Poet and linguist. Was imprisoned for three and a half years in Malawi without trial and without charge. His works include Of Chameleons and Gods, The Chattering Wagtails of Mikuyu Prison and Skipping without Robes. Lives in exile. Currently works as a professional research fellow at the University of Leeds, UK. Holds a PhD in Linguistics from University College London.

Gabrielle Kirk McDonald, United States of America
President of the International Criminal Tribunal for the Former Yugoslavia. First African-American to hold position of federal district judge in Texas (1979-1988). Former partner with major law firm in Texas and professor of law. Graduated first in her class from Howard University School of Law, USA. Has received numerous awards and honors in recognition of her achievements.
(© Photo: Raphael Gaillarde)

Cecilia Medina Quiroga, Chile

Professor of International Law and International Human Rights Law at the University of Chile, Santiago. Previously, Professor of International Law and International Human Rights Law at the Law School, University Diego Portales, Chile. Vice-President of the UN Human Rights Committee. Lived in exile from 1973 to 1990. Visiting Professor at several academic institutions. Holds a PhD in law from Utrecht University, the Netherlands.

Hossein Mehrpour, Iran

Professor of law at the University of Shahid Beheshti, Teheran, Iran. Chairman of the Board for Follow-up and Supervising the Implementation of the Constitution. Former member of the Guardian Council of the Constitution. Author of various publications in the field of Islam and human rights. Holds a PhD in civil law from Teheran University, Iran.

Rigoberta Menchú Tum, Guatemala

Internationally acclaimed spokesperson for the rights of indigenous people. UNESCO Goodwill Ambassador for indigenous issues. President of the Menchú Foundation. Has received many honorary doctorates and international awards, including the 1992 Nobel Peace Prize, for her work in the field of social justice and ethno-cultural reconciliation as well as the 1998 Prince of Asturias Award on International Cooperation.

Joni Mitchell, Canada

Songwriter, singer, musician, poet and painter. Has produced 19 albums over 30 years. Her albums include Song to a Seagull, For the Roses, Court and Spark, Dog Eat Dog, Hits and Misses. Has inspired other singer-songwriters with her music. Has received numerous awards and honors, including two Grammy Awards for Best Pop Album and Best Artwork & Packaging for her Turbulent Indigo release.
(Photo: Nick Elgar / LFI/ABC Press)

Danielle Mitterrand, France

Founder of France-Libertés-Fondation Danielle Mitterrand, which defends human rights and fundamental freedoms. Widow of François Mitterrand, former President of France. Active in resistance during the Second World War. Author of four books. Has received several awards, including the prize from the North-South Centre in Lisbon. Honorary doctorates from Edinburgh University, UK, and University of Cape, South-Africa.

Les Murray, Australia

Poet. Lives and works in a rural valley to the north of Sydney. Travels around the world to read his poetry and to give lectures. The universal themes in his poetry are reached through precise observation of the natural, social and local world and by listening to the vernacular rhythms of his fellow Australians. Has won several international prizes, including the Petrarcha Prize in 1995 and the T.S. Eliot Prize in 1997.

Bishop Martinus Muskens, the Netherlands

Bishop of Breda, member of the Permanent Commission of the Netherlands Bishops Conference, and advocate of the poor in the Netherlands. Worked from 1970-1977 in Indonesia. Taught church history for fifteen years in Rome. Author of several publications. Studied missiology at Nijmegen University, the Netherlands.

Sadako Ogata, Japan

United Nations High Commissioner for Refugees. Previously Professor and Dean of the Faculty of Foreign Studies at Sophia University in Tokyo. Former Independent Expert of the UN Human Rights Commission on the human rights situation in Myanmar. Has published a number of books and articles on diplomatic history and international relations. Holder of a PhD from the University of California, USA.

Marten Oosting, the Netherlands

National Ombudsman of the Netherlands and President of the International Ombudsman Institute. Previously Professor of Administrative Law and Public Administration in the Faculty of Law, University of Groningen, the Netherlands. Author of various publications on aspects of his work. Studied sociology and law at Utrecht University, the Netherlands. Honorary doctorate from Twente University, the Netherlands.
(© Photo: Vincent Menzel)

Olara Otunnu, Ivory Coast

Special Representative of the UN Secretary-General for Children and Armed Conflict and President of the International Peace Academy in New York, USA. Formerly, Minister for Foreign Affairs of Uganda, Permanent Representative of Uganda to the United Nations and Chairman of the UN Commission on Human Rights. Active in many initiatives and organizations. Holds degrees from Makerere University, Oxford University and Harvard Law School.

William Pfaff, United States of America

Author and journalist. Columnist for The International Herald Tribune in Paris and for newspapers elsewhere in Europe and North America. His books include The Wrath of Nations (1993), Barbarian Sentiments (1989) and The Politics of Hysteria (1966). Received the Jean-Jacques Rousseau Prize in 1990.

Sonia Picado Sotela, Costa Rica

Vice-President of the Board of Directors of the Inter-American Institute of Human Rights. Former Ambassador of Costa Rica to the United States. First and only woman judge on the Inter-American Court of Human Rights (1984-1994). Author of numerous publications on human rights issues. Has received several awards for her work. Studied law at the University of Costa Rica.

Elisabeth Rehn, Finland

Under-Secretary-General, Special Representative of the Secretary-General in Bosnia and Herzegovina. Special Rapporteur for Human Rights in Former Yugoslavia. Former Minister of Defence and of Equality Affairs in Finland. Former presidential candidate. Has received several honors and awards. Holds a honorary doctorate from Abo Akademi and a BSc in Economics from Helsinki School of Economics.

Rendra, Indonesia
Poet. Founded his own theater group and has written several plays. Known as an electrifying reader of his own work and has been invited to read his poems at many international poetry festivals. Has received numerous awards for his artistic achievements and for his struggle for human rights and democracy through the arts. Studied at the American Academy of Dramatic Arts in New York City, USA.

Mary Robinson, Ireland
UN High Commissioner for Human Rights. Former President of Ireland. Former Reid Professor of Constitutional and Criminal Law at Trinity College, Dublin. Participated in numerous international activities relating to human rights and supported the work of international human rights organizations. Studied law at Dublin University and Harvard University.

Nigel Rodley, United Kingdom
Professor of Law at the University of Essex. Special Rapporteur on Torture of the UN Commission on Human Rights. Was the first Legal Adviser of the International Secretariat of Amnesty International. Has numerous publications concerning public international law and human rights to his name. Holds a PhD from Essex University, UK.

Nawal El Saadawi, Egypt
Psychiatrist, well-known feminist author and novelist. Author of various books including The Hidden Face of Eve, Woman at Point Zero, and the Fall of the Imam. As a result of her writings El Saadawi was dismissed from several jobs and detained in 1981. In 1991 the government closed down the Arab Women's Solidarity Association which she founded. Has been awarded several national and international literary prizes and honorary doctorates.

Pierre Sané, Senegal
Secretary-General of Amnesty International. Heads the International Secretariat of Amnesty International in London and serves as primary spokesman for Amnesty worldwide. Led Amnesty International's delegation at the UN World Conference on Human Rights in Vienna. Studied at various universities, including Carleton University, Ottawa, Canada.
(Photo: Willem Offenberg)

Helmut Schmidt, Germany

Honorary Chairman of the InterAction Council. Former Chancellor of the Federal Republic of Germany and previously, Minister of Defence, Minister of Economics and Minister of Finance. Joined the Social Democratic Party (SPD) in 1946 and held several positions, including Deputy Chairman of the party. Studied Economics in Hamburg.

Ahmad Shamlu, Iran

Writer and poet. In trouble both before and after the 1979 revolution and has been arrested and forced into hiding or exile more than once in his career. Worked as poet, journalist, film-maker and tv editor. Has published 19 volumes of poetry as well as many translations of world literature. Has received awards for his artistic work.

Goran Simic, Bosnia

Writer. His works include: poetry, essays, reviews, plays for children and radio plays. Previously editor of several literary magazines in the former Yugoslavia. One of the founders of PEN Bosnia-Herzegovina. Came to Canada in 1996 under the auspices of PEN Canada. Senior resident at Massey College, Canada. Has received several awards and prizes.
(Photo: Milomir Kovačević)

Max van der Stoel, the Netherlands

High Commissioner on National Minorities of the Organization for Security and Cooperation in Europe. Special Rapporteur on Iraq of the UN Commission on Human Rights. Former Minister for Foreign Affairs of the Netherlands. Has received several awards and honorary doctorates for his work. Studied law at Leiden University, the Netherlands.

Wisława Szymborska, Poland

Poet. Awarded the Nobel Prize for Literature in 1996. Worked as a poetry editor and columnist. Published sixteen collections of poetry. Her poems have been translated in several languages and have been published in many foreign anthologies of Polish poetry. Has received various awards and prizes for her work. Studied Polish literature and sociology at Jagiellonian University, Cracow, Poland.

Vedat Türkali, Turkey

Writer of poems, novels and plays. Worked in the film industry, wrote scripts and directed a number of films. Censorship and court cases have dogged most of his career. Arrested in 1951 and sentenced to nine years imprisonment. Has won several prizes and awards for his work. Studied in the Turkish Studies Department of Istanbul University's Literature Faculty.

Ted Turner, United States of America

Vice-Chairman of Time Warner Inc., the world's leading media and entertainment company. Oversees Time Warner cable network division, including CNN. Turner is an active environmentalist and sportsman. Has received numerous civic and industry awards and honors. Made a substantial contribution to support the goals of the United Nations.
(© 1996 TBS, Inc. All Rights Reserved. Photo: Mark Hill)

Lech Wałęsa, Poland

Trade union activist and politician. President of Poland (1990-1995). Chairman of Poland's first independent trade union Solidarność (Solidarity) from 1980-1990. Detained in 1981-1982. Awarded the 1983 Nobel Peace Prize. Has received various honorary doctorates, international awards and state honors. Author of two books and various publications.

Jaap Walkate, the Netherlands

Chairman of the Board of Trustees of the UN Voluntary Fund for Victims of Torture. Netherlands Ambassador to Pakistan. Previously Netherlands Ambassador to Peru. Held various positions at the Netherlands Ministry of Foreign Affairs in the field of human rights. Delegate to UN conferences. Honorary member of the medical society of the World Health Organization. Studied law at Leiden University, the Netherlands.

Halima Warzazi, Morocco

Expert of the UN Sub-Commission on Prevention of Discrimination and Protection of Minorities. Special Rapporteur on harmful traditional practices of the Sub-Commission. President of the Preparatory Committee of the World Conference on Human Rights (1991-1993). President of the Third Committee of the UN General Assembly (1966). Graduated in literature from Cairo University.

341

David Weissbrodt, United States of America

Member of the UN Sub-Commission on Prevention of Discrimination and Protection of Minorities. Fredrikson & Byron Professor of Law at the University of Minnesota. Works with several international human rights organizations in Minnesota. Author of several books, monographs and articles on human rights and immigration law. Received his AB from Columbia University and his JD from the University of California Law School, USA.

Harry Wu, China

Human rights activist. Executive Director of the Laogai Research Foundation. Spent 19 years in the Laogai, a forced labor reform camp, for expressing his political ideas. Arrested in 1995 by the Chinese government while entering China; expelled two months later under international pressure. Author of three books. Has received numerous awards for his activities.

Acknowledgements

This publication would not have been possible without the support of many people.

First, sincere thanks are due to the authors of the essays and poems for their enthusiasm and willingness to contribute to this commemorative book. We have enjoyed working with them. We trust that the final result will meet all expectations.

We are greatly indebted to the staff of the English Section of the Translations Department of the Netherlands Ministry of Foreign Affairs for their professional translation of many of the essays and in particular to Marion Alhadeff for her unfailing support and dedication.

We should like to thank Lawrence Gerner for the creative way in which he visualized each article of the Universal Declaration of Human Rights.

We owe a special word of thanks to our colleagues for their continuous encouragement and patience and to Esther van der Velde for her assistance.

The attention devoted to the publication of this book by the staff of Kluwer Law International is gratefully acknowledged. Lindy Melman and Peter Buschman deserve a special mention for their cooperation and support as does Antoon van Vliet for the creative design and lay-out of the publication.

The following people were responsible for translating the foreign-language poems:

Poem	Translation
'To Unknown Heroes' by Ina Brouwer	Barend van der Heijden, from Dutch
'The Autumn Melodies' by Afshin Ellian	Ernestine Hoegen, from Dutch
'The Red Jacket' by Anna Enquist	Lloyd Haft, from Dutch
'From the Years of Barbarism' by Agnes Gergely	István Tótfalusi, from Hungarian
'Song of the Full Moon' and 'Song of the Sun' by Rendra	Harry Aveling, from Indonesian
'The Banquet' by Ahmad Shamlu	Iraj Kaboli and Khashayar Shahriari, from Persian
'A Simple Explanation' by Goran Simic	Amela Simic, from Bosnian
'Tortures' by Wisława Szymborska	Stanisław Barańczak and Clare Cavanagh, from Polish
'Seventh Year' by Vedat Türkali	Moris Farhi, from Turkish

We conclude with the names of authors and publishers who granted us permission to reprint copyrighted poems:

Poem	Source
'Hollow Eyes, Bellies, Hearts' by Jimmy Carter	From 'Always a Reckoning' by Jimmy Carter. © Jimmy Carter. Reprinted by permission of Times Books, a division of Random House, Inc.
'From the Republic of Conscience' by Seamus Heaney	From 'New Selected Poems 1966 to 1987' by Seamus Heaney. Reprinted by permission of Faber and Faber. From 'Selected Poems 1966–1987' by Seamus Heaney. © 1990 by Seamus Heaney. Reprinted by permission of Farrar, Straus & Giroux, Inc.
'Seasons Greetings for Celia (BC)' by Jack Mapanje	Has appeared in 'Skipping Without Robes', Bloodaxe Books, 1998, UK.
'One Kneeling, One Looking Down' by Les Murray	First published in The Times Literary Supplement 1997.
'Song of the Full Moon' and 'Song of the Sun' by Rendra	First published in 'State of Emergency', Wild & Woolley, 1978, Australia. © Rendra.
'Tortures' by Wisława Szymborska	From 'View with a Grain of Sand: Selected Poems'. © 1993 by Wisława Szymborska, English translation by Stanisław Barańczak & Clare Cavanagh. © 1995 by Harcourt Brace & Company, reprinted by permission of the publisher. Reprinted by permission of Marek Bukowski.

The General Assembly

Proclaims this Universal Declaration of Human Rights as a